WITHDRAWN
SEP 2 0 2023
John Carter Brown Library

AMERICAN EXPLORATION AND TRAVEL

Teodoro de Croix

El Caballero de Croix

Teodoro de Croix

AND THE NORTHERN
FRONTIER OF NEW SPAIN, 1776–1783

FROM THE ORIGINAL DOCUMENT
IN THE ARCHIVES OF THE INDIES, SEVILLE
TRANSLATED AND EDITED

BY

ALFRED BARNABY THOMAS

·NORMAN·
University of Oklahoma Press

COPYRIGHT 1941 BY THE UNIVERSITY OF OKLAHOMA
PRESS, PUBLISHING DIVISION OF THE UNIVERSITY.
MANUFACTURED IN THE U.S.A. FIRST EDITION, JANUARY, 1941; SECOND PRINTING, MARCH, 1968.

To
Herbert Eugene Bolton

PREFACE

THE work of Don Teodoro de Croix, Caballero of the Teutonic Order and commander general of the interior provinces of New Spain, stands out significantly in the history of our West and northern Mexico. Although many data are available here in his translated report, the editor has made no attempt to give a comprehensive view of the whole range of his activities. Such a subject is too large for the limits of a single volume. The "Historical Introduction," accordingly, attempts only to define the conditions that influenced the solution of Croix's main problem: the defense of the interior provinces from Indian attack. Croix worked within a frame dominated by geographical influences, cultural conflicts between Indian and Spaniard, internal conflicts that arose either from historic conditions or from contemporary forces opposed to his efforts, and finally by events occurring within and beyond New Spain.

The General Report of 1781, presented here, is a detailed analysis of each of the provinces of his command: Texas, Coahuila, New Mexico, New Vizcaya, Sonora, and to a brief extent, California. As a whole, the document presents for its time the most comprehensive survey ever written of conditions in the area of our present Southwest and northern Mexico. From the total picture arises a view of Indian attack and destruction of Spanish civilization from Texas to California and from New Mexico to Durango. Implicit in the account of this struggle is a highly valuable indication of the location, range, names, habits, customs, practices, and psychology of the Indian groups which impinged on Spanish control in this vast region. On the Spanish side of the picture are clearly seen the internal conflicts between Croix and the local American-born Spaniards, Creoles, who as military officers or powerful landowners differed in their own interests with those of the king as represented by Croix.

Clearly reflected in Croix's writings are the significant international changes that affected the Spanish empire in the

PREFACE

late eighteenth century. His reports give a needed balance to modern interpretation of the effects of these international changes. The revolt of the thirteen English colonies, for instance, had a more decisive influence in northern Mexico than the acquisition of California and Louisiana had. It is customary to reverse this emphasis.

Finally, we see here the successes and heartbreaks of Croix himself. One senses his zeal to get his job done; one also finds praiseworthy his modesty. But the characteristics most clearly defined are his intellectual capacities and his stubborn honesty. No other figure who reached this North American frontier visualized the whole problem of Indian-Spanish conflict, saw the necessity for making vital changes in the mode of defense, or had the courage to attempt the remedies and unhesitatingly admit his mistakes, as Teodoro de Croix did.

The writer is under obligation to individuals and institutions for assistance in bringing this study to a conclusion. He is happy to acknowledge his indebtedness to the University of California for the Native Sons of the Golden West Fellowship, which permitted him to gather his first Croix materials in the Archives of the Indies, Seville, Spain, in 1925-26; and to the John Simon Guggenheim Foundation for a Fellowship in 1929-30, which enabled him to continue his studies in that archive and extend them to the Spanish Archives in Salamanca and Madrid and to the British Museum. Two grants-in-aid, one from the American Council of Learned Societies and the other from the Social Science Research Council, have enabled him to carry on investigations in the National Archive of Mexico in 1928 and 1937 respectively. The Research Council of the University of Oklahoma provided him with funds to purchase photostats from the Spanish Archives in New Mexico, from Harvard College Library, the Library of the University of Texas, and from the Bancroft Library, University of California. To Professor Herbert E. Bolton the writer wishes to extend his acknowledgments for the inspiration of his teachings; to Dr. Harvard Miller, Arizpe, Sonora, for hospitality during the writer's visit to Croix's capital; to Professor

PREFACE

Eduardo W. Villa, Director of the Archivo Histórico del Estado de Sonora, Hermosillo, for sending him valuable data on Croix; and to Don José de la Peña, of the Archive of the Indies, Seville, and Señor Rafael López, Chief of the Archivo Nacional de la Nación, México, for their repeated kindnesses.

ALFRED BARNABY THOMAS

Tuscaloosa, Alabama, December 1, 1940

CONTENTS

I. HISTORICAL INTRODUCTION

Geography, Indians, and Spaniards	3
The Administration of Teodoro de Croix, 1776–1780	16
Disappointments and Achievements, 1781–1783	58
Conclusion	64

II. GENERAL REPORT OF 1781 BY TEODORO DE CROIX

Province of Texas	72
Province of Coahuila	88
Province of New Mexico	105
Province of New Vizcaya	115
Province of Sonora	132
Province of California	230
Bibliography	247
Index	271

ILLUSTRATIONS

El Caballero de Croix	FRONTISPIECE
Map: The Northern Frontier of New Spain, 1776–1780	*facing* 82
Tables Showing Financial Condition of New Vizcaya and New Mexico, 1781	114
Table Showing Increase in Income from Sonora, 1778–1780	146
Croix's Capital: Arizpe, Sonora	178
Façade of Cathedral, Arizpe, Sonora	210

PART I
HISTORICAL INTRODUCTION

I

GEOGRAPHY, INDIANS, AND SPANIARDS

IN northern Mexico and the present American Southwest, Spain faced perhaps her most difficult colonizing problem in the Americas. The push northward began soon after the Cortesian conquest of the great Valley of Mexico. In spite of enormous difficulties between 1540 and 1700 five great areas were defined: Sonora, New Vizcaya, Coahuila, New Leon, and New Mexico, and early in the eighteenth century, Texas —the interior provinces of New Spain. Geographically the area, with the exception of the plains of eastern New Mexico and Texas, is a mountainous desert. In the west the Sierra Madre Occidental is the principal physiographic feature. Its counterpart to the east across the great V-shaped Chihuahua desert is the Sierra Madre Oriental. Together they sweep down to unite at the Isthmus of Tehuantepec and cradle, in the Valley of Mexico, the heart of the Aztec civilization. A double range running roughly east and west between Durango and San Luis Potosí separates the Valley from the Chihuahua desert, which, inclining to the north, ends along the Rio Grande.[1]

In the northwestern part of Mexico the parallel ranges of the Sierra Madre Occidental create the washboard landscape of Sonora. Interlaced among the Sonoran mountains are swiftly flowing streams that have eroded deep gullies on their way to the Gulf of California. The major exceptions to this drain-

[1] For references on the geography of northern and northwestern Mexico, see H. H. Bancroft, *Resources and Development of Mexico* (San Francisco, 1893); M. Orozco y Berra, *Apuntes para la historia de la geografía de México* (Mexico, 1884); Alexander Humboldt, *Essai politique sur le royaume de la Nouvelle-Espagne*, (Paris, 1827); Carl Lumholtz, *New Trails in Mexico* (New York, 1912); and *Unknown Mexico* (New York, 1902).

HISTORICAL INTRODUCTION

age system are the Rio Gila cutting the province across the north and emptying into the Rio Colorado, and the Rio San Pedro rising deep in Sonora and flowing northward into the Rio Gila. The other streams of importance, the Rio de Altar, Rio de Sonora, Rio de Yaquí, Rio de Mayor, and the Rio Fuerte, all debouch into the Gulf of California.

Scattered for the most part along Sonora's innumerable river valleys were primitive groups of Indians. At the mouth of the Gila River were the Yuman tribes; along its middle and upper course were the dreaded Gila Apache. More menacing to the province were the Seri along the barren coast of the Gulf of California, roughly from Guaymas to the mouth of the Altar River. North and east of them the restless Pimas Altos and Pimas Bajos maintained a casual but dangerous contact with the Gila while their own frequent rebellions threatened Spanish control. More friendly were the Opata along the Rio Sonora in the north central part of the province.[2]

Culture patterns of all these groups were primitive. The Gila had practically no agriculture. Although the Pima, Seri, Opata, Cocomaricopa, Piato, and others cultivated small patches along the river beds, the chase, some native plants such as the mesquite, and fishing supplied their wants.

The great province of New Vizcaya, bordered on the west

[2] For data on the north Mexican tribes, see H. H. Bancroft, *The Native Races* (San Francisco, 1883), I, Chap. V; M. Orozco y Berra, *Geografía de las lenguas y carta etnográfica de México* (Mexico, 1864; Ralph L. Beals, *The Comparative Ethnology of Northern Mexico Before 1750*, Ibero-Americana: 2 (Berkeley, 1932); John R. Swanton, "Indian Tribes of the Lower Mississippi Valley and Adjacent Coast of the Gulf of Mexico," *Bulletin 43*, Bureau of American Ethnology (Washington, 1911); Cyrus Thomas, "Indian Languages of Mexico and Central America," *Bulletin 44*, Bureau of American Ethnology (Washington, 1911); W. I. McGee, "The Seri Indians," *Seventeenth Annual Report*, Part I, Bureau of American Ethnology (Washington, 1898); Carl Sauer, *The Distribution of Aboriginal Tribes and Languages in Northwestern Mexico*, Ibero-Americana: 5 (Berkeley, 1934); Wendell C. Bennett, and Robert M. Zingg, *The Tarahumara* (Chicago, 1935); Carlos Basauri, *Monografía de los Tarahumaras* (Mexico, 1929); Leslie Spier, *Yuman Tribes of the Gila River* (Chicago, 1933). For Texas see Juan Agustín de Morfi, *History of Texas, 1673–1779* edited by Carlos Eduardo Castañeda (Albuquerque, 1935); Herbert E. Bolton, *Athanaze de Mézières and the Louisiana-Texas Frontier, 1768–1780* (Cleveland, 1914) and *Texas in the Middle Eighteenth Century* (Berkeley, 1915).

GEOGRAPHY, INDIANS, AND SPANIARDS

by the Sierra Madre Occidental, occupied practically all of the Chihuahua desert. The drainage system on this plateau in the north is chiefly in the Conchos River and its tributaries. This river, rising in the west central foothills of the Sierra Madre, empties into the Rio Grande some two hundred miles southeast of El Paso. In the south the Rio Nazas, with tributaries in Durango, drains off to the east into a sink in southern Coahuila known as Lake Parras. Everywhere throughout the plateau are small streams—arroyos, dry most of the year but raging torrents from occasional cloudbursts—that terminate in the rocky soil or innumerable lagoons. Among the most important of these fugitive streams are the Rio de Casas Grandes, the Rio de Santa Maria, and the Rio del Carmen, all in the northwestern part of the province.

On the east a vast, desolate, mountainous waste, the Sierra Madre Oriental, its northern front abutting on the lower Rio Grande, dominates the entire province of Coahuila. The main ranges are the Serranías del Burro, Sierra del Carmen, Sierra Hermosa de Santa Rosa, the Sierra de San Mateo, and others in the south. From the northern and eastern fronts innumerable arroyos drain into the Rio Grande. Through the deep canyon separating the Serranías del Burro on the north and the Sierra del Carmen and Sierra Hermosa de Santa Rosa on the south, flows the Rio de la Babia, frequently dry in its upper reaches. Emerging from the mountains, it becomes known as the Rio Sabinas, while its lower course to the Rio Grande is the Rio Salado. This is the principal drainage system in Coahuila. From the south are other streams which enter the Salado in Coahuila, notably the Rio Salado de los Nadadores. On the western side of the Sierra Madre Oriental, and extending somewhat into the Chihuahua desert, is the Bolsón de Mapimí, a huge, rugged depression, mostly desert, but in its southern extremity a marshy sink.

The single exception to the geography of the northern area is the province of Texas, although in its southwestern part, fringing the Rio Grande opposite New Vizcaya and Coahuila, are barren hills and in places high, rough sierras. Northward

HISTORICAL INTRODUCTION

are the rolling plains watered by small streams and broad gulf-bound rivers.

In this vast area—the Chihuahua desert, Coahuila, and southwestern Texas—ranged innumerable bands of Apache. Within New Vizcaya itself, in the Sierra Madre Occidental, were the fierce Tarahumara Indians in touch with the Gila (on the north), who raided the extensive district north of Chihuahua and south to Durango. Along the banks of the Conchos River were the Conchos Indians, who were decidedly more friendly to the Spaniards. The greatest menace was the Apache. Having their principal habitat in this area on the northern side of the Rio Grande were the Natagée, Mescaleros, and Lipan Apache. The Natagée dwelt nearer El Paso and regularly moved back and forth, north to make a union with the Gila in southern New Mexico and south to raid northern New Vizcaya and El Paso itself. Southeast of them were the Mescaleros, the mescal eaters, whose residence was principally in the mountains of southwestern Texas whence they crossed the Rio Grande to attack Chihuahua on the west and, taking refuge in the Bolsón de Mapimí, raided the haciendas and towns as far as Saltillo. Occasionally they attacked as far south as Durango. Below them along the lower reaches of the Rio Grande were the Lipan. These dwelt on the plains and in the mountains on both sides of the Rio Grande. In company with the Mescaleros they frequently carried their raids into New Vizcaya, but primarily confined their attacks to the eastern side of the Coahuila mountains in the neighborhood of Monterrey, or turned north to destroy life and property in Spanish Texas among the missions and settlers near San Antonio.

Intruding into this picture in Texas were the Indians of the North and the Comanche.[3] The latter, emerging from the Rocky Mountains in the early eighteenth century, swept down across the Texas plains during the middle of the century driving the Apache before them and raiding the New Mexi-

---

[3] Alfred B. Thomas, *Forgotten Frontiers: A Study of the Spanish Indian Policy of Don Juan Bautista de Anza, Governor of New Mexico, 1777–1787* (Norman, Oklahoma, 1932), 57 ff. (Hereinafter cited: Thomas, *Forgotten Frontiers*.)

can and Texas settlements. By 1776 the Comanche were crossing the Rio Grande to attack the Lipan as well as the Spanish settlements. The invasion of the Comanche into south Texas invited a possible alliance between them and the Gulf Karankawa, dreaded for their cannibalistic proclivities.[4]

New Mexico, then including present Arizona, presented a picture little different from that of northern Mexico. The western boundary was the Colorado River into which flowed the Gila which drained the Mogollón and other sierras in southern New Mexico. Cutting along the eastern side of the province is the Rio Grande del Norte bordered on both sides almost continuously by barren sierras. In the central part of the province are mesas with wide stretches of desert broken here and there by arroyos dry for the most part of the year. Across the northern part of the area is the high wall of the Rocky Mountains.

In the mesa region, encircled by the Apache, lived a peaceful agricultural people, the Pueblo Indians. The Navajo in the northwest attacked them and, allied with the Gila in the south, reached into Sonora and New Vizcaya. Beyond the Navajo in the mountains were the Ute, who made long forays into the province. On the eastern side of the Rio Grande were various groups of Apache, the Jicarilla, the Sandia, the Organo, and others who, in alliance with the Natagée, swept in and out of the area almost at will. In the south, in the Mogollón range, dwelt other Apache bands who attacked the Spanish caravans passing up and down the river and raided El Paso and the presidios in northern New Vizcaya and Sonora.[5] The Spanish settlements from Santa Fe south to El Paso fought a never ending battle with these various groups of Apache. Finally into the picture of Navajo, Apache, and Ute activities the Comanche pushed down through the plains of west Texas.[6]

Into this northern desert and mountainous area occupied

---

[4] Archivo General de Indias, Seville, Spain, 103–3–24, El Caballero de Croix to José de Gálvez, No. 8, Arispe, October 3, 1781. See below, pages 72–76, ¶ 1–10. (Hereinafter cited: A.G.I.)

[5] Thomas, *Forgotten Frontiers*, 3–19.

[6] *Ibid.*, 57 ff.

HISTORICAL INTRODUCTION

by scattered groups of Indians of a decidedly inferior cultural level, the Spaniards moved from the Valley of Mexico in the late sixteenth century. The northern geography determined their routes. One branch advanced northwestward along the Pacific slope; a second went directly north into the great Chihuahua desert area; while the third pushed to the northeast between the Gulf and the Sierra Madre Oriental toward the lower reaches of the Rio Grande.

In the Valley of Mexico the Spaniards had found Aztecs with notions of government, carrying on agriculture, and adequately housed; in short, having conquered a people more or less attached to the soil, they had little difficulty in making their occupation extraordinarily effective. However, the different geographic and cultural conditions of the Indians of the north created a type of society that differed sharply from that of the valley. In the north a principal incentive to the Spaniards at first was the exploitation of silver mines. Needed in transportation, workings, and travel were donkeys, mules, and horses. To supplement the food supply cattle were introduced along with goats, sheep, chickens, and other fowls. In the sheltered valleys and near streams, cattle and other herds multiplied rapidly to create a new wealth, the cattle range industry. To protect the mining settlements and guard strategic spots selected for occupation, the Spaniards established military detachments known as presidial troops. Finally, the Church, solicitous for the salvation of all humanity, sought the conversion of the Indians, and in distinction from the practice in the Valley of Mexico of establishing churches in populous Indian villages, the fathers founded missions and tried to attract the Indians thereto. The great northern area emerged accordingly as a mining, cattle, military, missionary and Indian frontier society.[7]

This society, however, was governed by the prevailing ideas of social organization that dominated the colonial period of Hispanic America. Its basic economic character found its ex-

[7] Herbert E. Bolton and Thomas M. Marshall, *The Colonization of North America, 1492-1783* (New York, 1925), 75.

GEOGRAPHY, INDIANS, AND SPANIARDS

pression in large land grants, called haciendas, to the privileged members of the Spanish aristocracy. Because of a juridical conception developed in the Middle Ages in Spain, the subsoil rights were reserved. These could be granted to the same individual or to another, usually of the aristocracy, so that both areas suitable for grazing and mountainous regions passed into private hands, from which the king, of course, drew his share, usually a fifth. Likewise the Church received outright vast tracts of land for purposes of its support, deficiencies otherwise met by the King's treasury.

The cattle ranges were managed by superintendents, while the sheep herders, cowboys, and the servants attached to the administration of the property and the upkeep of the *casas,* or residences, of the owner and the superintendent, were largely drawn from the mestizos, offspring of Spanish and Indian unions principally fostered through the missions.[8] On the lands of the Church the same social blends existed. In the mining settlements there was a larger percentage of Spanish workers, brought originally from Spain to conduct the operations, whose places were gradually taken over in the manual branches by condemned prisoners, runaway Indians or Indians seized on the ground of being cannibalistic, and by the mestizo group available in nearby towns and haciendas.[9]

The last economic factor for consideration is the towns, some of which had become fairly large by the end of the eighteenth century. They had grown up either as distributing points for mines and haciendas, as capitals of the provinces, or had sprung from nearby mining settlements such as Chihuahua, Durango, Saltillo, Arizpe, Monterrey, El Paso, and others. In the towns were congregated predominant middle-class groups engaged in trade, commerce, manufacturing, in-

[8] Considerable data on the details of hacienda life in the late eighteenth century are found in Juan Agustín de Morfi, *Viaje de Indios y diario del Nuevo México,* edited by Vito Alessio Robles (Mexico, 1935). See particularly pp. 85–91. (Hereinafter cited: Morfi, *Viaje.*)

[9] J. Lloyd Mecham, *Francisco de Ibarra and New Vizcaya* (Durham, 1927), Chap. VIII; Hubert H. Bancroft, *History of Mexico* (San Francisco, 1883), III, 579, 597, speaks of German and Spanish miners being imported for technical work.

HISTORICAL INTRODUCTION

dustry, and other related activities. The population was generally mixed Indian and Spanish, with the mestizo group dedicated to the menial tasks.

Elements of conflict of a profound nature existed throughout the society. Everywhere Indians emerging from the security of their mountain retreats raided towns, mining camps, haciendas, and defenseless shepherds and cowboys tending their herds. Indians sought cattle, a new source of food, hides for clothing, and leather for a variety of uses in their primitive hand industries; and horses, first introduced into the Americas by the Spaniards. These latter animals increased the effectiveness of Indian warfare, extended their hunting range, and had culture value, increasing the wealth and importance of the man who owned one. A variety of ornaments, particularly those to be found on church altars and in private homes on the haciendas and in the smaller towns, had their attraction also, but the garnering of these was incidental to the main objective of attack—the acquisition of horses and cattle. The constant murder and rapine that accompanied the attack was primarily incidental and rarely premeditated, except in cases of revenge for fancied or real wrongs committed by the Spaniards.

To meet the devastation of life and property, caused primarily by the projection of Spanish society into the Indian culture of the area, the Spaniards created two principal techniques, the one preventive, the other punitive. They first tried to make peace by treaties with the Indians. However, the ineffectiveness of this procedure rested in the sheer impossibility of the Spaniards to establish peace with such a vast variety of practically independent groups. Another weakness arose from the difficulty of impressing upon primitive groups the supposedly sacrosanct character of this purely European invention. Finally, the hard necessity of existence frequently forced the Indians to replenish their food supplies, while instances of advantages taken by more sophisticated Spaniards in technicalities hidden from Indian understanding, brought reprisal.

GEOGRAPHY, INDIANS, AND SPANIARDS

A second technique was that of conducting campaigns into the Indian country in efforts to recapture animals, rescue prisoners, or retaliate upon Indian rancherias in the hope of discouraging future raids. This procedure was equally fallible. Considering the needs of the vast Spanish empire in North and South America, presidial troops were simply not available in sufficiently large numbers to provide adequate defense of all the villages, towns, and cities. Because the great distances constricted transportation over mountainous trails, it was extremely difficult to keep what troops there were supplied with powder, ammunition, and weapons. The necessity of recruiting untrained troops and subaltern officers from mestizo elements added a weakness not germane to the regular colonial army.[10] Lacking, also, on this desolate frontier was an adequate complement of well trained officers more imperatively needed in other regions where the Spaniards had to defend themselves against other Europeans. Because of this defective military condition, there were lack of discipline and training, and practical ignorance of strategy and operation of war. Father Morfi, commenting on Croix's review of the presidials at Aguaverde, tucked away in the fastness of the Coahuila mountains, remarked that the soldiers did not understand how to load their guns and that the bullets did not fit the muzzles.[11]

Besides these flaws in the regime itself, the Indians added to the Spanish difficulties of defense by raiding the horse herds of the presidios. Here the scarcity of fodder and the bareness of the country made it necessary to pasture the horse herd, whose guard, drawn from the few presidials available to defend the fort itself, was often too weak to resist a sudden at-

---

[10] A.G.I., Audiencia de Guadalajara (hereinafter cited: A.G.I., Guad.), 253, Croix to Gálvez, No. 735, Arispe, April 23, 1782, ¶ 56–58. (Hereinafter cited: Croix, General Report, 1782.) See also, Harvard College Library, Sparks Mss. 98 (VI), No. 2389, Croix to Gálvez, No. 3, Confidential, Chihuahua, March 29, 1779, ¶ 98. [NOTE: This number 2389 refers to the item as listed in James Alexander Robertson, *List of Documents in Spanish Archives Relating to the History of the United States ... in American Libraries* (Washington, 1910). Hereinafter this number will be given for the convenience of the student.]

[11] Morfi, *Viaje*, 241.

HISTORICAL INTRODUCTION

tack and stampede. With the horses gone, the presidials were reduced to foot and had to wait, sometimes for months, for a new supply of animals. The result was, as Croix himself said, that the king was spending huge sums of money on troops who could only defend themselves and do nothing toward protecting the neighboring countryside, much less make campaigns against the Indians.[12]

In the second place, when mounts were available and supplies of ammunition and weapons plentiful for a campaign, the Indians from concealed positions in neighboring hills would watch the departure of the troops. While the soldiers headed for the point where scouts had last reported the Indians, the latter swooped down on the undefended settlement left behind. Homecoming troops with no victory to their credit frequently were greeted by blackened ruins and their murdered women and children.

The transportation of supplies—food, clothing, all kinds of equipment besides weapons and powder—needed at the presidios and frontier settlements exposed the Spaniards to similar dangers at the hands of the Indians. Thus a train of mules, sent south from the frontier line to one of the centers of supply, required, besides the drivers, an armed escort. Not only were these cordons frequently attacked and destroyed, but the settlement or presidio, temporarily weakened, lived in haunting fear, often justified, until the return of the defenders with the necessities of existence.[13]

Closely associated with this chaotic discipline was the inefficiency of administration within the presidios. The provision for paying the wages and salaries of the troop and officers and for allotting money for the purchase of supplies and horses necessitated the establishment of central disbursing offices far within northern Mexico to avoid Indian attack. To them mule trains were dispatched from the presidios twice

[12] A.G.I., Guad, 253, Croix de Gálvez, No. 458, Arispe, January 23, 1780, ¶ 75–90. (Hereinafter cited Croix, General Report, 1780.)
[13] Charles Wilson Hackett (ed.), *Historical Documents Relating to New Mexico, New Vizcaya and Approaches Thereto, to 1773* (Washington, 1926), II, 219–27. "Extract of a paper which Don Lope de Sierra wrote in regard ... to Nueva Vizcaya," on p. 223.

yearly to secure the sums appropriated for presidial upkeep. Occasionally Indians got the money. When, however, the funds for salaries and wages came intact to the presidio, the disbursement of it rested in the hands of the captain and paymaster. Because of the scarcity of competent individuals for such positions, irregularities crept into the handling of the accounts. The comparatively rare inspections by superior officers from the central government frequently resulted in nothing more than the dismissal of the offending officers at the moment, without the application of a remedy to the fundamental difficulty. Thus the soldiers were rarely paid; equipment they were supposed to keep up with wages they were supposed to receive fell into disrepair.

When funds were available, the paymasters were under obligation of purchasing supplies on the semi-annual trips to Chihuahua and other central points. The merchants in the towns coöperated in raising prices upon the arrival of the paymasters. Frequently a liaison was established between a particular paymaster and a merchant or group of merchants; in other cases the paymasters failed to distinguish between their own funds and those of the presidios in the various gambling resorts or houses of ill fame into which they chanced to stumble.[14] In such cases, however deplorable, the temptation to relax is understandable among men exiled to distant and dreary lives on the frontier, as much the victims of the system as of their own frailty.

The effects of this arrangement, conditioned by the exigencies of the frontier, were disastrous to the soldiery at the presidios. The most conscientious paymaster was defenseless in the face of the unfair practices of the merchants, from whom he had to buy his provisions. To the high prices of goods he was compelled to add the items of drivers' wages, freightage, and losses incident to the trail, and these costs determined the price to the soldier of the individual items on the list of goods posted for sale in the presidio. His meager wages failed to secure the bare necessities for himself and family, so

[14] Croix, General Report, 1782, ¶ 201.

HISTORICAL INTRODUCTION

that he fell into debt; was inadequately fed, equipped, and housed; and as a result developed a morale shot through with insubordination or, at most, sullen obedience.[15]

Quite apart from the problems developed as a result of Indian attack, the northern frontier suffered from conflicts in the higher ranges of the political and economic order. The wealthy, aristocratic, Creole landowners, accustomed to ruling their domains as absolute monarchs, were jealous of interference from the central government in the provinces.[16] Governors and other high officials sent into the area, anxious to justify their administration in the eyes of their superiors, did not hesitate to reclaim lands for the king or support petitions of local communities and others who sought to recover lands wrested from them by the Creoles. Endless litigation arose between the latter and the central authorities on measures proposed from time to time by high army officers, always Spaniards, to solve the basic problem of Indian attack. The Creole attitude was further stiffened by the fact that, adequately defended in their own huge *casas* if they lived in the country, or enjoying the security of the larger cities, they had little interest in the Indian raids on lonely herders or inhabitants of the smaller villages and towns, and less in the larger demands of an empire that reached beyond their own domains.

In conflict, too, with the central authority was the Church. Constant bickering characterized the relations between the local priests and the presidial captain and soldiery who, infringing the rights of the padre's mission Indians, attempted to deprive them of lands or made more personal attacks. Higher up, the governor and the bishop waged endless war over questions of jurisdiction involving land, taxes, and control of the Indian communities which furnished the Church with important income and the governor with a source of labor supply in the royal mines, or in his own. Paralleling this

---

[15] Harvard College Library, Sparks Mss. 98 (III), No. 2146, Croix to Gálvez, No. 38, México, April 25, 1777, ¶ 39–40.

[16] A.G.I., Guad., 284, Croix to Gálvez, No. 891, Arispe, March 24, 1783. See also Croix to Gálvez, No. 3, above page 11, footnote 10.

GEOGRAPHY, INDIANS, AND SPANIARDS

conflict was that carried on by the Church with the powerful Creole landowners over identical issues.[17]

International affairs affecting North America at the end of the eighteenth century influenced adversely the solution of the Indian problem on this vast frontier. Spain's participation in the Seven Years' War had secured for her Louisiana. This territory extending indefinitely north of the Texas province necessitated the diversion of needed funds to establish peaceful relations with the new groups of Indians in the area. The most pressing problem was that of winning over the north Texas groups and establishing peace between them and the Comanche. This work at very considerable cost was successfully carried out by Athanaze de Mézières between the years 1769 and 1779.[18] Because of the resulting alliance between the Comanche and Spaniards in Texas, greater pressure was put upon the Apache to the east and south; this in turn sharpened Apache attack upon the northern frontier of Mexico.

In the far West the expansion of Russia along the Pacific Coast necessitated the Spanish occupation of California, an undertaking which coincided with that of the settlement of Louisiana. Here the north Mexican frontier was looked to for men, supplies, and equipment, both for new towns and the establishment of the California missions.[19] Moreover, means of communication with California, found by way of the Gila valley, necessitated alterations in the Sonoran end of the frontier line, which in effect advanced the Spaniards into the very heart of the Gila Apache country. These new burdens of California and Louisiana, aimed at holding back foreign invasion, were a dead weight in any solution of the internal Indian problem.

[17] The most detailed and satisfactory study of the conflict between the ecclesiastical and secular authorities in a Spanish colonial province is that of Frances V. Scholes, "Church and State in New Mexico, 1610–1680," *New Mexico Historical Review*, XI, Nos. 1–4 (January–October, 1936), and XII, No. 1 (January, 1937); also Scholes, "Problems in the Early Ecclesiastical History of New Mexico," *New Mexico Historical Review*, VII, No. 1 (January, 1932).

[18] Herbert E. Bolton, *Athanaze de Mézières and the Louisiana-Texas Frontier, 1768–1780* (Cleveland, 1914).

[19] Herbert E. Bolton, *Outpost of Empire* (New York, 1931).

HISTORICAL INTRODUCTION

THE ADMINISTRATION OF TEODORO DE CROIX, 1776-1780

EARLY PLANS

BY 1776 the threatened collapse of the entire northern frontier of Mexico, sapped by maladministration, increasing Indian attack, and the recent acquisitions, demanded attention. Acutely aware of the menace during the previous decade, the Spanish authorities included a survey of the problem as part of the general reorganization of New Spain attendant upon the acquisition of Louisiana and the proposed occupation of California.[20]

The survey, known as the Rubí Inspection, covered the years from 1766 to 1768 during which the Rubí conducted an examination of the frontier from eastern Texas to Altar in Sonora, paying particular attention to the problem of relocating the presidios to provide a more efficient defense against Apache invasion from the north. To a council of war held in Mexico City in 1769, Rubí submitted his recommendations, or *Dictámenes*,[21] which were subsequently incorporated in a Royal Regulation dated September 10, 1772.[22] The principal feature of the *Dictámenes* and the Regulation was the provision for the alteration of the sites of certain presidios.

To carry out the royal orders, Viceroy Bucareli commissioned Don Hugo O'Conor in 1772. By 1776 this officer, with the rank of commander inspector, had decided upon the exact sites and had transferred the presidios to their new locations, besides finding time to direct general campaigns against the Apache. However, in spite of an extensive correspondence he carried on with Bucareli touching the problems of internal

---

[20] Herbert I. Priestley, *José de Gálvez, Visitor-General of New Spain, 1765-1771* (Berkeley, 1916).
[21] A.G.I., 103–4–15, Superior Gobierno. Año de 1771. No. 1, Pral. Testimonio de los Dictámenes ... (Hereinafter cited: Rubí, *Dictámenes*).
[22] A.G.I., 106–4–24, Reglamento é instrucción para los presidios ... 10 de Setiembre de 1772.

THE ADMINISTRATION OF CROIX

presidial administration and the protection of the horse herds, nothing was done to alleviate any fundamental difficulties.[23]

The year 1776 brought a crisis on the northern frontier. The continued decline of the provinces there was apparent to the Council of the Indies, if not to Bucareli. Moreover the advance into California and the acquisition of Louisiana territory from France gave the interior provinces an importance not hitherto attached to them. Accordingly, after long discussion in the king's council, the northern region was amputated from the viceroyalty and placed under a single military government to be known as the Commandancy-General of the Interior Provinces of New Spain.[24] For the office of commander general, Charles III appointed Teodoro de Croix on May 16, 1776, in recognition of his long services and more recently for the distinguished merit displayed as castellan of the port of Acapulco.[25]

Don Teodoro de Croix, Caballero of the Teutonic Order, was born on June 20, 1730, in the castle of Prévoté, near Lille, France, the ancestral home. At the age of seventeen he entered the Spanish army and went to Italy as an ensign of Grenadiers of the Royal Guard. In 1750 he transferred to the Walloon Guard, ranking a lieutenant in 1756. In the same year he was decorated in Flanders with the Cross of the Teutonic Order, which gave him the title of Caballero. In 1760 he was made a colonel in the Walloon Guards; by 1765, a captain in the Vice-regal Guard. As such he accompanied his uncle, the Marqués de Croix, Viceroy of New Spain, to Mexico in 1766. In the same year the viceroy appointed him governor of Acapulco. Between December, 1766, and 1770 he served as inspector of

---

[23] O'Conor's own survey of these difficulties is in his "Papel Instructive," O'Conor to Croix, México, July 22, 1777, with Croix to Gálvez, No. 79, México, July 26, 1777. A.G.I., Guad., 516.

[24] A.G.I., Guad., 252. Informe dado por el Señor Marqués de San Juan ... 1768 sobre la creación de una capitanía general. ... This includes the correspondence of Viceroy Croix, Visitor Gálvez, the Duke of Alba, Arriaga, and the Plan para la erección de un Gobierno y comandancia general. ...

[25] A.G.I., Guad., 301. Charles III to José de Gálvez, Aranjuez, May 16, 1776. The appointment included jurisdiction over only the provinces of New Vizcaya, Sonora, Sinaloa, and California. Croix's instructions (see footnote 27, below) added Texas, New Mexico, and Coahuila.

HISTORICAL INTRODUCTION

the troops of the kingdom of New Spain with the rank of brigadier. In 1771 Croix left Mexico with his uncle, arriving in Spain in 1772 after a five months' stay in Havana. Here he remained until 1776.[26]

The instructions Charles III gave Croix conferred upon him practically viceregal powers[27]—direct dependence upon the royal person, the exercise of the royal patronage, the general-superintendency of the royal treasury, "just as the viceroys of those dominions have managed their offices according to the laws of the Indies." Some limitation was put on Croix's authority, however, by the fact that the king reserved to Bucareli a certain control over California's development, while Croix was directed to stimulate the growth and progress of that province.

This attempt of the king to give both officials authority in the same area resulted in confusion, so that Croix's powers were not defined until a specific case arose in the following August. At Querétaro, Croix opened a packet of twenty-four letters from Governor Neve, Father Serra, and Captain Rivera, which demanded among other things an increase of troops, means of populating suitable spots between San Diego and Monterrey and between the latter and San Francisco, and the establishing of a fort on the Santa Barbara Canal with troops necessary to occupy this post.[28]

Not feeling himself yet sufficiently familiar with California, Croix forwarded the twenty-four letters to Bucareli, whose intimate contact with the province might result best for the service.[29] Bucareli promptly returned the packet and in rather

[26] Domingo de Vivero, *Galería de retratos de los gobernadores y virreyes del Peru, 1532–1824* (Barcelona, 1909), I, 157–58.

[27] The king's instructions are found in A.G.I., Guad., 242, accompanying Consejo de Indias, No. 5. The king to Croix, San Ildefonso, August 22, 1776. For another copy see Simancas, Guerra, 7049, Pedro de Nava to Don Juan Manuel Abarez, Chihuahua, April 4, 1797, enclosure No. 2.

[28] A.G.I., 104–6–17, Croix to Gálvez, No. 89, Querétaro, August 23, 1777.

[29] Croix to Bucareli, Querétaro, August 15, 1777, in R. Velasco Ceballos, *La administración de D. Frey Antonio María de Bucareli y Ursúa* (Mexico, 1936), Publicaciones del Archivo General de la Nación, XXIX, I, 349–50. (Hereinafter cited: Ceballos, *Bucareli*.) A copy of Croix's letter to Bucareli here accompanies a copy of Croix's account to Gálvez cited in footnote 28 above.

lordly fashion informed Croix that "neither was your lordship nor am I authorized to separate from our commands any part of the provinces which the king put under our care."[30] Croix's interest in the efficient administration of the provinces rather than in his prerogatives stands in sharp contrast to Bucareli's refusal to succor California and seek a definition of powers later.[31] The latter promptly wrote Madrid asking for approval of his action. California waited meanwhile. In reply to Croix's letter recounting the impasse, Gálvez stated that in regard to California, Croix should take action in all matters requiring the exercise of governmental measures, but that measures directed to provide supplies and other necessities to maintain California were in the province of the viceroy.[32]

The king's instruction also failed to make clear the principal objective of the new command. Article Twelve stated: "In consideration of the basic reason that I have had for the new establishment of the office which I have conferred upon you, which is to secure the conversion of the numerous nations of heathen Indians who live in the northern part of North America you will dedicate your first attentions and activities toward converting them...." However, Article Ten read: "Your first objective and care must be directed toward the defense, stimulation and extension of the enormous territories included in the district of your command." Since Croix put the emphasis of his work on this latter article, the instructions of the king dealing with defense are particularly important. Specifically the new commander general was directed to utilize the militia to aid in pacifying the country and to establish in the various companies order and discipline. Secondly, the king emphasized the importance of founding well-organized settlements both near the presidios and along the frontiers. Finally, insistence was upon the strict observance of the Regulation of Presidios of September 10, 1772.

[30] Bucareli to Croix, Mexico, August 27, 1777, in Ceballos, *Bucareli*, I, 350-53.
[31] For Ceballos' interpretation of Bucareli's action, see Ceballos, *Bucareli*, II, xxvi.
[32] Gálvez to Croix, Madrid, December 23, 1777, with Croix to Gálvez, No. 89. See above, footnote 28; see also, Bucareli to Gálvez, México, July 27, 1778, in Ceballos, *Bucareli*, I, 436–37.

HISTORICAL INTRODUCTION

To acquaint himself with the frontier problems Croix was advised to devote time in studying the archives in Mexico City and to inspect the provinces in person. At Arizpe, Sonora, he was to establish his capital and a mint, hear petitions, report by letter monthly, and prepare each six months a concise account of the state of the provinces under the four branches of government: justice, policy, treasury, and war.[33] In more personal matters Croix was directed to maintain a bodyguard, provided with a salary of twenty thousand pesos a year, and laid under strict injunction to refuse dinners or presents from subordinates, public bodies, or private individuals.[34]

Crossing the Atlantic on the Nuestra Senora del Rosario, Croix disembarked at Vera Cruz on December 7, 1776. On the twenty-second he paid his respects to Bucareli in Mexico City.[35] During the next eight months Croix devoted himself to the problem of organizing his command, familiarizing himself with frontier conditions, and working out plans for defense of the provinces. In accord with royal orders Bucareli instructed the governors of the provinces to direct their reports to the new chief.[36]

As his principal lieutenant on the frontier, Croix appointed José de Rubio commander inspector. Antonio de Bonilla, specifically named in Croix's instructions, became the secretary of the commandancy. Pedro Gallindo Navarro occupied the post of auditor. Several clerks completed the office staff. Later Father Morfi became Croix's personal chaplain.[37]

---

[33] For a peculiar attitude toward this report of Croix, published hereinafter, and his other two reports of 1780 and 1781, three of the most significant documents touching the northern frontier of this period, see Charles E. Chapman, *The Founding of Spanish California* (New York, 1921), 410–11.

[34] Croix reprimanded the *cabildo* of San Francicso de Patos for proposing to provide lodgings for him (Morfi, *Viaje*, 149); see also Vito Alessio Robles, *Bibliografía de Coahuila, histórica y geográfica* (Mexico, 1927), 187–88 (Monografías, bibliográficas Méxicanas, No. 10).

[35] Archivo General de la Nación, México City, Bucareli, Tomo 86, 16, Bucareli to Gálvez, No. 2638, Mexico, December 27, 1776. (Hereinafter cited: A.G.N.)

[36] *Ibid.*, 16–17.

[37] A.G.I., Guad., 516, Croix to Gálvez, No. 1, México, February 25, 1777 (Rubio); Article 10, Instruction, page 18, footnote 27 above (Bonilla); A.G.I., Guad., 267, Croix to Gálvez, No. 88, México, July 27, 1777 (Morfi); and Morfi, *Viaje*, 21.

THE ADMINISTRATION OF CROIX

In the provinces no fundamental change in the administrative organization was contemplated or made. O'Conor had requested his release because of ill health, while captains of various presidios submitted petitions for change of status, retirement, promotion, etc. Thus Croix was able to appoint new officers to command the presidios of Tubac, Altar, San Carlos, and San Elezario.[38] In Sonora, Anza, returning from California, was appointed commander of the armed forces.[39] In New Mexico Governor Mendinueta had resigned. There Croix recommended Pedro Garibay,[40] but the king had already conferred the honor upon Anza for his distinguished California services. The office of superintendent of the hacienda Croix deferred in assuming until the more pressing obligation of restoring peace in the provinces was accomplished; consequently, this administrative side of his command did not exist.[41] He did, of course, prepare periodically detailed financial statements of provincial conditions.

While organizing his staff, Croix was studying frontier affairs. It was not until March 31, however, that Bucareli delivered some of the archives, some one hundred and fifty-six documents bearing principally upon more recent happenings.[42] Meanwhile reports of the deplorable conditions constantly reached the new commander. On January 18, 1777, Crespo, governor of Sonora, wrote Bucareli that the Pima and Seri were committing outrages and that he feared these Indians might ally with the Apache. Likewise, Father Ximenez Pérez wrote from Querétaro that the Sonora missionaries feared a general revolt.[43] On February 26, Croix relayed to Gálvez news of constant attacks upon New Mexico by the Co-

[38] A.G.I., Guad., 516, Croix to Gálvez, No. 5, México, February 25, 1777.
[39] See service record of Governor Anza, 1752-1783, in Thomas, *Forgotten Frontiers*, facing p. 353.
[40] A.G.I., Guad., 516, Croix to Gálvez, No. 17, México, February 26, 1777.
[41] A.G.I., Audiencia de México (hereinafter cited: A.G.I., Aud. de Méx.), 1378, Bucareli to Gálvez, No. 2786, México, February 27, 1777. Ceballos, *Bucareli*, I, 343-48 has only Bucareli's letter of remission.
[42] Harvard College Library, Sparks Mss., 98 (III), No. 2145, Croix to Gálvez, No. 37, México, April 25, 1777.
[43] A.G.I., 104-6-18, Croix to Gálvez, No. 32, México, March 24, 1777. Copies of both Crespo's and Ximenez's letters accompany No. 32.

manche, Ute, Navajo, and Apache.[44] New Vizcaya also provided its quota of deaths and robberies.[45]

With these events in mind Croix received, at the end of March, Bucareli's instructions for guidance.[46] It was plain from the viceroy's comments, restricted largely to the work of O'Conor, that he considered the provinces to be in a promising condition. "Indisputably," the viceroy wrote brightly, "the condition of the frontier, the quality and the discipline of the troops of the presidios have been ameliorated. The injuries that the citizens suffer are fewer and much less frequent . . . ."[47] For the most part the instructions included a restatement of Bucareli's orders to O'Conor during the past four years, a summary of O'Conor's replies, and conclusions based upon what the viceroy believed summed up the situation.

A month later, with the results of his study, the constant reports of the provincial governors, and the instructions of Bucareli before him, Croix outlined his first plans.[48] It was plain that he had little confidence in Bucareli: "Thus, most illustrious lord," he bitterly exclaimed to Gálvez, "I look upon a dismal stage. Although some try to persuade me that the provinces under my command have taken on a better aspect than that which they had in 1771 . . . . I cannot reconcile these favorable reports with the adverse ones that are frequently proffered in this capital and with those sent from the Interior Provinces . . . . It would please me greatly if the first ones were true, but on the other hand the second ones frighten me . . . for I see the greater disasters which they foreshadow . . . ."[49]

Prefacing his proposal for operations, Croix made an analysis of Indian hostilities in relation to the presidial line established by O'Conor and the condition of the troop garrisoning the frontier posts. In Texas, the Lipan seemed the most ser-

[44] Data with Croix to Gálvez, No. 17, see above, page 21, footnote 40.
[45] A.G.I., Guad., 516, Croix to Gálvez, No. 31, México, March 24, 1777.
[46] A.G.I., Aud. de Méx., 1378, Bucareli to Gálvez, No. 2819, México, March 27, 1777.
[47] *Ibid.,* ¶ 17.
[48] See above, page 14, footnote 15, Croix to Gálvez, No. 38.
[49] *Ibid.,* ¶ 46.

THE ADMINISTRATION OF CROIX

ious problem, but he was faced with conflicting reports of whether peace should be sought with them or with the Indians of the North.[50] Coahuila represented a more grave affair. There the Mescaleros, Lipan, Indians of the North, and Natagée were the enemy. The general opinion he recorded was that the policy of friendship was destroying the province. Not only did the Apache harry the settlements, but their hostility to the Indians of the North was encouraging the latter into the province.[51]

With regard to the location of various presidios, reference to the map convinced Croix that suppression of some and the transference of certain others to the frontier, such as the presidios of Mapimí, El Gallo, San Bartolomé, and Conchos, were lamentable errors. This action had exposed the areas formerly protected by the forts, but did nothing to stem Indian invasion.[52] Supporting this analysis, Croix referred to the fact that Captain Don Joseph Berroterán, an official whose vast knowledge of the frontier geography was well known, had opposed the move and warned of the dangers now evident. "I am greatly surprised," wrote Croix, "that, in the preparation of Article 15 of the Royal Instructions, inserted in the presidial regulation of September 10, 1772, the accounts of the explorations of Captain Don Joseph Berroterán were not borne in mind and that, although he dispatched these opportunely, his recommendations opposing locating the presidios on the banks of the Rio Grande were not given much weight."[53]

Specifically, Berroterán in his report to Viceroy Revillagigedo on April 17, 1748, had stated that "from the juncture of the rivers Conchos and Norte [to the east] there is not a suitable place on the banks [of the Rio Grande] upon which a presidio could be built, because of the scarcity of pastures . . . and even if this river afforded the most desirable resources, presidios built upon it twelve leagues apart could not impede the entrance of the many Indians on the northern side of the

[50] *Ibid.*, ¶ 1–2.
[51] *Ibid.*, ¶ 2–9.
[52] *Ibid.*, ¶ 10–16.
[53] *Ibid.*, ¶ 17.

HISTORICAL INTRODUCTION

Bolsón [de Mapimí]."[54] In spite of this information, Julimes was placed at the confluence of the Conchos and Rio Grande; Cerro Gordo, twenty-eight leagues down stream but not on the river's banks; San Saba, thirty leagues further beyond; while La Babia, about forty from the latter, was not near the stream but twenty leagues back in the mountains.[55]

In regard to Sonora, the chief problems there, Croix pointed out, were as elsewhere, Indian difficulties. The Gila Apache raided constantly and were threatening alliance with the Pima and Seri, whose restlessness was giving Anza much concern. Equally serious were the Seri and Piato whose coastal position and relations with the Tiburones and Papago were a threat to the flank of the Spaniards. The other problem was the establishment of the proposed contact with California via the Gila-Colorado route.[56]

In New Mexico, the invasions of the Indians were among the most serious along the northern frontier. The Comanche warred in all directions; the Apache came up from the west and south; while the Ute and Navajo battered the settlements on the north and west.[57] The defense consisted of the presidio of Santa Fe, a militia of Indians and Spaniards ill-equipped with arms and horses,[58] without instruction and discipline. "I am persuaded," Croix wrote Gálvez, "that if we lose the important barrier of New Mexico, which I pray God may not happen, the Indians would be masters of that immense country, and accustomed to living by robbery would indubitably approach us. If today an army is needed only to make war on the numerous and vagrant Apache, what force would be necessary to curb the other nations?"[59]

With this picture of aggressive Indian attack, Croix indicated the weakness of the defense. The troops were not skill-

[54] *Ibid.*, ¶ 18.
[55] *Ibid.*, ¶ 19.
[56] *Ibid.*, ¶ 27–34.
[57] *Ibid.*, ¶35–37.
[58] It became necessary at this time to send New Mexico fifteen hundred horses. Harvard College Library, Sparks Mss., 98 (III) No. 2160, Croix to Gálvez, No. 43, México, May 26, 1777. Thomas, *Forgotten Frontiers*, 383; note 89 should read 1777.
[59] See above, page 14, footnote 15, Croix to Gálvez, No. 38, ¶ 42.

ful in handling firearms; knew nothing of subordination or discipline; lost their horses, wore out their uniforms, arms, and harness; and frequently hungered. Indeed, Croix felt the line of presidios itself was contributing to the ruin of the provinces since the troops, engaged either in constructing buildings or guarding their posts and reconnoitering the countryside, left the interior areas unprotected. The great distances between the forts made it easy for the Indians to evade the presidial forces and raid the hinterland. The supply system also had broken down. Bankruptcy, arising from a dishonest or incompetent paymaster, had left the troops without food, clothing, and ammunition.[60]

With the salients of the frontier problem outlined, Croix offered his solution. The first obligation was to ward off the hostilities along a vast frontier of fifteen hundred miles garrisoned with less than two thousand men. Since the inability of these to protect the settlements was patent, he recommended a minimum increase of two thousand men. Behind the presidial line he proposed a string of fortified towns so that in reality the frontier would have a double line of defense. He preferred, however, to scrap the existing presidial line since "instead of drawing the line of presidios through the diameter as was wished, it would have been better to put it around the circumference," thereby excluding the waste land of the Bolsón de Mapimí from the area to be defended. But for the time being Croix realized the mistaken line would have to be maintained.[61] Supplementing this program, Croix next advised allying with the Indians of the North against the eastern Apache. By catching the latter between the pincers of the two forces, he believed surrender of the Lipan and others could be forced. Their collapse would automatically weaken the western Apache, particularly the Gila against whom the Spaniards would have to await his arrival on the ground.[62]

Before attempting any correction of the troop Croix counseled waiting until Rubio forwarded his reports of the inspection of the presidios. However, he did recommend that the

[60] *Ibid.*, ¶ 40–45.   [61] *Ibid.*, ¶ 48–52.   [62] *Ibid.*, ¶ 56–58.

HISTORICAL INTRODUCTION

distributing center for paying the troops be moved from Los Alamos to Arizpe in Sonora, and the one at San Luis Potosí, supplying Texas and Coahuila, to Monclova. As to the administration of the quartermasters in the presidios, he proposed that some alteration of the existing organization would have to be made. This general problem, however, like that of defense, had to await his personal inspection of the province.[63]

During the next three months, dolorous accounts from the frontier kept pouring in. In May Governor Ugarte of Coahuila wanted to round up the Lipan and deport them overseas as the only cure for the provinces.[64] Rubio, reporting from New Vizcaya, described as typical the condition of the third company of the Flying Corps stationed at Janos, a key presidio. All their guns and pistols, he wrote, were either broken or rusty, the soldiers totally ignorant of their use; they had no swords, only lances, while their horses were underfed and undersized.[65] Governor Barri, of New Vizcaya, wrote in similar vein from Durango. Anza, in Sonora, forwarded a letter from Standard-Bearer Limón at San Ygnacio to the effect that most of the San Bernardino troop were unmounted and without a single grain of powder or balls, and that he had requested from superiors these and other necessities such as clothing, wages, and tobacco, "since they are miserable and without any human support outside of what is absolutely necessary for the maintenance of forty men."[66] Moreover, Anza himself reported new attacks, murders, losses of mules and horses at the hand of the Pima and Seri.[67] From California Governor Neve, backed by Father Serra and Captain Moncada, put in a plea for reënforcements.[68]

Reporting this black picture to Gálvez—Apache successes

---

[63] *Ibid.*, ¶ 59–65.
[64] Harvard College Library, Sparks Mss., 98 (III) No. 2188, Croix to Gálvez, No. 48, México, May 26, 1777. See also A.G.I., 516, Croix to Gálvez, No. 47, México, May 26, 1777.
[65] Rubio to Croix, Chihuahua, May 25, 1777, with A.G.I., Guad., 516, Croix to Gálvez, No. 72, México, July 26, 1777.
[66] Anza to Croix, San Miguel de Orcasitas, May 23, 1777, with Croix to Gálvez, No. 72. See above, footnote 65.
[67] A.G.I., Guad., 516, Croix to Gálvez, No. 76, México, July 20, 1777.
[68] A.G.I., 104–6–17, Croix to Gálvez, No. 89, Querétaro, August 23, 1777

THE ADMINISTRATION OF CROIX

everywhere, the troop badly managed, unsupported, without discipline, their arms useless, and the settlers in panic—Croix summarized his measures for defense, though he despaired of bringing immediate relief to the harassed provinces.[69] In New Vizcaya he redistributed the troops. Between Cadena (near Mapimí) and Ancón de Carros he placed the First Flying Company. On the frontier he created two divisions of the presidial force so that a detachment of 150 men were to be constantly engaged in offensive and defensive operations to protect the interior country. Near Chihuahua he stationed the Second Flying Company.[70] Later he supplemented these measures with orders to Rubio to form a militia system.[71] For Sonora he proposed to order Governor Ugarte of Coahuila to take over Anza's command when the latter left for New Mexico.[72] For California he asked the viceroy to send supplies urgently requested from there.[73]

With these preliminary plans under way, Croix left Mexico City on August 4 for the frontier.[74] At Querétaro he halted from the twelfth to the twenty-eighth to answer his mail. Here news reached him from Anza of the rebellion of the Seri and the Opata occasioned by the failure of O'Conor to pay them for their services in the general campaign of 1775 and by the burdens imposed by the religious. Croix gave Anza full power to take any measures against the Seri and directed him to compensate the Opata at once. To the Father Provincial at Xalisco he sent a sharp request for him to "moderate the zealous indiscretion of his religious and have them confine themselves to the strict limits of their apostolic ministry."[75]

Overwhelmed by this new revolt and the appalling conditions revealed in the steady stream of letters from frontier of-

[69] A.G.I., Guad., 515, Croix to Gálvez, No. 80, México, July 26, 1777.
[70] Harvard College Library, Sparks Mss., 98 (III) No. 2165, Croix to Gálvez, No. 59, México, June 26, 1777.
[71] A.G.I., Guad., 515, Croix to Gálvez, No. 65, México, July 26, 1777.
[72] Croix to Gálvez, No. 76. See above, page 26, footnote 67; also A.G.I., Guad., 516, Croix to Gálvez, No. 77, México, July 26, 1777.
[73] Croix to Gálvez, No. 89. See above, page 26, footnote 68.
[74] Diary of Croix, Mexico to Durango, with A.G.I., Guad., 516, Croix to Gálvez, No. 118, Hacienda de Patos, November 20, 1777.
[75] A.G.I., Guad., 515, Croix to Gálvez, No. 90, Querétaro, August 23, 1777.

HISTORICAL INTRODUCTION

ficials, on August 23 Croix requested of Bucareli the increase of two thousand men, already proposed to Gálvez.[76] The viceroy's sharp refusal[77] of this needed complement brought to the surface the smoldering antagonism between these two high officials who divided the government of New Spain.

CROIX VERSUS BUCARELI, THE BUREAUCRAT

BUCARELI'S animus against Croix originated with the king's decision to create the Commandancy-General. This act Bucareli evidently interpreted as a reflection upon his administration since his optimistic picture of provincial conditions patently did not deceive the king and his council. Thus the order to receive the new commander general, who was to deprive the viceroy of half of his territorial jurisdiction and exercise practically viceregal powers, must have been a shock to Bucareli. He tendered his resignation.[78] Charles III, however, reassured his viceroy of his royal confidence and urged him to reconsider. Bucareli did so,[79] unfortunately for Croix and the well-being of the interior provinces. Undoubtedly had an official as experienced in frontier affairs as Bernardo de Gálvez[80] been appointed viceroy at this time, Croix would have had support in frontier problems instead of the opposition of a man who, in regard to this northern frontier, was essentially an armchair executive filled with petty resentment.

A second factor influencing Bucareli's attitude toward Croix was his parsimony and his contempt for the Mexican

---

[76] Croix to Bucareli, Querétaro, August 22, 1777, enclosed in A.G.I., Guad., 515, Croix to Gálvez, No. 98, Querétaro, August 23, 1777. Published in Ceballos, *Bucareli,* I, 355–68.

[77] Bucareli to Croix, México, August 27, 1777, in Ceballos, *Bucareli,* I, 368–72.

[78] Ceballos concludes, and the writer agrees, that Bucareli's resignation arose out of the situation described above (Ceballos, *Bucareli,* II, xxvi, and I, 409, note 1).

[79] Bucareli's letter of resignation, not available, was dated September 26, 1777 (Ceballos, *Bucareli,* I, 409). For Bucareli's answer to the king's request to reconsider, see Ceballos, *Bucareli,* I, 410–11. The archival location, not given by Ceballos, is A.G.N., Bucareli, Tomo 90, 1–2, Bucareli to Gálvez, No. 2851, México, August 26, 1777.

[80] For an admirable study of Gálvez, see John Walton Caughey, *Bernardo de Gálvez in Louisiana 1776–1783* (Berkeley, 1934), 61–69, who gives details of Gálvez' service on the northern frontier.

population predominant in the provinces. His basic objective was economy; alleviation of human suffering at no time entered his calculations.[81] Croix's plea for two thousand men consequently was quite beyond the vision of this viceroy, so meticulous in keeping his prerogatives intact and his budget balanced. A third factor was that Croix early exposed the incompetence of O'Conor, Bucareli's appointee, and thereby reflected upon the viceroy's judgment. This was unforgivable.

Evidence of Bucareli's lack of coöperation appears early. Croix, upon his arrival in Mexico, had asked for the files of the interior provinces. Bucareli had responded after several months by turning over only those documents that covered the period of O'Conor's administration.[82] Croix ultimately had to appeal to Spain for a royal order to force Bucareli to provide the older materials necessary for a comprehension of the fundamental causes of provincial decline.[83] So dilatory was Bucareli that Croix had to leave for the frontier without the papers which were later forwarded to him, almost a full year after news of his appointment reached Bucareli, and nine months after his request for them.

Similarly, Bucareli delayed several months in supplying the king's commanded instructions for Croix's guidance. This document, dated March 31, turned out to be a mere summary of the materials already turned over, namely Bucareli's various instructions to O'Conor and the latter's reports from the frontier.[84] Upon this data Bucareli based his recommendations and conclusions which, by this time it was apparent to Croix, in no wise conformed with the reports from his frontier staff and other provincial officials, notably Anza in Sonora, Mendinueta in New Mexico, Ugarte in Coahuila, and Neve in California.[85] Two months later Croix received from O'Conor himself a *papel instructivo,* which likewise portrayed very in-

[81] A scholarly analysis of this aspect of Bucareli's administration is in Ceballos, *Bucareli,* II, vii–cix.
[82] See Croix to Gálvez, No. 37, page 21, footnote 42, above.
[83] Bucareli acknowledged the royal order on November 26, 1777 (Ceballos, *Bucareli,* I, 382–84).
[84] Bucareli to Gálvez, No. 2819, page 22, footnote 46, above.
[85] See above, pages 20–24.

adequately, though in places revealingly, the actual conditions of the command as he left it. The paper, however, did convey significant information to Croix on the habits and methods of frontier Indian warfare.[86]

Under these circumstances, when Croix arrived in Querétaro and found news of the Seri revolt, he wrote Bucareli in paralyzing detail of the conditions reported by Anza and others, and asked for an immediate increase of two thousand men to meet the crisis.[87] To Croix's fifty-four paragraph letter, Bucareli replied briefly and cavalierly. He intimated that Rubio and others named by Croix had given a picture altogether too black and that Croix had been carried away by complaints of individuals. These, he pointedly suggested, after Croix had seen the provinces himself at first hand, he would be able to recognize as based merely upon the expected seasonal Indian attack! Finally, shocked at contemplating the expense of recruiting and equipping two thousand men, estimated at six hundred thousand pesos annually, he refused to place such a burden upon the royal treasury, especially since O'Conor had considered the present troops sufficient. In defense of his action, the viceroy referred to the importance of other *negocios publicos* specifying in particular the necessity of adequately defending Vera Cruz.[88]

Thoroughly aroused by Bucareli's stubborn refusal to open his eyes to realities, Croix appealed to the king. "I do not know," he wrote Gálvez, "whether the greatest enemy of them (the provinces) is the savage Indian or the impression which conjectural opinion and mistaken reports have made."[89] To Bucareli, Croix's reply was devastating. From Governor Barri, of New Vizcaya, Croix obtained a statement of the condition of this province between 1771 and 1776, approximately the period of O'Conor's administration. Enumerating all the alcaldias in New Vizcaya, Barri indicated on data from local

---

[86] O'Conor to Croix, México, July 22, 1777. See above, page 17, footnote 23.
[87] See above, page 28, footnote 76.
[88] See above, page 28, footnote 77.
[89] Harvard College Library, Sparks Mss. 98 (IV), No. 2202, Croix to Gálvez, No. 105 (Confidential), Durango, October 11, 1777, ¶ 4.

justices in each case the number of persons murdered by the Indians, those taken captive, haciendas and ranches abandoned because of Indian attack, and cattle, horses, mules, and other animals stolen. The totals were staggering: persons murdered, 1,674; persons captured, 154; haciendas and ranches abandoned, 116; livestock stolen, 68,256. Two notes added to the report stated that the figures did not include presidial officers and soldiers killed in battle; the many travelers murdered on the roads, as the latter's names and places were unknown; nor, finally, the huge number of mules and horses stolen from the presidial troops under O'Conor's jurisdiction, and from the haciendas and church lands near Chihuahua, O'Conor's capital. A second note warned that since the beginning of the year (1777), the hostilities had not only continued but were being pursued with increasing cruelty and force.[90]

This shot was so hot that Bucareli, resorting to the universal bureaucratic practice of passing the data on, reported briefly to Croix that he had asked O'Conor, now in Guatemala, for an explanation. Besides avoiding a direct reply, the subterfuge also enabled the viceroy to repeat his refusal for immediate reënforcements of one thousand men: "With regard to the increase of troops upon which you insist, I can add nothing to my letter to you of August 27 last."[91]

If Bucareli believed Croix intended to cease firing, he was mistaken; the opportunity to comply exactly with the royal instructions to keep the viceroy informed was too good. Enroute to Monclova from the Hacienda de Avinito on October 16, he renewed his bombardment with more reports from Anza.[92] Tucson, the latter reported, was without meat, butter, and candles; the cornfields of the mission of San Ygnacio were destroyed by the Indians; the captain of Santa Cruz presidio reported its crops burned, the settlers' houses fired, and the

[90] Croix to Bucareli, Durango, September 27, 1777, enclosing Barri's data (Ceballos, *Bucareli*, I, 373–77). A copy of Barri's data is also found in A.G.I., 103–4–16.
[91] Bucareli to Croix, México, October 15, 1777 (Ceballos, *Bucareli*, I, 377).
[92] A.G.I., Guad., 516, Croix to Gálvez, No. 123, Hacienda de Patos, November 24, 1777.

settlers scattered; the justice of Rio del Sonora was refused reënforcements, the troops being sent to protect various missions; the governor of the port of Guaymas announced that the Seri had taken all the horses there. From a dozen other points in Sonora the story was the same. Anza begged of Croix reënforcements at once so that "in some manner the torrent of so many misfortunes which menace us may be stemmed."[93] Writing Bucareli, Croix asked: "I could reach there in a few days and would go at once, but what good would my presence do lacking troops to make my plans effective and fruitful? I can only repeat my requests until the goodness of your Excellency forwards the increase of troops I have solicited."[94]

At last Bucareli felt compelled to order the rifle company at Guadalajara to proceed immediately to Sonora and promised to raise two flying companies indicated by Croix in an earlier communication. He took a shot, however, at Bonilla, on Croix's staff, by demanding Croix to inquire of that officer why he had reported to O'Conor in 1775 the excellent condition of the troops there and why a troop so robust then was not now in a better condition.[95]

After Croix had returned from his inspection of Coahuila and Texas, he wrote Bucareli on February 8, 1778, telling him that he had read both Bonilla's and O'Conor's report on Sonora. These officers, he commented, had recognized the excellent qualities of the troops but they also adverted to their defects, which from his trip along the frontier he now realized were general. It must have been a bitter pill for the viceroy when he wrote: "If the province of Sonora is in the same deplorable condition that I have seen today in those of Texas and Coahuila and part of New Vizcaya, I not only emphasize as very necessary the increase of two thousand men for the

[93] Anza to Croix, San Miguel de Orcasitas, September 1, 1777, with Croix to Gálvez, No. 123. See above, page 31, footnote 92.

[94] Croix to Bucareli, Hacienda de Avinito, October 16, 1777, with Croix to Gálvez, No. 123. See above, page 31, footnote 92.

[95] A.G.I., Aud. de Méx.. 1380, Bucareli to Gálvez, No. 3354, México, November 26, 1777, enclosing Bucareli to Croix, México, November 12, 1777. A small part of these extensive reports is published in Ceballos, *Bucareli*, I, 378-82; see also Croix's report to Gálvez, on this addition of troops, A.G.I., Guad., 276, Croix to Gálvez, No. 150, Valle de Santa Rosa, February 15, 1778.

THE ADMINISTRATION OF CROIX

whole frontier, but I consider that even this force will be inadequate."[96]

Croix then launched into a detailed analysis of the provinces he had seen and the condition of Sonora based on the reports of Bonilla and O'Conor cited to him by Bucareli himself. He had no trouble in establishing that both these officers had recommended to Bucareli an increase of more than one hundred and fifty Opata for Sonora, and intimated that had he permitted this increase, the province would now have a better aspect.[97] Croix felt that O'Conor was inefficient and supplied Bucareli with the facts. In New Vizcaya, O'Conor's principal residence, there were the worst weaknesses among the troops and many bankruptcies among the presidial paymasters. Pointing out that the king had kept officers of merit and rank in the provincial governments to aid O'Conor, who also had at his disposal two adjutant inspectors to share the work, Croix asked what good were these officers? O'Conor had not coöperated with them. On the contrary, with the exception of Mendinueta of New Mexico, they had been able to contribute nothing to the improvement of the troops because O'Conor gave them very little authority in this respect. Moreover, against all of them, Crespo of Sonora, Mendinueta of New Mexico, Fayni of New Vizcaya, Ugarte of Coahuila, and Ripperdá of Texas, O'Conor had made unpleasant accusations. That these men were not the incompetents O'Conor tried to prove was sufficiently evident, Croix thought, from Bucareli's own subsequent recommendations for their various promotions.[98]

Bucareli's reply to this document is not available. However, in forwarding a copy to the king, the viceroy stated that Croix was reporting "the deplorable and very sad condition in which he had found Sonora, New Vizcaya and Coahuila

[96] Croix to Bucareli, Valle de Santa Rosa, February 8, 1778 (Ceballos, *Bucareli*, I, 385).
[97] *Ibid.*, 388.
[98] *Ibid.*, 388–89. For O'Conor's attack on Ripperdá and O'Conor's unreal understanding of frontier problems, see Bolton, *Athanaze de Mézières*, 42–63, which also has Ripperda's defense wherein he indicates frontier difficulties so evident to Croix.

HISTORICAL INTRODUCTION

..." and that "... I have indicated to the Commander General that I shall take particular care that the necessary resources shall not be lacking for his needs while there are funds in the treasury."[99]

Four months later Bucareli, having heard from O'Conor regarding Barri's report of losses in New Vizcaya, undertook a vigorous defense of the erstwhile commander inspector. Criticising the report as lacking details of where and when the murders and robberies occurred, he stated that reports of officials on the frontier during the years in question did not justify the data furnished by the justices. It is significant, however, that Bucareli himself failed to specify whose reports, and give names and dates upon which he based his own statement. Finally, he defended O'Conor on the ground that Barri had never adverted to the losses mentioned in reporting to Mexico City on the state of the province.[100] This charge hardly reflects credit upon the integrity of Bucareli, who himself appointed Barri to the governorship of New Vizcaya, which the latter did not assume until eighteen months before O'Conor left the frontier.[101] Thus Barri could hardly have been expected to render reports of a province he was not commanding. Moreover, O'Conor established his headquarters at Chihuahua, while Barri functioned at Durango in the south, so that reports of Indian attacks in the province fell largely to O'Conor and not to Barri, who specifically said he was unaware of the extent of the attack in the jurisdiction of Chihuahua and excluded that from his totals which otherwise must have been even greater.

It is not without interest that at the same time Bucareli, so ardently defending O'Conor and blocking reënforcements for Croix, was himself soliciting from Spain authority to increase the frontier troops in New Leon and New Santander, pro-

[99] Bucareli to Gálvez, México, March 27, 1778 (Ceballos, *Bucareli*, I, 384–85).
[100] Bucareli to Gálvez, México, July 27, 1778 (Ceballos, *Bucareli*, I, 405–6).
[101] Barri was relieved of the governorship of Lower California on December 27, 1774 (Ceballos, *Bucareli*, I, 184–86). Neve arrived in March, 1775, and Barri left for San Blas on March 26. [H. H. Bancroft, *History of the North Mexican States and Texas* (New York, n.d.), I, 739].

vinces under his administration. The expense of these he wrote Gálvez, "does not seem to me a consideration, but even if it were, I consider it indispensable since the line of presidios does not ward off the injuries as was considered when its establishment was resolved upon."[102] Croix could not have put the case better!

CROIX'S INSPECTION OF THE NORTHERN FRONTIER, 1777–1778

FROM the hacienda of Avinito, Croix wrote Anza on October 16 giving him wide discretionary authority to proceed against the Indians and renewing his request to the viceroy for reënforcements.[103] A month later in Monclova, Croix called a council of war to which he invited Governor Ugarte and the provincial presidial captains. After a careful survey of the extent and nature of the attacks of the Nagatée, Mescaleros, and Lipan, known as the eastern Apache, the council agreed that a general campaign requiring three thousand men should be made against these Apache.[104]

Proceeding on his journey, Croix next inspected the presidio of San Juan de Bautista del Rio Grande and thence to San Antonio. Here a second council of war was held in January to integrate the policy determined upon at Monclova with the conditions existing in Texas.[105] Attending were the governor, Don Domingo Cabello, informed local officials, and

[102] Bucareli to Gálvez, México, January 27, 1779 (Ceballos, *Bucareli*, I, 445–47). For Croix's report, see A.G.I., Guad., 270, Croix to Gálvez, No. 316, Chihuahua, December 28, 1778.

[103] Croix to Gálvez, Hacienda de Avinito, October 16, 1777, with Croix to Gálvez, No. 123, see above, page 31, footnote 92. See also Harvard College Library, Sparks Mss. 98 (IV), No. 2215, Croix to Gálvez, No. 119, Hacienda de Patos, November 24, 1777, in which Croix gives an account of his first investigations, impresses on Gálvez the need of the troop increase and a method of doing this. See also A.G.I., Guad., 270, Croix to Gálvez, No. 279, Chihuahua, September 23, 1778.

[104] Bolton, *Athanaze de Mézières*, II, 147–63 has the proceedings of the Monclova council. Croix again emphasized the need of troops in a letter to Gálvez enclosing copies of letter from officials testifying to the sad condition of the province; see A.G.I., Guad., 516, Croix to Gálvez, No. 137, Saltillo, November 27, 1777.

[105] Bolton, *Athanaze de Mézières*, II, 163–70 has the proceedings of the San Antonio councils.

HISTORICAL INTRODUCTION

Croix's staff. Texas presented a special situation because of the intrusion of the Comanche from the north, and because of the recent acquisition of Louisiana territory west of the Mississippi in 1763. The Spanish authorities had as a result of Rubí's inspection directed Athanaze de Mézières, a former French Indian agent, to win over the Texas Indians to Spanish allegiance. Between 1769 and the meeting of the council in January 1778, de Mézières had succeeded among the northern groups, generally called the Indians of the North. With these considerations in mind, the San Antonio council agreed that de Mézières should consult with the governor, Ripperdá, on the best method of allying the Comanche to attack the Apache coincident with the general campaign to go forward from Coahuila, New Mexico, New Vizcaya, and Texas.

On his return from Texas, Croix inspected the presidios at Aguaverde and Monclova.[106] From the latter place he branched off to the west towards Chihuahua, a route that took him through the rugged Coahuila Mountains. His first stop was for the inspection of the presidio of La Babia. From here he moved over the main range and came down to the Rio Grande to the presidios of San Saba. From the latter he went on to check San Carlos farther west along the river and there turned directly west to reach Chihuahua in April of 1778.[107]

In Chihuahua during the months of June and July, Croix held his third council of war[108] at which were gathered some of the most distinguished soldiers of the northern frontier. Colonel Anza; Governor Mendinueta, vacating the office in New Mexico; Governor Barri, New Vizcaya; Governor

---

[106] The presidio had been moved from the town of Monclova nearer the Rio Grande but continued to be called the presidio of Monclova (Morfi, *Viaje*, 239).

[107] On his arrival at Chihuahua, Croix dispatched to Gálvez an extract of all his operations (A.G.I., Guad., 267, Croix to Gálvez, No. 170, Chihuahua, April 3, 1778). Impressed with the immensity of his command, Croix felt impelled to write Gálvez urging the need of an adjutant inspector (A.G.I., Guad., 270, Croix to Gálvez, No. 341, Chihuahua, January 23, 1779).

[108] A.G.I., Guad., 267, Croix to Gálvez, No. 159, Valle de Santa Rosa, February 15, 1778. For the councils of war see A.G.I., Guad., 276, Croix to Gálvez, No. 217, Chihuahua, June 29, 1778, which contains proceedings of the general council, while A.G.I., Guad., 267, Croix to Gálvez, No. 236, Chihuahua, July 27, 1778, deals with New Mexico.

THE ADMINISTRATION OF CROIX

Ugarte, Coahuila, on his way to replace Anza in Sonora; Commander Inspector Rubio; various captains of New Vizcaya presidios; and local prominent citizens—these discussed the Indian problem.

The council devoted itself to the whole frontier exclusive of Sonora.[109] Since the principal enemies of New Vizcaya were the Mescaleros and Lipan, who were likewise the chief problem of Texas and Coahuila, it was agreed that the general campaign recommended by the other two councils be carried out against the Lipan, and steps be taken to win over the Mescaleros to the Spanish side in the hope of splitting the Indian forces. The alliance projected in Texas with the Comanche was also approved. Finally, feeling that the frontier troops were too few either to conduct the campaign or to protect sufficiently the presidios and settlements, the council recommended the addition of eighteen hundred men. To support their position they referred to the campaign of 1775 in which 1228 men participated. On that occasion frequent flank raids were made by the Apache on the towns.

Until the troops could be so increased the council detailed what should be done in each of the provinces of Texas, New Mexico, Coahuila, New Vizcaya, and Sonora. For Texas they suggested that a ban be placed on supplying arms to the Lipan and on trading with them; that the Lipan buffalo hunts be curbed; and that the Comanche and the Lipan be discouraged from coming to San Antonio at the same time.[110] In regard to New Mexico, the council called upon Brigadier Don Pedro Fermín de Mendinueta to indicate the operations possible both with the present troop and with the proposed increase.[111] Touching Coahuila, the members of the council adopted the policy previously recommended at Monclova, namely that until the troops had been increased, friendship with the Lipan and eastern Apache should be cultivated and the troops now available distributed according to the orders of the command-

[109] See above, page 36, footnote 108. Croix to Gálvez, No. 217, 1.
[110] *Ibid.*, Encl. No. 1, Fourth Session, June 15, 1778, point 18, province of Texas.
[111] *Ibid.*, province of New Mexico.

er general.[112] In regard to Sonora, Anza was to submit a report in the terms asked of Mendinueta, in relation to the new establishments proposed on the Colorado and Gila rivers. These the commander general was to keep in mind in connection with the reconnaissance he was to make in the province and the councils he was to hold there.[113]

Finally, the council recommended that the operations of the troops of each province were to be integrated with those of the troops in the neighboring provinces, and that separate councils should be held in each province for the best government affecting the troops, the arrangements of their interests, recruiting, Indian auxiliaries, erection of new settlements, and other matters. The proceedings of this and the Monclova and San Antonio councils were to be transcribed and sent to the king so that in case the troops could not be augmented, his Majesty might permit the presidios of El Príncipe, Norte, San Carlos, San Saba, San Antonio de la Babia, Santa Rosa, and Monclova to be returned to their former sites, as well as any others that the commander general might indicate, for better protection of the settlements.[114]

Reporting the proceedings of the councils to the Minister of the Indies, José de Gálvez, Croix requested 378 light troops for the presidios of New Vizcaya, Coahuila, New Mexico, and Sonora to replace the militia and to reinforce the flying companies until there could be spared the necessary two thousand men to carry out the campaign and adequately protect the settlements.[115]

In the proposed plan for the campaign against the eastern Apache, El Paso occupied a key position. For this reason Croix took steps to strengthen the settlement. Rubí, in his inspection of 1767, had recommended the establishment of a post at Robledo near present Fort Selden, New Mexico, some miles north of El Paso.[116] Likewise, Rubí had considered mov-

---

[112] *Ibid.*, province of Coahuila.
[113] *Ibid.*, province of Sonora.
[114] *Ibid.*, province of New Vizcaya.
[115] *Ibid.*, 2. Croix also reported the armaments needed for his program (A. G.I., Guad., 276, Croix to Gálvez, No. 202, Chihuahua, May 1, 1778).
[116] Rubí, *Dictámenes*, ¶ 11. See also, below, footnote 118.

THE ADMINISTRATION OF CROIX

ing the presidio of El Paso south to Carrizal. El Paso itself could be adequately protected by a militia organized there, and the post at Robledo could be established with some soldiers from Santa Fe and settlers from El Paso.[117] The presidio at Carrizal was set up in 1773, but the militia units in El Paso were still in an unsatisfactory condition when Croix assumed command and nothing had been done toward establishing Robledo.[118]

With the projected campaign in mind, Croix called a council of war in July, 1778, to complete the work proposed by Rubí and commanded by the king. Since Anza was leaving Chihuahua after this meeting to assume his post as governor of New Mexico, the council recommended that he complete the militia organization of El Paso and examine the possibilities of a post at Robledo.[119] In September Anza placed the El Paso militia on a footing of two companies of forty-six Spaniards and thirty Indians, and forty-seven Spaniards and thirty Indians respectively.[120] In regard to Robledo, having reconnoitered the spot, Anza advised against the site as insecure from Indian attack and inadequate for the support of a settlement. In its place he suggested the abandoned pueblo of Socorro. Croix considered this not authorized by the king's instructions and concluded in the end to leave at their post the presidials supposed to be detached from Santa Fe and keep the settlers at El Paso to strengthen that settlement.[121]

With the work of the councils over by the end of July, Croix devoted himself to the program decided upon in the juntas, and particularly to the defense of New Vizcaya before he should leave for Sonora. By the following March, 1779, success was attending the policy of alliance, war, and peace. In Texas the nations of the north made peace with the authori-

[117] *Ibid.*, ¶ 11.
[118] Alfred B. Thomas (ed.), "Antonio de Bonilla and Spanish Plans for the Defense of New Mexico, 1772–1778," in *New Spain and the Anglo-American West* (Lancaster, Pennsylvania, 1932) I, 189, ¶ 26.
[119] *Ibid.*, 187, note 24.
[120] *Ibid.*, 187. See also A.G.I., Guad., Croix to Gálvez, No. 298, Chihuahua, October 23, 1778.
[121] *Ibid.*, 188. Croix to Gálvez, No. 236, has the proceedings of this council of war. See above, page 36, footnote 108.

HISTORICAL INTRODUCTION

ties and dissolved their alliance with the Comanche.[122] Plans were made for a campaign against the Carancaguacas.[123] The Xarame offered submission.[124] In Coahuila the separation of the Lipan from the Mescaleros progressed, and the Lipan themselves were grievously attacked by the Indians of the North. In spite of this favorable beginning, Croix felt that Coahuila was still seriously affected by past attacks.[125] In New Vizcaya, the attacks were continuing, but the Chafalote, Natagée and Mescaleros had asked for peace at the frontier posts.[126] In Sonora the forces sent Anza had succeeded in a temporary control of the Seri, though the Gila were still a menace.[127]

The most satisfactory aspect of the program was Croix's success in raising by one way and another an increase in troops for practically all the presidios. The force was a lightly armed troop from his own provinces which provided an increase of nineteen men for each presidio except Santa Fe, which had added thirty-five; San Antonio, thirty-four; and Sonora, which received an additional 120 raised by the viceroy under Croix's pressure at the time of the Seri revolt. In all, the force totaled 580.[128] For these new recruits, Croix had distributed throughout the presidios a handbook on penal laws and instructions to officers for the training of the new troops in maneuvers and handling of weapons. In order to check up on the results and direct improvements, he designated certain presidial captains to conduct inspections in all the presidios.[129]

---

[122] Croix to Gálvez, No. 3, ¶ 7. See above, page 11, footnote 10.
[123] *Ibid.*, ¶ 9.
[124] *Ibid.*, ¶ 10.
[125] *Ibid.*, ¶ 17. See also A.G.I., Guad., 270, Croix to Gálvez, No. 337, Chihuahua, January 23, 1779.
[126] *Ibid.*, ¶ 30.
[127] *Ibid.*, ¶ 32.
[128] *Ibid.*, ¶ 37–40. The plan for the distribution of the troops is in A.G.I., Guad., 276, Croix to Gálvez, No. 171, Chihuahua, April 3, 1778. For New Mexico, Croix originally proposed an increase of thirty-eight troops and two officers (A.G.I., 103–4–18, Croix to Gálvez, Valle de Santa Rosa, February 15, 1778). The report of Mendinueta, November 3, 1778, is translated. See below, page 20, footnote 36.
[129] See above, page 11, footnote 10. Croix to Gálvez, No. 3, ¶ 450–52.

THE ADMINISTRATION OF CROIX

In New Vizcaya Croix strove to create a militia. To secure funds he levied upon the population an excise tax and asked for voluntary donations. The results exceeded his expectations so that he estimated more than one hundred thousand pesos would be available before he left for Sonora. This burden had not resulted in the slightest move to petition the government although he evidently antagonized the wealthy Creoles. He reported to Gálvez: "In Mexico there are some wealthy subjects who owning the most valuable haciendas in New Vizcaya cause well known injuries to the population of the province and serious prejudice to the rest of the king's vassals. It can be that these owners have not been shown their real interests so that it is not strange that my measures regarding militias should occasion them disgust. . . ."[130]

From New Mexico, Texas, and Coahuila he expected little, assuming some financial aid would be necessary to organize the militias there.[131] In general while conditions had not improved, they had not worsened. To guarantee their future, he again implored Gálvez for two thousand men: "I have spoken of the impossibility of keeping up the defense of that frontier, so extensive, with the small number of troops that are stationed there. The mismanaged government, the lack of observance of the Articles of the Regulation; the corrupt, greedy management of the business affairs, the lack of instruction, discipline, the vices, confusions and extravagances have put them in a state of uselessness. Lastly, with reference to the panic and terror that the hostility of the Indian enemy has caused these inhabitants, I beg your excellency the help of two thousand men . . . All this I have proved and substantiated with . . . testimonies of facts. . . ."[132]

If these reënforcements were not forthcoming, he concluded, he would be forced to reduce his operations to a defensive war that would threaten greater decadence, since the present force was unable to guard the key points on the frontier and punish attackers, while the Indians, encouraged by

[130] *Ibid.*, ¶ 54, 59.
[131] *Ibid.*, ¶ 63. See below, page 24, footnote 58.
[132] *Ibid.*, ¶ 77–80.

HISTORICAL INTRODUCTION

these signs of weakness, would become even bolder.[133] The only hope of improving the provinces and controlling the savages was offensive warfare, athough even that might not guarantee results until certain defects among the frontier officials were corrected. Reform at this point promised difficulties:

"The first is the lack of good officers .... there are very few who comply with their obligation and also very few who give any hope of improving their behavior and conduct. They openly embrace all the abominable excesses of drunkenness, luxury, gambling and greed, but under cover and away from the forts, vices have a free rein. This sets a bad example for the troop. They do not observe orders, hide the truth so that from their reports it is not possible to appraise either favorable or adverse news, nor is it possible to take a stand against this without hazarding authority ... With all these faults I see myself forced to suffer and even to be courteous to the good and bad alike, to the former because it is just and to the latter because promotion may correct his habits and because I have no others to whom to turn."[134]

In New Vizcaya, also, Croix initiated his policy of constructing new settlements. The first, San Juan Nepomuceno, in the region known as Chavarria, got under way in the latter part of 1778.[135] To protect it, the presidio of San Buenaventura was moved to the region, a transfer in fact demanded by the presidio's force and the chaplain who protested that he had scruples about baptizing with the putrid water available there. Moreover, Croix pointed out that the new presidio would not alter the line but make defense easier, protect the population of the valley of San Buenaventura better, and it would be able to assist, if necessary, the presidio projected for the valley of Casas Grandes and yet be within touch of Janos and Carrizal.[136]

On April 26, with New Vizcaya organized, Croix advised

[133] *Ibid.*, ¶ 84–90.
[134] *Ibid.*, ¶ 96–97.
[135] *Ibid.*, ¶ 65.
[136] A.G.I., Guad., 275, Croix to Gálvez, No. 297, Chihuahua, October 23, 1778, 1–2. See below, page 55, footnote 174.

THE ADMINISTRATION OF CROIX

Gálvez of his plans for an early departure for Sonora.[137] However, early in May he fell sick.[138] Shortly thereafter he moved his headquarters to the Pueblo de Nombre de Dios, some twenty leagues from Chihuahua, in the hope that the thermal baths there would relieve his attack. However, for a time he steadily became worse until paralysis rendered useless both his hands and arms. Convinced that death was approaching, Croix received the holy sacraments and drew up a statement to enable his auditor, Pedro Galindo y Navarro, and Antonio de Bonilla, the secretary, to certify his signature made by a stamp until he should recover, or in case of death, until a successor, not provided for in his instructions, should take over.[139] From the symptoms reported by his attending physician, Dr. Santiago Augier, Croix seemed to be suffering from lead poisoning complicated by malarial attacks.[140] Fortune favored him so that by the end of August, although still without complete use of his arms, he believed he would be able to travel by October.

In the midst of his convalescence at Nombre de Dios, Croix received a major setback in his broad plans to relieve the province, when a royal order, dated February 20, 1779, arrived directing him to avoid open war with the Indians wherever possible and resort to suave and gentle means of winning them to royal allegiance.[141] With no choice but to obey, Croix im-

[137] A.G.I., Guad., 267, Croix to Gálvez, No. 386, Chihuahua, April 26, 1778.
[138] A.G.I., Guad., 267, Croix to Gálvez, No. 394, Pueblo de Nombre de Dios, June 23, 1779.
[139] A.G.I., Guad., 267, Croix to Gálvez, No. 404, Pueblo de Nombre de Dios, July 23, 1779.
[140] *Ibid.*, 9–10, has the physician's report, who certified in part as follows: «Dn. Santiago Augier, Doctor en medicina, y cirujia, por la universidád de Montpellér, ... certifico ... que ... el Dn. Teodoro de Croix ... se halla ... sin impedimento alg.no ... y unicamente le assiste el de no poder escrivir, y firmar de su Propio Puño, nacido de una perlesia producida de resultas de un dolor colico de los Pintores Oplumberos, que ha padecido durante un par de meses seguidos, y que ha sido complicado, aunq.e contra lo ordinario el principio de una calentura Erratica, seguida p.r una doble terciana, y terminada p.r una Fiebre depuratoria, laqual privacion de movimiento, segun anuncia su convalecencia ... Doy la pres.te que firmo en la mision de Nombre de Dios, á 8 de Julio de 1779. D. or Santiago Augier.»
[141] Archivo de San Francisco el Grande, Vol. 33, XI, 1779, 33–39 (University of Texas Library. Copia de Rl. orden de S. M. comunicada por el Exmo. Sor. Dn. José de Gálvez á el Sor Comandante Gral. Don Teodoro de Croix... El Pardo, February 20, 1779).

HISTORICAL INTRODUCTION

mediately dispatched letters to the governors of Texas, Sonora, Coahuila, and New Mexico commanding compliance with the royal wish. Replying to Gálvez, he intimated his disappointment, but still hoped that the two thousand men requested could be sent him as they would be sorely needed for defensive purposes while he was attempting to persuade the Indians to give over their attacks and settle down near the presidios and frontier towns.[142]

With a heavy heart at the prospect of reorganizing his whole program, Croix left Chihuahua on September 30 for his future capital at Arizpe, Sonora. If he was comforted by the thought that the king might grant his request at last for reënforcements, he was soon to suffer his greatest disappointment. Somewhere along the road to Arizpe, a messenger overtook him with a letter from Gálvez announcing that Spain had declared war upon England on June 21. Realizing the empire's necessity for troops to support Bérnardo de Gálvez in the reconquest of Florida and to protect the Gulf coast and Caribbean possessions, Croix immediately withdrew his request for the two thousand men.[143]

Arrived in Arizpe on November 13, via Janos and the *camino real* that ran west through Fronteras, he was received in the cathedral with ceremonies befitting his high rank.[144] Establishing himself in one of the larger residences,[145] he threw himself into the task of revising his program, the two main pillars of which, offensive war and reënforcements, were now sacrificed to meet the exigencies imposed by the English

---

[142] Harvard College Library, Sparks Mss. 98 (III) Croix to Gálvez, No. 405, Pueblos de Nombre de Dios, July 23, 1779.

[143] Croix, General Report, 1782, ¶ 17–18.

[144] Bancroft Library, University of California, Bancroft Ms. 57326. Diario del ... Mascaró gives Croix route to Arispe; regarding the ceremonial, see Archivo de la Iglesia de Arispe, Sonora Mexico, No. 5. Ceremonial para el recivimto. de Sres. Comandtes. Grales. y la procede una real declaración sobre lo mismo. The King, Aranjuez, February – 1794. This document indicating the ceremonial in use for Nava refers to the fact that Croix had altered the usual form on his arrival; just how is not stated. Shortly after his arrival in Arispe, Croix received news of his raise in rank to that of field marshal, the royal order dated Aranjuez, June 24, 1779, A.G.I., Guad., 267, Croix to Gálvez, No. 481, Arispe, February 23, 1780, in which Croix returns his thanks.

[145] The writer on a visit to Arispe was shown a large residential building which local tradition reports was Croix's headquarters.

THE ADMINISTRATION OF CROIX

war and the king's new humanitarian, but economical, policy of war solely for defense.

NEW PEACE POLICY AND REORGANIZATION OF THE PRESIDIAL LINE

New Peace Policy

THE basic problem for Croix under the new dispensation was that of reorganizing the presidial line and buttressing it with reforms within the presidios and a defensive line of military settlements. However, he immediately took steps to seek peace in the provinces with the various frontier groups. In Texas he found himself handicapped by the untimely death of Athanaze de Mézières, who had been designated to persuade the Comanche into an alliance.[146] These Indians and the Indians of the North were becoming restless from strictures on the Louisiana barter in hides, riding horses, and captives, in exchange for guns, powder, balls, knives, hatchets, mirrors, vermilion, and other trinkets. Moreover the authorities in Texas feared their possible alliance with the Karankawa cannibals along the coast. The hostility of the Comanche underlay a series of terrible raids that depopulated cattle ranches and farms and drove the settlers into the larger towns. The only bright spot in Texas was the terrific attack of the Comanche upon the Lipan which drove that tribe to seek peace with the Spaniards in Texas and Coahuila.[147]

To meet the onslaught upon Texas, Croix ordered its governor, Cabello, to overlook these infractions to induce the Comanche to sign a peace treaty and attempt to break up the alliance between them and the other Indians of the North and the Taguacanas.[148] The governor accordingly dispatched Don Nicolas de la Matte to visit the Taguacanas and Taovayas. However, Croix reported to Gálvez that the only means of keeping the Comanche and the Indians of the North in peace was to guarantee the supply of goods they were accus-

[146] See above, page 35, footnote 105.
[147] See below, Croix, General Report, 1781, pages 72–76, ¶ 1–10.
[148] *Ibid.*, pages 75–80, ¶ 10–27.

HISTORICAL INTRODUCTION

tomed to get from Louisiana. Otherwise, he added, they would become allies of the English traders who were already finding their way across the Mississippi and along the Red River.[149]

The objective of Croix's policy of winning over the Comanche rested with Governor Anza of New Mexico. In 1779, soon after entering upon office, Anza conceived the idea of invading and attacking the Comanche in their country northeast of New Mexico. His plan of campaign, brilliantly conceived and executed, resulted in 1779 in the first crushing defeat of these Indians at Spanish hands. Carried out in two major actions, the attack occurred near Pueblo, Colorado, of today. After this battle the Comanche came to Santa Fe to seek peace. However, this objective was not completely achieved to the satisfaction of both Comanche and Spaniard until 1786, three years after Croix had left the command of the interior provinces.[150]

In Coahuila Croix, having found it impossible to carry out the general campaign against the Lipan and Mescaleros, directed his energies to establishing peace with these two powerful Apache groups. By the spring of 1780 he had made a treaty with the Mescaleros and had laid plans to persuade them to settle in pueblos near the frontier settlements.[151] This measure, essentially an alliance between the Mescaleros and the Spaniards, coincided with the onslaught of the Comanche upon the Lipan in Texas in the fall of 1779, so that the latter, confused by the two developments, hastened to seek peace with the Spaniards also.[152] They were also doubtless influenced by the successful campaigns of the governor of Coahuila, Don Juan Ugalde, who utilized Mescalero allies to attack the Lipan in that province. In any event, by the spring of 1780, peace treaties were concluded with the Lipan, which temporarily relieved the pressure of hostility on Coahuila.

In New Vizcaya, with the Mescalero peace assuring for the time being some protection to the frontier establishments,

---

[149] *Ibid.*, page 81, ¶ 29.
[150] Thomas, *Forgotten Frontiers*, 57–83.
[151] See below, Croix, General Report, 1781, page 96, ¶ 88.
[152] *Ibid.*, page 91, ¶ 68.

THE ADMINISTRATION OF CROIX

Croix brought to a successful conclusion his program for the erection of the military settlements behind the frontier presidios. The settlement of the towns begun in October, 1779, was largely completed by the following May. From Namiquipa to Coyamé 274 officers, sergeants, and soldiers, with their families, had been established. In all of them the construction of defenses had been begun, and grain, hay, oats, and other crops had been planted and grown. Between Janos and San Elezario 130 men were patrolling the frontier, while provincial pickets were established at El Parage and Cerrogordo to assure safety on the highway from the Rio de Nazas to Chihuahua.[153]

In Sonora Croix found a very complicated situation. The Seri, who had risen in revolt in 1777, soon after he had assumed command of his duties, had been with great difficulty put down by Anza, who had been appointed to the position of military governor of the province by Croix. When Anza attended the council of war in Chihuahua in 1779, he made it plain that the Seri and other rebellious tribes were by no means safely under control, and that they had understandings with the Gila Apache, who attacked from the north and who also in turn were allied with the Navajo in New Mexico. Added to the difficulties of preserving the existence of the province, was the unfortunate location of the presidios of Fronteras in the canyon of San Bernardino and Tubac at Tupson. Besides the pressing need of remedying these conditions, Croix was under obligation to provide adequate protection to the route opened up between Sonora and California by Anza in 1776 along the Gila River, the very heart of the Gila Apache country.[154]

Reorganization of the Presidial Line

Approaching the problem of reorganizing the presidial line, Croix conceived the elements as (1) rearranging the line to make the presidios more effective; (2) buttressing them with

[153] *Ibid.*, pages 116–21, ¶ 166–84. See also A.G.I., Guad., 278, Croix to Gálvez, No. 520, Arispe, May 23, 1780.

[154] See below, Croix, General Report, 1781, pages 133–41, ¶ 228–66.

HISTORICAL INTRODUCTION

a secondary line of frontier settlements from which militia could be drawn to support military action and provide food supplies for the presidios; (3) protecting the presidial horseherds from Indian raids; and (4) making needed reforms in the internal administration of the presidios.

Upon the basis of his study in Mexico, his long journey through the frontier provinces, and the investigations of the three councils of war, Croix analyzed the weaknesses in the presidial line established by O'Conor. In all, these comprised seventeen presidios located approximately equidistant from each other from Texas to Sonora. In the latter province there were: Altar, Tubac, Terrenate, and Fronteras; in New Vizcaya, Janos, San Buenaventura, Carrizal, San Elezario, El Príncipe, La Junta de los Rios Conchos y Norte, and San Carlos; in Coahuila, San Saba, Babia, Aguaverde, Monclova, San Juan Bautista del Rio Grande, and Bejar, at San Antonio, Texas.[155]

In Sonora, Croix sensed the error in moving Tubac to Tucson, located in a corner of the province where it could not protect the settlements from the Seri, Pima, or Apache, nor extend aid to Santa Cruz, that is, Terrenate. This post, in a good position to defend the province, was, because of its distance from its neighbors, exposed to Indian attack which had taken a large toll of lives. The moving of Fronteras to the canyon of San Bernardino was particularly unfortunate, since the presidio could not protect the frontier, was exposed on all sides to attack, and could not communicate readily with its neighbors, Janos, as mountainous territory intervened. In Fronteras, on the other hand, was a valley that produced good crops, supported herds, and could serve as a base for operations against the Apache. The result was that the valley of Fronteras was losing its settlers, while a defenseless San Bernardino was un-

---

[155] The map of the frontier made by Rubí's engineer La Fora shows the location of these posts. See Bolton, *Guide to the Materials for the History of the United States in the Principal Archives of Mexico* (Washington, 1913), item No. 1138, p. 365. Another copy is in the Departmento de la Guerra, Madrid. Photostatic copies may be found in the Library of Congress, Manuscript Division, and in the Bancroft Library, University of California, Berkeley. For further details see Thomas, *Forgotten Frontiers*, note 4, p. 371.

able to attract them. Finally, the arrangements for the security of Sonora had been delayed by the discovery of a route to California by Anza in 1774, which had necessitated finding a new frontier line along the Gila to the Colorado. Croix therefore found Sonora in grave danger of collapsing under the raids of the Apache from the north and uprisings among the Seri and others in the interior, while the presidios established were failing to offer a defense against either.[156]

In New Vizcaya the presidio of Janos was the best located on the line for defensive purposes. San Buenaventura had been moved to Velarde, but had been returned to its original and better location in the valley of its name where abundant food supplies were being developed for itself, Janos, and Carrizal. Carrizal had been satisfactorily occupied as a result of the transfer of the presidial company from El Paso. San Elezario was well placed. However, the presidio of El Príncipe, which had been added by O'Conor to divide the distance of eighty leagues between San Elezario and the presidio of Las Juntas, was a serious error. It was poorly situated to ward off Indian invasion into New Vizcaya, had inadequate resources in its neighborhood to support a settlement, and, located in a deep canyon, was unable to give or receive assistance when needed in coöperation with Las Juntas and San Elezario. The presidio of Las Juntas, at the mouth of the Rio Conchos where it flowed into the Rio Grande, was very useful in defending the province and its own neighboring missions, in gathering forces for campaigns against the eastern Apache, and in communicating with Coahuila. Farther down stream was the presidio of San Carlos which had been transferred from Cerrogordo, far within the province. Its position resembled that of El Príncipe, besides having the added disadvantage of being unable to develop, for lack of good land, a supporting settlement.[157]

In Coahuila there were three presidios useless for adequate defense. The first, in the Big Bend region, was the presidio of

[156] Croix, General Report, 1780, ¶ 518–23.
[157] *Ibid.*, ¶ 24–29.

HISTORICAL INTRODUCTION

San Saba.[158] The most isolated garrison on the line, it could hardly provide for its own defense, lacked adequate pasturage for its horse herd, and had failed as a base for missionary conversion of the Apache. Equally hopeless was the situation of La Babia, far up a canyon, surrounded by mountains, unable to lend or receive assistance, and offering absolutely no impediment to the Apache, who easily found their way around it among the canyons and into the provinces of both New Vizcaya and Coahuila. On the eastern slope of the northern Coahuila mountains was the presidio of Aguaverde, which had been moved there from the valley of Santa Rosa. Its fault was that the Mescaleros there were peaceful, that the abandonment of the Santa Rosa valley exposed it to attack from the Apache coming in from the west, and finally, nearby was the presidio of Monclova. The removal of the presidio of Monclova from Monclova, the capital of the province, exposed that city and its nearby haciendas and settlements to attack. San Juan Bautista on the Rio Grande, near present Guerrero, was, in Croix's opinion, like Janos, excellently situated. It served its purpose of defending the frontier here from invasion and acted as an important link in the communication with Texas.[159]

Viewing New Vizcaya and Coahuila together, Croix concluded that the preisdios of El Príncipe, San Carlos, San Saba, La Babia, and Aguaverde were ineffectual since the Lipan and Mescaleros could find their way around them and attack the two provinces far within. Indian raids were unimpeded since towns and valleys, from which the presidios were withdrawn to be moved to their isolated posts, were exposed to attack and therefore gradually abandoned.[160]

With the weaknesses of the presidial line made clear, Croix proceeded to put into effect the necessary measures to eliminate these and strengthen the provinces in general. Sonora, the key province in relation to New Mexico, New Vizcaya, and California, was a primary object of Croix's concern. Soon after his assumption to office, he appointed as commander of

[158] *Ibid.*, ¶ 30. [159] *Ibid.*, ¶ 29–35. [160] *Ibid.*, ¶ 59–68, 70–73.

the armed forces Anza, who promptly quelled the Seri revolt. But at the Chihuahua councils, Anza had warned of the precarious condition of Sonora so that with his transfer to New Mexico, Croix fell back upon the able governor of Coahuila, Don Jacobo Ugarte y Loyola, to act as military governor in place of Tueros, who had relieved Anza.[161] Ugarte had reached Sonora only a few months before Croix's arrival and consequently had not been able to do more than gather information on the status of the province. With this information before him, Croix concluded that the first objective should be the reorganization of the presidial line to break up the alliance between the Apache and the Seri.[162] Accordingly he commissioned Ugarte to conduct reconnaissances of the frontier terrain to determine the most suitable location for the presidios, and to decide what posts along the Gila and San Pedro rivers would best protect the route to California.[163]

Ugarte submitted with his own, the plans of his engineer, Rocha, who had accompanied him. Guided by additional data from the activities of Bonilla, O'Conor, Father Díaz, and others who had previously made similar investigations, Croix organized what was essentially a new frontier line for Sonora.[164] He established a new presidio at Babispe made up of Opata Indians, Spanish allies in Sonora. He removed the presidio of San Bernardino, that is, Santa Rosa de Coro de Guachi, to Fronteras, and transferred the presidio of Santa Cruz de Terrenate to Las Nutrias. As to Tucson and Altar, he decided to leave them on their sites and proposed to establish a new presidio in La Estancia de Buenavista. Tucson was necessary for keeping open communication with the route to California via the Rio Colorado, while Altar could oppose the invasion of the Apache into that part of Sonora and prevent their alliance with the Seri.[165]

To control these latter Indians, Croix reëstablished the pre-

[161] See below, Croix, General Report, 1781, page 144, ¶ 281.
[162] *Ibid.*, pages 146 f., ¶ 290–92.
[163] *Ibid.*, pages 147–51, ¶ 293–309.
[164] *Ibid.*, pages 150 f., ¶ 307–10.
[165] *Ibid.*, pages 154–216, ¶ 319–508.

sidio at El Pitic, in the west central part of the province. The post originally there had been transferred in 1748 to San Miguel de Orcasitas. When, after the uprising of 1776-77, its return was clearly demanded, Croix dispatched Engineer Manuel Mascaró to reconnoiter the region with a view to constructing the necessary fortifications and laying out the fields for cultivation. For the support of the presidio Croix had settlers gathered and furnished three thousand pesos for the expenses of the establishment.[166]

Croix's instructions to protect the route to California had been given him with the idea of transferring the presidios of Orcasitas and Buenavista to points on the Colorado and Gila rivers. But the Seri uprising and Ugarte's subsequent report, after his reconnaissance of the frontier, that no suitable spots existed either on the Gila or San Pedro Rivers delayed the execution of the idea. In the meantime, Croix established two small settlements at the junction of the Gila and Colorado rivers and transferred from Buenavista, Altar, and Orcasitas a subaltern officer, a sergeant, two corporals, and eighteen men to garrison the spot, accompanied by Father Garcés and Father Juan Díaz. These he provided with utensils, stock, and other necessary tools for cultivating the lands, and with rules and regulations for maintaining proper relations with the Yuma Indians there.[167]

For defense of Sonora Croix placed in the various frontier presidios flying companies and other units, 476 men under the command of Captain Don Joseph de Vildosola, and required him to use his judgment in the execution of defensive and offensive operations. In the interior of the province he established at various points, particularly at Buenavista, El Pitic, and Altar, 172 men.[168] As part of the defensive program and

---

[166] *Ibid.*, pages 216 f., ¶ 508–14.
[167] *Ibid.*, pages 219–23, ¶ 521–35.
[168] *Ibid.*, pages 224–27, ¶ 539–52. Croix also provided for the reviews of the presidios of Tupson, Altar, Orcasitas, and Fronteras: A.G.I., Guad., 277, Croix to Gálvez, No. 592, Arispe, December 23, 1780 (Orcasitas); A.G.I., Guad., 272, Croix to Gálvez, No. 591, Arispe, December 23, 1780 (Altar); A.G.I., Guad., 272, Croix to Gálvez, No. 589, Arispe, December 23, 1780 (Fronteras); A.G.I., Guad., 590, Croix to Gálvez, No. 590, Arispe, December 23, 1780 (Tupson).

THE ADMINISTRATION OF CROIX

for the stimulation of trade and commerce of Sonora, Croix ordered Governor Anza to find a land route between New Mexico and Sonora. It was thus hoped that a convenient pressure upon the Gila Apache from both sides would insure safe communication for the exchange of the products of El Paso and New Mexico, such as wine, vegetables, and other foods, for the silver of Sonora. Anza carried out the expedition in November, 1780, and reached the presidio of Las Nutrias where he met Vildosola. The route so opened, however, was not satisfactory to Croix as it came into Sonora too far to the east. Consequently he ordered a new survey in the hope of shortening the march by 150 leagues. But other matters in New Mexico as well as in Sonora intervened, so that the attempt was not repeated while Croix was in command.[169]

With little difficulty Croix was able to readjust the basis of his program laid down in New Vizcaya before receiving the order for defensive war and before news had reached him of the hostilities with the English. His major reform consisted in creating two divisions of the presidial line. The first included the presidios of Janos, San Buenaventura, and Carrizal, so that with the troops called the Flying Corps, these three could patrol constantly the intervening areas between them. South of Janos he established a garrison in the valley of Casas Grandes. Together the four units amounted to 335 men, the larger part of which could be assembled in less than thirty-six hours at a central point.[170]

The second division of the line included the presidio of San Elezario and the settlement of El Paso, in conjunction with Carrizal. There the combined forces amounted to 199 men who could, with the Flying Corps, patrol the areas intervening between them, proceed when necessary against the Apache in the nearby mountains, and provide escort for the caravans to and from New Mexico.[171] Croix also continued his program of developing local militias.[172]

[169] Thomas, *Forgotten Frontiers*, 30–41.
[170] Croix, General Report, 1780, ¶ 127–31. Flying Corps were small detachments of mobile, lightly armed and mounted troops.
[171] *Ibid.*, ¶ 132–34.
[172] *Ibid.*, ¶ 114–22.

HISTORICAL INTRODUCTION

From this point—Carrizal—to Coahuila, all the presidios excepting that of Las Juntas were helpless against invasion. He recommended ultimately abandoning San Carlos, San Saba, and La Babia, but delayed action to use them as a base for campaigns projected into the territory of the Mescaleros and Lipan. In Coahuila he ordered the presidio of La Babia transferred to protect the valley of Santa Rosa, and the presidio of Aguaverde to the Villa of San Fernando de Monclova, the capital of the province. This shortened the line in Coahuila, tightened up the defense at critical points, and tied the well-placed presidio of San Juan Bautista into a coördinated plan.[173]

In the second place, as part of this arrangement on the frontier, Croix continued the creation of militia units throughout New Vizcaya and Coahuila, and the erection of a line of military settlements behind the two divisions in the former province and behind the presidial line in Coahuila, with the added feature of providing, in the vast area between Las Juntas and the Coahuila frontier, an extension of the military settlements, west and south of the Bolsón de Mapimí, to run in a huge semicircle from Chihuahua to Cuatro Ciénegas, a short distance west of Monclova.

The militia was to serve a double purpose—to provide the principal defense of the military settlements and to supply the Flying Corps used in conjunction with the presidial patrols. Their creation Croix successfully carried through, except near Saltillo, by persuading the various towns of Coahuila and New Vizcaya, as well as wealthy landowners, to contribute the necessary funds so that with the king, who maintained the presidios, the burden of expense would be divided. The line of settlements also had two functions—a defensive one, and one of providing food supplies for the militia and the troops of the presidios. The first line of military settlements began at Namiquipa, just south of the presidio of San Buenaventura, and extended northeast through the Rancho de Mala Noche, Majalca, Pueblo of San Gerónimo, Hacienda de Ormigas, Chor-

[173] *Ibid.*, ¶ 135–42.

THE ADMINISTRATION OF CROIX

reras, El Pueblito, and El Coymé, where it terminated about eighteen leagues from the presidio of Las Juntas. Thus the frontier line from Janos to San Elezario had its parallel of military settlements, which also supported Las Juntas.[174]

The second line branched off from Chihuahua in a semicircle that began at Dolores and curved southeast through Ancón de Carros, Santa Rita, Guajuquilla, Las Canas, Pelayo, San Juan de Casta, and Calabazillas. From this point it passed in front of Parras and El Saltillo and then turned north toward the Villa of Monclova to end at Cuatro Ciénegas near the valley of Santa Rosa.[175]

In New Mexico, Anza vigorously pushed forward Croix's plan of reorganization. As part of this work Anza had made the well-known Miera map[176] of the province, which carries the information that each town was to have at least twenty families gathered in from the countryside exposed to Apache and Comanche attack. While details are lacking concerning how extensive the reorganization was, there is evidence to indicate that progress was made at Encinal, Albuquerque, Cañada, Taos, and possibly at Ojo Caliente. In Santa Fe, however, Anza's attempt to transfer the Genízaros in the barrio of Analco to the frontiers, probably near Albuquerque, and raze the buildings on the northern side of Santa Fe River, caused some of the settlers to go to Croix in Arizpe. The commander general, apparently convinced of just grievances on the settlers' part, ordered Anza to desist until he had adequate proof that his proposals were justified.[177]

As part of the presidial reorganization, Croix undertook to solve the problem of conserving the soldiers' horses by stabling them. He pointed out that the Indians could easily stampede pastured herds; that it was difficult to get new allotments because of the long distance between the presidios and the ranges in the interior of Mexico; that with the horse herd

[174] *Ibid.*, ¶ 143–45. Croix also took steps to establish a new town at Janos (A.G.I., Guad., 275, Croix to Gálvez, No. 330, Chihuahua, December 28, 1778).
[175] *Ibid.*, ¶ 146–49. For Croix's general reports on the militia, see A.G.I., Guad., 281, Croix to Gálvez, No. 595, Arispe, January 23, 1781.
[176] Miera's map is published in Thomas, *Forgotten Frontiers,* facing p. 87.
[177] *Ibid.,* note 59, 379–80.

gone, the presidial forces on foot could not carry on their frontier duties; and that frequently, because of this loss, some forces were inactive for periods of from three to six months. He contended further that the practice of putting them out to pasture made the animals in many cases unfit for duty as the forage was insufficient to maintain their strength.[178]

To remedy this condition, Croix proposed the construction of stables as part of the presidial establishment. In this way, by extending the walls of the presidio to include a large enclosure, haylofts and granaries could be built in the upper part and the horses kept within the corral. During the spring they could be pastured by day to feed and in winter months they could be kept strong and healthy on hay, oats, and other dry feed. Furthermore, he recommended the substitution, for the undoubtedly picturesque customs of racing, bullfighting, and other useless activities, of regular cavalry maneuvers and the use of the horses in patrolling the open lands between the presidios to condition the horses for campaigns.[179]

In order to test his idea, Croix dispatched a questionnaire to the various military leaders of the provinces, governors, captains of presidios, and even civilians experienced with frontier conditions. In his query, Croix tried to impress upon the recipients that the unusually large number of animals employed in a typical campaign was unnecessary. Ordinarily, he stated, one hundred men used six horses and two or three mules apiece to ride, transport their equipment, and carry food supplies. Such a large body made almost impossible any surprise attack upon the Indians in their own territory. Even if such a raid upon the rancheria were not disputed, the Indians usually circled around and stampeded the horse herd.[180]

As part of this military weakness, Croix also criticized the use of the long, heavy, four or six ply leather coats which the presidials wore as a protection against arrows and lances. A

---

[178] Croix, General Report, 1780, 74–90. See also, Croix, General Report, 1782, ¶ 393, Part I, items 1–20. For Croix's investigation of the problem see A.G.I., Guad., 517, Croix to Gálvez, No. 737, Arispe, April 23, 1782.
[179] Croix, General Report, 1782, ¶ 393, Part II, items, 1–35.
[180] *Ibid.*, ¶ 393.

soldier's campaign equipment, which consisted of a gun, sword, lance, and a bulky three or four ply leather coat, also drew his criticism. Urging imitation of the lightly-equipped and fast-moving Indian, he felt that the gun and the sword would always be superior to the enemy's arrows and lances, whereas the heavy coats were more frequently a shroud than a protection.[181] Croix's main conclusions from these facts were that the number of horses in the presidial horse herds should be radically reduced; that with animals well fed and well cared for, and the soldiery lightly equipped, campaigns could be made more rapidly, and surprise could be more successfully utilized.

Twenty-one replies in answer to the questionnaire found ten in agreement and eleven opposed to the reform.[182] The main contention of the opposition was that the desert condition of the country demanded liberal changes of mounts on extensive campaigns and correspondingly large allotments of horses. In his comment to Gálvez, Croix easily disposed of this objection by pointing out sensibly that a small number of horses would not eat so much grass around the various oases in the desert. Thus a few animals well fed would be vastly more useful on campaign than a huge body of horses half-starved before the enemy was even located.[183] The real reason for the opposition to reducing the horse herds was not concealed from Croix, namely, that most of the leading frontier figures to whom the questionnaire was addressed were conducting a profitable business by supplying horses to the presidios through arrangements with ranch owners farther within Mexico. The constant losses to the enemy created a large and steady demand for the animals with fortunes entailed in the trade.

To obviate the abuses in the paymaster's office, Croix proposed a system of adjutant paymasters. Under the prevailing system the paymaster was absent from the presidio from three to six months each year to gather provisions and to collect the

[181] *Ibid.*, ¶ 38–49.
[182] *Ibid.*, ¶ 395.
[183] Croix to Gálvez, No. 737. See above, page 56, footnote 178.

appropriation at the remote centers where the money was kept. The funds for New Mexico and New Vizcaya were maintained at Chihuahua, those for Coahuila and Texas at San Luís Potosí, and those of Sonora at Los Alamos. During the absence of the paymaster the supplies of the presidio became disordered; frequently his cashier proved dishonest. The paymaster hardly had time to attend to the detail of his office on his return, making out reports, and settling the accounts for the individual soldier. As a result the records of the office were so disorganized that no check could be made upon the paymaster, and finally, willingly or not, he himself became involved with merchants who exploited him.

As a remedy, Croix proposed that an adjutant paymaster always remain at the presidio. Moreover, Croix suggested that the goods bought by the paymaster be strictly checked on his return against previously compiled lists of the garrison and family heads. Unfortunately, the recommendations affecting stabling the horses and reorganization of the paymasters' office did not reach the Council of the Indies until late in 1782, and Croix was transferred to Peru before the Council had completed its study of the proposal. Subsequent alterations in the status of the commander general's office placed it under the viceroy, who delayed further the consideration of the adjutant-paymaster project.[184]

DISAPPOINTMENTS AND ACHIEVEMENTS
1781–1783

BY the end of 1781 Croix had reorganized the defense forces of the frontier and had taken steps to insure the protection of the route to California. The maturing of his plans for the improvement of internal presidial administration coincided with the marked success of his campaign against the Indians of New Mexico, Sonora, and New Vizcaya. On the whole the outlook for the immediate future was bright.

[184] Croix, General Report, 1782, ¶ 50-369.

DISAPPOINTMENTS AND ACHIEVEMENTS

However, the last year and a half of his administration was destined to be filled with events that, while they did not fundamentally alter his program, marred the record of success that had previously accompanied his efforts.

The first blow fell with the arrival of news in Arizpe that the small garrison and settlement on the Rio Colorado had been massacred in an uprising of the Yuma. The cause of the unhappy affair Croix attributed primarily to the unfortunate misrepresentation of the resources of the spot made by Anza and Father Garcés in their reports to Bucareli.[185] The immediate reasons arose out of the failure of the Rio Colorado officers to establish satisfactory relations with the Yuma, and out of the inability of Croix adequately to provide a sufficiently strong presidial force to guarantee the safety of the settlement. This last condition, of course, is to be considered, as Croix considered it, in the light of the total demands for adequate protection of a frontier that extended almost two thousand miles, and in the necessity the king placed upon Croix of keeping expenses at a minimum.

The heart of the trouble was probably the fault of the Spaniards themselves who occupied the lands of the Yuma on the Colorado. "The Spanish paid small regard to the rights of the natives in allotting lands, and their cattle ruined the Yuma crops. When provisions were exhausted, the Yuma refused to supply them, unless at exorbitant prices, and the Chiefs of the Yuma, even Palma, began to incite the people against the settlers."[186] Garcés himself, in an excess of religious fervor, undertook to prevent the Yuma's war with a neighboring tribe. The missionaries urged upon Croix a new departure in colony making, namely, permitting the missionaries, soldiers, settlers, and Indians to live in close association. This departure both Díaz and Garcés assured Croix would succeed, as the Yuma were accustomed to individual property in land![187] The last straw was the arrival at the Colorado settlements of the Rivera expedition on its way to California. To condition his horses be-

[185] Chapman, *op. cit.*, 413. See below, page 220, footnote 139.
[186] Chapman, *op. cit.*, 142.
[187] *Ibid.*, 408–9.

fore the arduous trip across the desert, Rivera had permitted both his horses and cattle to forage on the Yuma's land. The animals had destroyed the mesquite plants, which were so important a source of food to the Yuma.[188] In July the Yuma rose, killed Rivera and his men, raided the two settlements, and murdered Fathers Garcés and Barreneche.[189]

In Coahuila Croix was faced with a doubly unpleasant sitution. Early in 1782 two wealthy Creole landowners, the Marqués de Aguayo and Don Lucas de Lasaga, living in Mexico but owning extensive haciendas in the neighborhood of Parras and Saltillo, made strong representations to the king to the effect that Croix was keeping the troops of the frontier inactive, and that as a result the Indians were making devastating raids upon their properties. They further complained that during the time of O'Conor that official had been very industrious in his defense of the frontier and their losses correspondingly less.

Gálvez sent Croix a summary of the charges and a royal order to take the offensive against the Indians. Croix easily answered the objections raised by the two Creoles and pointed out that he had anticipated the royal order by commanding his subordinate in both New Vizcaya and Coahuila to engage the savages. As to the record of O'Conor, Croix referred to extensive Indian raids in the very area that the Marqués and Lasaga claimed were so peaceful. And he bluntly stated that since this was true, the reports of these massacres and raids in O'Conor's time had perhaps not been sent to the king with the same veracity which had distinguished his own accounts of these things. What really furthered Indian raids in this area, Croix further demonstrated, was that the Marqués and Lasaga had made it a point of honor to resist the imposition of taxes that he had devised for the purpose of creating a flying squadron to protect Parras and its vicinity. As to his own measures to defend the area to minimize this failure of the Marqués and Lasaga, he had several months before the arrival of the royal order commanding offensive warfare ordered

[188] *Ibid.*, 413.   [189] *Ibid.*, 413. See below, page 128, footnote 69.

DISAPPOINTMENTS AND ACHIEVEMENTS

the troop commanders in both New Vizcaya and Coahuila to proceed against the Apache.[190]

In the second place, the governor of Coahuila, Don Juan Ugalde, who had evinced his opposition to Croix's program of keeping the horse herds of the presidios in stable, had initiated a series of campaigns in the fall of 1782, the failure of which demonstrated the truth of all Croix's contentions, namely, that it was impracticable to operate in the mountains with a large horse herd, that the animals became incapacitated for any further duty, that the settlements were exposed to Indian attack during the absence of the troop, and that the Indians were emboldened by their success in eluding attack. In spite of these considerations Ugalde had invaded the Bolsón de Mapimí with a detachment of 213 men, including officers and an auxiliary force of Lipan. After six months of hard campaigning the net result was the capture of one warrior and ten women and children, who were coming to make peace, the death of one Mescalero, and the capture of one woman in a rugged place in the mountains of the Sierra del Pino, the death of four others in another engagement in which Ugalde also recovered 154 animals, but with the loss of one soldier and the wounding of six others. In addition the Spanish horse herd was so worn out that Ugalde was forced to ask remounts at the same time he had the temerity to demand of Croix twenty-four horses for each soldier for the next year.[191] In his account of the failure to Gálvez, the annoyed Croix demanded what would be the number of animals incapacitated if Ugalde had twenty-four for each of the two hundred odd men on the campaign just ended! Finally, added to the unfortunate results of the expedition was the fact that while Ugalde was seeking the Apache in one direction, they had entered the province in another to kill and rob in the territory of Mapimí, Cuencamé and San Juan del Rio. Croix intimated strongly to Gálvez that Ugalde would have done better to have devoted his efforts to

[190] Croix to Gálvez, No. 891. See above, page 14, footnote 16.
[191] Ugalde to Croix, Santa Rosa, March 9, 1783, No. 1. Summary of Ugalde's Fourth Campaign, with A.G.I., Guad., 284, Croix to Gálvez, No. 925, Arispe, June 2, 1783.

HISTORICAL INTRODUCTION

protecting the settlements and energetically attacking the invaders where they made their appearance rather than attempting to dislodge them from the Bolsón de Mapimí, where attacks on the Indians had always been of momentary importance.[192]

In view of the results of this campaign and Ugalde's insubordination and negligence in having left the province exposed, Croix ordered the removal of the governor.[193] In April, 1782, he sent Lieutenant Colonel Don Pedro de Tueros to govern Coahuila and coöperate with Commander Inspector Neve in putting the local troops in condition to attack the Apache as commanded by the new royal order.[194]

In the other provinces of the north, Croix was enjoying the success his efforts there could lead him to expect. In New Vizcaya, a Mescalero chieftain, for years a border menace, presented himself, largely due to Ugalde's attacks on the Mescalero rancherias in Coahuila, at El Paso in July, 1782, begging for peace. Croix acceded to his petition with the understanding that he and other Indian chiefs who were responsible for the raids on Mapimí and Cuencamé would surrender. Upon fulfillment of the agreement Croix was able to rid the frontier of 137 Apache, among whom were three principal chieftains, and send them into the interior under guard.[195] This action for the time being ended Indian raids on the Coahuila-New Vizcaya frontier.

In the interior of New Vizcaya Croix saw on the other hand the completion of his primary and secondary lines of defense. Besides the seven presidios, manned with 686 men, he had created the First, Second, Third, and Fourth Flying Companies composed of a total of 564 men. In addition there was the Flying Company of the Villa of Saltillo made up of one

[192] Croix to Gálvez, No. 925, Arispe, June 2, 1783. See above, page 61, footnote 191.

[193] A.G.I., Guad., 282, Croix to Gálvez, No. 835, Arispe, October 7, 1782; and A.G.I., Guad., 283, Croix to Gálvez, No. 851, Arispe, November 4, 1782.

[194] A.G.I., Guad., 283, Croix to Gálvez, No. 849, Arispe, November 4, 1782; A.G.I., Guad., 283, Croix to Gálvez, No. 850, Arispe, November 4, 1782; A.G.I., Guad., 283, Croix to Gálvez, No. 852, Arispe, November 4, 1782.

[195] A.G.I., 105-5-3, Croix to Gálvez, No. 881, Arispe, February 24, 1783. See also A.G.I., Guad., 282, Croix to Gálvez, No. 836, Arispe, October 7, 1782.

DISAPPOINTMENTS AND ACHIEVEMENTS

hundred units, taken from the pickets of Cerrogordo and El Pasage. Thus the soldiers available for the first-line defense of New Vizcaya totaled 1,350. In addition Croix had created the Provincial Militia Corps of New Vizcaya, distributed throughout the province as follows: at San Carlos, two squadrons and seven companies, each containing forty-three men for a total of 301 at Príncipe, three squadrons and ten companies; at Durango, one squadron and three companies; at San Juan Bautista, two squadrons and eight companies; at San Gabriel, one squadron and three companies; at Santa Rosa de Cosiguriachic, two squadrons and six companies; and at Santiago, two squadrons and seven companies. While the total of all the companies is not given except in that of San Carlos, assuming the usual number of forty-three men for each company, the militia units available for defensive purposes would have been 1,892 men, or a total of militiamen and soldiers for the entire province of 3,242 men. To this first line of defense is also to be added the military strength provided in the two cordons of military settlements which Croix established that extended from Namquipa, near San Buenaventura, northeast to a point eighteen leagues from the presidios of Las Juntas, and from Dolores, near Chihuahua, southeast to Quatro Chénegas near the valley of Santa Rosa.[196]

Between 1781 and 1783, Texas and New Mexico presented no special problems to Croix. In Texas, the military forces were concentrated in two presidios, one at San Antonio de Bejar and the other at Bahía del Espíritu Santo, each composed of ninety-six units.[197] While nothing had been done to curb the attacks of the Comanche, the peace established with the Lipan and Mescaleros and in New Vizcaya contributed temporarily to the well-being of the province. The Comanche problem, however, was on the way to solution in New Mexico where Governor Anza, after his victory over that tribe in 1779, had been working toward bringing about peace with these powerful Indians. The results of his work did not ap-

---

[196] A.G.I., Guad., 284, Croix to Gálvez, No. 936, Arispe, June 23, 1783.
[197] *Ibid.*, Estado de las tropas ... provincias de Texas.

pear, however, until 1786, when he signed a treaty with them.[198] Also in New Mexico, Croix had directed Anza to relieve the sufferings of the Moquí Indians who, starving as a result of a prolonged drouth, were moved in large numbers to various pueblos along the Rio Grande during 1781 and 1782.[199]

In Sonora, Croix himself directed the reorganization of the province. After the unfortunate Yuma massacre, a council of war acting upon the reports of various investigators, among them Neve and Ugarte, reported to Gálvez that the banks of the Colorado and Gila did not offer suitable sites for presidios. Consequently the program of extending the frontier to the Gila, projected some ten years before, was now definitely abandoned.[200] In defense of the province Croix had, just before his release from office, established a total of 498 presidials distributed among the six presidios of the province. Besides these he had created the presidial company of Opata Indians at San Miguel de Babispe, a unit composed of eighty-four soldiers, and a presidial company of Pima Indians at La Estancia de San Rafael de Buenavista, located at the pueblo of San Ignacio, amounting also to eighty-four soldiers. Croix further had at his disposal a picket from the regiment of dragoons of Spain, composed of fifty men, and the company of Catalonian volunteers numbering eighty-three.[201]

CONCLUSION

IN comparison with his distinguished contemporaries on the northern frontier, Anza, Bérnardo de Gálvez, de Mézières, and Ugalde, Croix faced a problem continental rather than provincial in character. His achievements, while not so spectacular, were equally significant in buttressing the empire in North America. It is an easy matter, as some have done, to

[198] Thomas, *Forgotten Frontiers*, 57–83.
[199] *Ibid.*, 329–32.
[200] Croix to Gálvez, No. 870. See above, page 59, footnote 185.
[201] Croix to Gálvez, No. 936. See above, page 63, footnote 196.

CONCLUSION

seize an isolated failure, such as the Yuma massacre, and brand Croix as incompetent. It is something else to visualize the difficulties of defending a frontier area of several hundred thousand square miles from uncontrollable Indian groups, with a budget limited by the demands of an empire intercontinental in extent. It is also interesting to dilate upon a Russian "danger," when the nearest representatives of the Czar were floundering along the Alaskan coast. The danger, too, from the English to these interior provinces has been over-emphasized. While it is true some fair-haired sons of England found their way into the wilds of what was later to be Oklahoma, and the Indians of North Texas were casting covetous eyes upon these strangers' beads and bullets, the real problem of that frontier was control of the Indians effected there largely by de Mézières. A half-century later the Mexicans learned to their grief that there was an Anglo-Saxon danger in that sector, but in the late eighteenth century it was remote. Indeed, Bérnardo de Gálvez, operating east of the Mississippi River in 1779, was able to regain Florida from the vaunted English.

The real threat to Spain's northern interior possessions was not an international one; it was the Indian. Croix, to be certain, had letters from Minister Gálvez warning of Russians, but he had only to look out of his window to see the ruins blackened by Apache barbarity. With a choice between imaginary foreigners and real, live Apaches, the practical-minded Croix naturally devoted his energies to the problem that stared him in the face.

Croix's efforts to repair the damage of Indian hostility and two and a quarter centuries of maladministration must be conceded a modicum of recognition. It is true that he had certain definite realities with which to work. In spite of the failure of the authorities in the past to provide adequate defense against Indian invasion, though the possibility of such an achievement is highly doubtful in view of the geographical barriers and the low level of Indian civilization in the area, the genius of Spanish colonization had dotted northern New Spain with cities and towns, introduced extensive mining developments, created a cattle range industry, and extended, by the heroic efforts of the padres, the civilizing work of the Church. In the wake of these European cultural forces flowed trade and commerce, in turn limited by the fundamental factors of geographical and Indian barriers.

With these realities before him, Croix had the imagination and ability to visualize his problem and utilize the resources at hand. Not content with armchair administration he made the gruelling inspection of his vast command. Upon that and his own researches he constructed his program of action. To support it he had the diplomacy and force of character to wring taxes from the unwilling traders and Creole landowners to support his military establishment. The war with the English deprived him of royal funds upon which he had depended, and of the two thousand men he had asked for to buttress his presidial organization. Nonetheless he accepted the reverses cheerfully and worked with the materials under his hands. Thus in New Vizcaya, besides injecting new life into the presidios, he set up patrols between these forts, created a line of military settlements, and organized the militia of New Vizcaya. The results are best seen in the steady mounting of the wealth produced during his administration.[202]

In Sonora he reorganized the presidial line, improving the location of the various posts to make them self-supporting, organized other presidial establishments at Babispe and La Estancia de Buenavista, augmented the militia forces, put down the threat of Seri rebellion, and temporarily staved off the Gila raids. In Coahuila he tightened the defenses of the provinces by a more intelligent distribution of the presidial forces, notably in transferring the useless Babia presidial troops, and in protecting the fertile valley of Santa Rosa. He succeeded in time in making peace, since punitive war was banned, with all the tribes from lower Rio Grande to the Gila country. In Governor Anza he had an administrator who knew how to execute his policy. After Croix had left the command,

[202] A.G.I., Guad., 283, Croix to Gálvez, No. 853, Arispe, November 4, 1782.

CONCLUSION

Anza brought the powerful Comanche into peaceful alliance with the Spaniards and utilized them, with the Ute, in temporarily crushing the Gila in the south.

Over the entire area Croix created a military establishment more extensive than ever before achieved on the northern frontier. From Texas to Sonora 4,686 men, either militia or presidials, were under arms.

Against this successful record was the unfortunate Yuma massacre with the sacrifice of the brave Garcés. Croix's attempts to cure the weaknesses of the paymasters' offices in the presidio and to stable the soldiers' horses reached only the paper stage. But here the cumbersome machinery of Spanish administration moved too slowly to give him the necessary authority before his term of office expired.

The diligence of Croix in the duties of his office is manifest from his enormous correspondence, of which his three extensive reports of 1780, 1781, and 1782 are the most outstanding. Besides the nine hundred-odd communications he dispatched to Gálvez Croix sent out and received an uncounted number of letters to the viceroy; to presidial, militia, and other commandants; to governors, inspectors, subinspectors; church and civil authorities. Together these throw light upon the economic, social, political, and military organization of northern New Spain, upon the relations of the Spaniards and Indians, and upon Indian culture itself. In short, the literary record of Croix is one of the major contributions to western American history in the late eighteenth century. Though his work and its value have heretofore been little appreciated in the history of North America, his king, Charles III, rewarded this faithful servant with his choicest gift—the office of Viceroy of Peru.

THE AFTERMATH

WITH Croix's departure from the frontier, the main lines of his policy were abandoned. His immediate successor, Neve, died within a few months after assuming the office of commander general. José Antonio Regel succeeded him as ad interim commander-general until Jacob Ugarte y Loyola was appointed in 1784. However, in 1785, the authorities in Spain decided to divide the commandancy-general into three districts and return its general administration to the authority of the newly appointed viceroy, Bérnardo de Gálvez, who died in the fall of the following year, 1786. These rapid changes paralyzed the work of Neve, Rengel, and Ugarte in carrying out Croix's policy. Two and a half years later, 1789, the French Revolution in Europe, the threatening interest of the United States in Florida and at the mouth of the Mississippi River, and a controversy with England over Nootka Sound in the north Pacific diverted needed military personnel and funds from the remote frontiers of northern Mexico. Thus the reforms necessary for meeting Indian invasion in Spain's interior provinces of North America, which Croix so laboriously and faithfully had worked out, evaporated in the larger conflicts which eventually destroyed Spain's control everywhere in the new World.

PART II

GENERAL REPORT OF 1781 BY TEODORO DE CROIX

II

Number 8   *341 folios*

My dear Sir: I proposed to your Excellency, under date of April thirtieth last, a general report of the state of these provinces in all their branches. Although I thereupon realized it would be a work necessarily diffuse and prolix, I was convinced of the possibility of compiling and forwarding it complete to your Excellency within a few days. But as I could work on it only at odd times, interrupted repeatedly by more important daily business, and being therefore unable to finish it in the short time which I had planned, it appeared to me better to make the report in sections. In this way only, then, could I fill in the gaps of my reports sent by mails, believed lost or intercepted by the English. This consideration has been the principal purpose of the work indicated above.

I had proposed to divide it into five sections, referring in the first to the particular condition of each province, the most noteworthy occurrences during the time of my government, my decisions, their results, and possible remedial measures distinguishing feasible measures and those of difficult execution.

This first part ought to be, as it is in fact, preliminary to the second, which must be restricted to general considerations of the Department of War, amplifying and clarifying the statements which I made to your Excellency in my letter No. 458 of January 23, '80, concerning the line of presidios, settlements, arrangement of the troops, management of their interests, reduction of their allowance for cavalry, creation of the militia, and the division of the Commandancy-General.[1] There will

[1] See above, page 12, footnote 12.

be set forth in the third, fourth, and fifth, everything else pertaining to missions, treasury, political and economic government, whose branches have the closest relations with that of war. I would have preferred to unite them in one summary, but now it is not possible because time is flying while grave affairs are multiplying in this command. I shall observe the order proposed in the formation and preparation of my reports.

It is certain that these separate remissions offer some inconveniences, since they bring to a head too soon a work incomplete in itself so that no synthesis can be formed, and they are set forth at the risk that the parts following may be digressive, prolix, and wearisome, if the information turns out to be incomplete in the future examination of the papers which vouch for and support it. But as the foundation of the plan is none other than reference simply to the condition in which I took over the provinces, the state in which they are now, and that which I conceive proper to improve their condition, there is no doubt that the superior goodness of your Excellency may deign to overlook the faults and defects of my reports, perceiving the worthy and sincere zeal which actuate them in obeisance to the royal service and with the greatest desire to please your Excellency. Under these considerations I begin the first report.

PROVINCE OF TEXAS

¶ 1.

THIS province consists of an informal villa, two presidios, seven missions, and a shifting population that hardly contains four thousand persons of both sexes and of all ages, who occupy the immense deserted country which reaches from the abandoned presidio of Los Adaes to that of San Antonio de Bejar.[2] It would not be worthy of the name of the

[2] Archivo Historico Nacional, Madrid (hereinafter cited: A.H.N.), Estado, 3883, Croix to Gálvez, No. 265, Chihuahua, September 23, 1778, includes a census of Texas which gives a total of 3103. The totals given by Morfi agree with this census, from which they were undoubtedly taken. His total 3803, is doubt-

province of Texas, or New Philippines, or the strain which its conservation inflicts, if to the excellent resources of its fertile soils, abundant rivers and minerals, there were not added the hope of converting to religion and vassalage the innumerable barbarous nations which inhabit it, and averting the fears arising from the proximity of foreign colonies; the hope of reciprocal benefits with Louisiana, which time can offer; and the necessity of sustaining the weak dominions of Texas as a safeguard to those of Coahuila and New Santander.

¶ 2. For all these considerations, if there is a real remedy for the hostilities which the interior provinces of New Spain suffer from, it must be framed and arranged in my opinion upon Texas. I have looked upon that province always with the greatest attention, and I am justly delighted with the peace and tranquility which that territory enjoyed up to the month of July of last year.

¶ 3. The Indians of the North maintained the peace and carried out in the early months of '79 a vigorous invasion against the Lipan.[3] They were so intimidated that there was left nothing for them to do but to submit to the necessity of living under our protection and favor. They presented themselves humbly and obsequiously to the governor of the province and gave up their robberies and the extensive slaughtering of the wild herds of cattle.

¶ 4. To break up a considerable number of Lipan rancherias, whose inhabitants made this attack in the neighborhood of the Arroyo del Cíbolo, merely the threat of punishment of a party of thirty-two men from the presidio of Bejar, commanded by Lieutenant Joseph Menchaca, was sufficient. A single hint from the governor of Texas sufficed for these Indians to deliver more than thirty riding horses which they had stolen from the settlers of San Fernando. This instance has few parallels. A sergeant and nine of our men met at considerable dis-

---

less a copyist error for on his own figures it should be 3103 (Morfi, *History of Texas,* Part I, p. 103, note 3).

[3] A.G.I., Guad., 270, Croix to Gálvez, No. 360, Chihuahua, February 22, 1779.

CROIX'S REPORT OF 1781

tance from their settlement numerous bands of Lipan and were well received and entertained. The same fortune attended another detachment of twenty men which met three hundred Indians of the North on the banks of the Rio de Guadalupe. Finally, from January of '79 to June of '80, there has been neither any particular hostility in the province of Texas, nor any victims known save a soldier and five shepherds or herdsmen killed by Comanche and Carancaguazes.[4]

¶ 5. The invasion of the Northerners into the Lipan rancherias resulted in the loss of three hundred members of that nation, some killed and some taken captive. These campaigns were made in revenge for their own injuries and for the important incentives of enmity and rancor between the two nations. This is the move to be desired, as, flowing from the just, skilful, and suitable measures of the government, the reciprocal destruction of our enemies might be achieved without their being able to understand, or complain openly of, our principles and without exposing the troops of the king.

¶ 6. All this is clear and evident in the extensive and well-stated reports of the governor of the province, Don Domingo Cabello, for the events, from July of '80 until today, refer to incessant attacks of the Comanche, so horrible and bloody that, if they continue with the same steadfastness, the desolation of the province will be consequent, irremediable and immediate, and (as the governor believes) very few vassals of the king may remain to contemplate this misfortune.[5]

¶ 7. It is suspected and it is believable that some of the Nations of the North may have united with the Comanche. One notices among the Lipan a docile disposition to aid us against their old enemies. However, they are beginning to exchange their enforced humility for what robberies they can, and to solicit, by whatever means possible for them, peace and friendship with the above nations. Finally, it is suspected that some of them have an understanding and coalition with the

---

[4] A.G.I., Guad., 267, Croix to Gálvez, No. 540, Arispe, June 23, 1780.
[5] For an account of some of these activities, see A.G.I., Guad., 267, Croix to Gálvez, No. 652, Arispe, June 30, 1781.

PROVINCE OF TEXAS

inhuman Carancaguazes of the seacoast near the presidio of La Bahia where the latter frequently attack, surfeiting their cruelty upon the unhappy shipwrecked.

¶ 8. The Comanche have always made attacks in the province of Texas, but the frightfulness with which they now execute them can be attributed fundamentally to the following causes. A small band of them who were coming with peace to the new settlement of Bucareli was attacked by the settlers, ignorant of the purpose of the Indians, and two perished in the encounter. Another band of sixteen Comanche, who were attacking the neighborhood of the Villa of San Fernando, had an encounter with a detachment of forty-eight men from the presidio of Bejar. Ten of the enemy and two of our men met death. The troops and settlers of New Mexico, with the aid of the Ute and Jicarilla Apache, have persecuted and punished them with rigor. Certainly it is not strange that the Comanche, insatiable (as are all Indians) in their vengeance, unable to resist the forces of New Mexico allied with the brave Ute and treacherous Jicarilla, and urged by the necessity of providing themselves with horses for their bison hunts, give vent to their cruelties and natural inclination to steal and commit murder in the province of Texas where they find less resistance, greater helplessness, and cowardice in some settlers who have become accustomed to living in the bosom of peace.

¶ 9. Neither will the alliance of the Comanche with the rest of the nations of the north be strange, since they are related with the Taovayaces and, as I understand, all these Indians are of the same origin, divided into bands, like that of the Apache, without any difference other than that some of the former are always on the move and some bands of the latter have a fixed domicile in formal settlements and villages.[6]

¶ 10. The suspicions, then, that the Nations of the North attack in the province of Texas in union with the Comanche, are well founded and I mentioned them in paragraph eighty-one

---

[6] For a discussion of the various tribes of Texas, their relationships and customs, see Bolton, *Athanaze de Mézières*, I, 17–122; see also Morfi, *History of Texas*, Chap. II.

of the report of March 29, '79.[7] They complained bitterly of the deceased Lieutenant Colonel Don Athanaze de Mézières because he did not visit and make presents to them all on his last journey to San Antonio de Bejar, and because the promises of this official had not been fulfilled. They are particularly sensitive over the failure of their barter with the Louisiana merchants in hides, riding horses, and captives, in exchange for guns, powder, balls, knives, hatchets, mirrors, vermilion, and other trinkets. This form of commerce they call *treta*.[8]

¶ 11. These positive resentments being deeply engraved in the inconstant, mistrustful, and greedy hearts of the Indians of the North moved them without doubt openly to break the peace they were maintaining in good faith, since lesser reasons would be sufficient to incline them towards war, which is their real profession and the one in which they can satiate their avarice and lust for spilling human blood.

¶ 12. The same incentives animate the cowardly spirit of the Carancaguazes (Karankawa) of the coast. They have already made themselves dreaded by reason of the repetition of their outrages and because two wicked apostates, or fugitives, from the Mission of Rosario, close to the presidio of La Bahia, govern and direct them.

¶ 13. The most notable injuries which these Indians have caused on the coast are the treacherous murders of the officers and the crews of three vessels which had the misfortune of anchoring and being lost in the port of Matagordo. One of them was on its way from New Orleans under the command of Don Luis Landrin; of the other the point of departure and destination is unknown; it is believed that the latter may be one of the transports of troops destined for the expedition against Pensacola.[9] [MARGINAL NOTE: The third shipwreck referred to in this paragraph has not occurred. The news which

---

[7] Croix to Gálvez, No. 3. See above, page 11, footnote 10.

[8] For data on these Texas–Louisiana relations, see Bolton, *Athanaze de Mézières*, II, *passim*.

[9] Reference is made to Bernardo de Gálvez' attack on Pensacola.

PROVINCE OF TEXAS

they sent the governor was mistaken. This he learned later in a letter of June 13 of this year. Rúbric of Croix.] Within the province they assaulted at night the mission of Rosario, carrying off twenty-two persons. (The captives' names I do not list because they are of the same race as the aggressors.) They commit frequent robberies successfully, for they are familiar with the environs of the presidio of La Bahia and its missions.

¶ 14. But these injuries are not comparable to those which the Comanche inflict. The province is overrun with these Indians, now alone, or as allies of the Nations of the North; at the moment not a foot of land is free from hostility. Its fruits of the field are despoiled, cattle ranches and farms that the happy days of peace had built up are rapidly being abandoned, and the settlers in terror are taking refuge in the settlements, nor do they venture to leave their neighborhood without a troop escort.

¶ 15. The new settlement of Nuestra Señora del Pilar de Bucareli was attacked by the Comanche while suffering from a calamitous inundation of the river on whose banks it was recently established. The settlers saw themselves obliged to abandon it, seek asylum among the friendly nations, and flee to the old abandoned mission of Nacodoches. There they subsist in the greatest danger and with no support save that, risky and intermittent, which the presidio of San Antonio de Bejar can supply them over the great distance of one hundred and twenty-five leagues, although they are but fifty leagues from the post of Natchitoches, attached to the Louisiana government, whose infantry garrison is needed for its own defense.[10]

¶ 16. The above presidio of Bejar and the Villa of San Fernando, capital of the province, are built, in spite of their long establishment, with huts and little wooden houses which a wind and rain storm largely destroyed last year. They have neither walls nor stockade to protect them from the attacks of the Indians.

¶ 17. In the five contiguous missions is a small number of In-

---

[10] See Bolton, *Athanaze de Mézières*, II, 259–61, 271, 289, 304, 309–10.

dians taken in force from the coast of the Colony of New Santander. Consequently they contribute little to the defense of the province and some frequent annoyance by running away to the homelands where they were born.[11]

¶ 18. Finally, it is not possible for the presidial companies of Bejar and La Bahia to attend to so many urgent and distant matters. If they were in a perfect condition, they would be without doubt respected by the enemy. The consequences are the sly, unpunished hostilities of the Comanche or the open threat of the Indians of the North whenever so inclined, or those of the Lipan Apache who can subsist only by robbery, and those of the vile Carancaguazes.

¶ 19. Such is the sad situation of the province of Texas. Its governor, Don Domingo Cabello, describes it extensively in repeated representations, proposing the extermination of the Lipan and Carancaguazes, and the means of restraining the Nations of the North by increasing troops in the province of his command up to the number of five hundred men to be taken from the garrison of Havana and transported in small boats to the coast of San Bernardo. But although I recognize the need of the assistance, I advert also to the exact causes and considerations which make it difficult now.

¶ 20. The governor has solicited this aid since the time he was an infantryman, when he recognized the real dangers to the territory of Texas. In this official report he has assumed the responsibilities under which his honor and office place him.

¶ 21. With this object in mind, I put the company of Bejar upon the footing of one hundred men and that of Bahia on the footing of sixty-three men, adding thirty-three units to their old allowance. These the king was pleased to approve. I, without means or powers for a larger increase, was not able to do more, nor can I do anything else than to advise the governor, with the convenience which the great distance from this capital to the province of Texas permits, of the measures which I have considered proper to avert the ruin of that terri-

[11] Morfi, *Viaje,* 225–30 describes these missions. See also Morfi, *History of Texas,* Chaps. V, VIII–X.

tory. However, my elementary commands have been executed with felicity under the intelligence, zeal, and knowledge of the governor, even before he had received them.[12]

¶ 22. As soon as this chief communicated to me the first news of the hostility of the Comanche, under date of July 17, '80, I replied to him on September 23 following. Therein I stated that I understood the grave evils threatening the province and that the small forces which garrisoned it would not be able to remedy them; but that, although I might wish to increase the staff because of necessity and of my zealous desires, it was morally impossible. The same urgencies existed in all the provinces of my command, so that the latter would be ruined if I should take their garrisons away to aid Texas. Furthermore, his Majesty, in the very recent royal order, commanded me absolutely to minimize the present costs because of the many and large expenses which the just war with the English was causing.

¶ 23. Convinced that at the time this important matter did not demand immediate attention, I had itemized in the general increase of forces the presidial companies of his command. I was persuaded that this aid would be sufficient for a respectable defensive war, if the unfortunate condition of the troops, their administration, instruction, and discipline were altered according to the means repeatedly advised so that we could use them in useful, safe maneuvers and operations, and as far as possible similar to those of the Indian enemies.

¶ 24. I was convinced that it was necessary to satisfy the complaints and quiet the unrest of the Nations of the North by honestly overlooking the injuries lately received, and by gentle persuasion which they could never attribute to our weakness, but to our desires of conserving peace for convenience and benefit of the Indians themselves. To achieve these ends, it appears proper to me that either through the captains of the militias of the pueblo of Bucareli, Don Antonio Gil

---

[12] A.G.I., Guad., 276, Croix to Gálvez, No. 154, Valle de Santa Rosa, February 15, 1778; A.H.N. Estado, 3883, Croix to Gálvez, No. 68, México, July 26, 1777.

Ybarbo, or the commander of Natchitoches, or by means of some particular emissary of confidence, some suitable present should be made to the Taovayaces and Tagaucanas nations, the most quarrelsome and warlike; that the emissary should inform himself carefully of the condition and of the ideas of these Indians; that he should persuade them of the benefits of peace; and if he should find the Comanche receptive to it, he should extend it to them at once. On the other hand, he should attempt skillfully to break the alliance of the Comanche with the Taovayaces and Taguacanas; that in the case that these three nations, or the last two, should embrace peace, he should proceed at once to make and ratify it under honorable capitulations possible of fulfillment on our part.

¶ 25. When the governor received these resolutions, he had already forestalled them in all respects, having so commissioned Don Nicolas de la Matte, settler of Louisiana, who by a fortunate coincidence, was in the presidio of Bejar.

¶ 26. The complete instructions which the governor gave to la Matte, as well as the spirit, honor, zeal, efficiency, and knowledge of the nations and understanding of some of their languages which this emissary possesses, promise the best results.

¶ 27. He set out from Bejar in November of the year '80, and on the last day of February found himself near the pueblos of the Taguacanas and Taovayaces. He had with him two faithful and expert interpreters, citizens of Louisiana, but now established in the province of Texas, the customary presents, and the intention of reaching New Mexico whence he must report to me.

¶ 28. These are, most excellent sir, the only measures which can be taken to ward off the desolation of the territories of Texas, but the funds of gratification of the presidial companies of Bejar and La Bahia cannot support their demands: the annual presents which the Indians expect, the particular expenses which they cause when they come to visit the governor, and the incidental ones on the account of the Lipan.

¶ 29. These indispensable presents will be useless if the Nations of the North lack barter and trade. They cannot be made at the expense of the king without his royal permission; to obtain that involves many considerations, and safeguards, and besides the routine of preparing a file of papers of detailed proceedings. If it must be continued by private traders, the war with the English may impede it.[13] Its reëstablishment will have to be delayed because of the necessary interchange of my reports with the governor of Louisiana and his replies, as I do not consider it proper that trade should be carried on by the settlers of the province of Texas.

¶ 30. By no means until war is concluded, can anything advantageous be done to keep the greedy nations of the Indians of the North content and quiet. I shall always see myself applying superficial remedies that will only serve to minimize the hostilities during some seasons, with the risk that the same remedies may stimulate fickleness, lack of confidence, and pride of these nations.

¶ 31. While they remain quiet, the Lipan will cause no especial anxiety in the province of Texas. It will not be necessary to change the governor's treatment of them; one can control the attacks of the Carancaguazes.

¶ 32. I have not been able to execute the campaign projected against these Indians, which I announced to your Excellency in letter No. 268, September 27, '78,[14] and in paragraph 9 of the secret communication of March 29 of the year following.[15] The reasons appear in an extensive file of papers in the possession of the assessor and of which I shall give an account to your Excellency when it is in condition. I shall do the same with the proceeding itself. It is relative to all matters touching hostilities of the Comanche, the perfidy of the Lipan, the unrest of the Indians of the North, the propositions and petitions of Governor Don Domingo Cabello.

[13] A.G.I., Guad., 278, Croix to Gálvez, No. 487, Arispe, February 23, 1780; *Ibid.,* Croix to Gálvez, No. 488, Arispe, February 23, 1780.
[14] A.G.I., Guad., 270, Croix to Gálvez, No. 268, Chihuahua, September 23, 1778.
[15] See above, page 11, footnote 10.

¶ 33. I believe that nothing is more difficult for this chief than the conservation of the peace with the Indians of the North and the Lipan. As the attendance of both at San Antonio de Bejar is unavoidable, a very delicate situation will supervene. As already noted, this obliges him to avail himself of means doubtful or impossible of success: warding off lamentable encounters, making the Indians happy and dispelling their suspicions of our friendships, to which, although barbarians, they are usually prey. They notice that we extend it to all without taking sides in the aggravations which the Northerners and Lipan cause one another, and that we overlook the attacks and robberies which they make upon the province by buying their friendship with presents in place of proceeding to their punishment. But it is apparent that the governor has managed until the present time these difficult affairs with the greatest zeal, prudence, skill, and felicity. Not only have I considered it fit to leave him free to exercise his powers, but I have had them extended so that he might do everything that appears best according to cases and events which occur, giving me an account of the results. Having set forth the just recommendation of his merit, I am submitting it to your Excellency so that the piety of the king may be pleased to dispense to this interested party the grace which may be his sovereign pleasure.

¶ 34. In the meantime, I shall conclude the particular report concerning the province of Texas, setting forth in brief statements the only means of contributing to its well-being.

¶ 35. The means are nothing more than what was agreed upon in the councils of war[16] which I remitted to your Excellency, but they demand the increase of troops and the necessity of representing to his Majesty that the Lipan Apache are not worthy of the sovereign piety his royal Catholic spirit dispenses them in the royal order of February 20 of '79.[17]

¶ 36. I would set forth the simple explanation of this means with brief, congruent reasons, if I considered the support of larger forces possible. These being out of the question, I think

---

[16] See above, pages 35, 36, 39, footnotes 104, 105, 108, 121.
[17] See above, page 43, footnote 141.

PROVINCE OF TEXAS

it necessary to maintain peace with the Nations of the North, to establish barter and commerce by the settlers of Louisiana with the permission of the government of Texas, to fix a quantity annually for presents and gifts at San Antonio de Bejar, to support and develop the pueblo of Nuestra Señora del Pilar de Bucareli, and to continue the principle of stirring up the mutual antagonism between the Nations of the North and the Lipan.

¶ 37. But the first is impossible while war with the English lasts; the second is insufficient; the third demands expenses; and the fourth is venturesome and can be dangerous to the province itself, and especially to those of Coahuila and the Colony of Nuevo Santander.

¶ 38. To free the province of Texas from the attacks of the Carancaguazes, there is no choice other than that of attacking by sea and land the small number of this nation and transporting it to an overseas destination. But neither the port of Vera Cruz nor that of New Orleans can, under the present system, provide boats and troops, nor should the troops of the province of Texas itself give preference to this matter in place of the more urgent ones in which they ought to engage themselves.

¶ 39. All these difficulties are for the present insuperable. Consequently there approaches either the risk of abandoning the province of Texas [or the necessity] of uniting at one or two points all its forces.

¶ 40. I would be of the opinion that the troop and settlers of the presidio of La Bahia de Espíritu Santo, the Indians of its missions, the garrison of the detachment of Arroyo del Cibolo, and the settlers of the new settlement of Bucareli should be incorporated into the Villa of San Fernando and in the five missions of its jurisdiction.

¶ 41. To convince one of the utility of this opinion it is sufficient to say that the united forces would conserve the dominion of the province and make themselves respected by all classes of enemies.

¶ 42. The Villa of San Fernando has whatever requirements can be desired for the establishment of a populous city even if it were not easy to embrace in its suburbs the five opulent missions, situated within a district of seven leagues.

¶ 43. The Indians are not capable of impeding an establishment so advantageous. Fortified, it could resist any feared invasion by neighboring foreign colonies.

¶ 44. Besides the progress which could result without doubt from the union of forces, new settlements would be erected with strong and competent colonists drawn from the capital. Finally, the dominion of Texas, assured of protection in the vast extent of its territory, would merit the name of Province. A result of those achievements would be the reducing of the numerous nations of barbarous Indians with the pious, prudent, and gentle means which the royal order of February 20 of '79 envisages. The respect of the Indians for some establishments, well ordered and advantageously situated for sustaining themselves, would be much more possible.

¶ 45. Brigadier Don Pedro de Rivera, in paragraphs 41 to 47 of the third part of his report, or project, which he presented to the viceroy, Marqués de Casafuerte, under date of December 7, '28,[18] considered useless the continuance of the presidio of La Bahía de Espíritu Santo. Lieutenant General Marqués de Rubí did not recommend it in that report which he made to Viceroy Marqués de Croix, under date of April 10, '68.[19] I do not consider that the operations in which the company of this presidio have been and are employed are worth the expense of 21,534 pesos, which their annual allotment amounts to.

¶ 46. At the time of its erection, the Indians of the coast were not worth noticing; today they make themselves respected. Now larger forces than those which the above company has

[18] Regarding Rivera in Texas, Charles W. Hackett, "Visitador Rivera's Criticism of Aguayo's Work in Texas," *Hispanic American Historical Review*, XVI (May, 1936), 162–72. See also Morfi, *History of Texas*, Part II, Index, especially the editor's notes.

[19] The report referred to here is the *Dictámenes*. See above, page 16, footnote 21. See also Herbert E. Bolton, *Texas in the Middle Eighteenth Century*, 106–8; and Morfi, *History of Texas*, Chap. X.

PROVINCE OF TEXAS

are necessary to subject them and are asked for. The presidio cannot stop the night attacks on the mission of Rosario, established a short league from the presidio, nor can it in any manner prevent the massacre of those shipwrecked on the coast, nor oppose with advantage the attacks of the Indians of the North, nor lend assistance opportunely to the presidio of Bejar and Villa of San Fernando, nor extend it to the Colony of New Santander. Finally, the terrain in which Bahia and its missions are situated does not provide the best resources for settlement, except the use of water from the river for irrigating the crops. This work, valued at more than seven thousand pesos, is made difficult because of lack of funds.

¶ 47. Governor Don Domingo Cabello has proposed, and sought my permission, to withdraw the detachment at the Arroyo del Cíbolo,[20] established in the neighborhood of the road from Bejar to La Bahia, because it does not have competent troops to garrison it, and because the site which it occupies is as exposed to surprise by the enemies as it is useless for settlement.

¶ 48. The wandering population of Bucareli does not serve Nacodoches according to the well-founded reports of the deceased Lieutenant Colonel Don Athanaze de Mézières.[21] It will be satisfactory in its original establishment upon the banks of the Rio de la Trinidad, but it needs support for diverting water, which fertilizes the fields, and for defending its settlers in a spot surrounded by enemies and far from the rest of the settlements of the province.

¶ 49. All that has been set forth favors my opinion of union of forces of the troops and settlers in the Villa of San Fernando and its missions, but at once the following difficulties present themselves: if the presidio of La Bahia is abandoned, who will impede the establishment of foreigners on the coast? How can the Indians of the missions of Espíritu Santo and El Rosario be persuaded to leave them? The Xaramanes will

[20] For data on the detachment at Cíbolo, see Bolton, *Athanaze de Mézières*, II, *passim;* Bolton, *Texas in the Middle Eighteenth Century*, III, note 12; and Morfi, *History of Texas*, Part I, 49, 50, 69, 79, 418–20.
[21] Bolton, *Athanaze de Mézières*, II, 304, 309–10.

85

re-apostatize and flee to the rancherias of the Indians of the North as the Indians of Rosario will among the Carancaguazes. The settlers of Bucareli retired, how shall we satisfy the complaints of the Indian allies who love and desire the neighborhood of the Spaniards? They will avenge this aggravation, and the communication with Louisiana will be closed to us. Finally, what concept will the barbarous nations form of the general and unseasonable abandonment? They will at once attribute it to cowardice and their boldness will increase.

¶ 50. I answer the first: that Bahia de San Bernardo is accessible only to small boats since it has hardly, at high tide, fourteen spans of water; the coast is swampy and likely to overflow, if credit is given to the information acquired since the year 1686 and the reconnaissance made by Brigadiers Don Pedro de Rivera and Don Diego de Ortiz Parilla.[22] But even if this be not certain, who will burden the governor of Texas with the repetition of reconnaissances and the measures for detaching competent bodies of troops, who at opportune times may examine the coast and dislodge foreigners who are attempting to establish themselves on it?

¶ 51. To the second, I state: that the small number of Indians gathered in the mission of Espíritu Santo and El Rosario does not merit much consideration since, if one attempts to transfer them to a better place with gentleness and skill, they will resent it; that even if there should be apostasy of some, that ought not to be surprising for even now they are capricious, yet return to their mission with the same serenity of spirit with which they undertook flight; and that if we place ourselves far away from the watering places where cattle, tame or wild, gather, it could not be at such great distance as to impede the union and march of settlers, with an escort of troops, to collect and butcher what might be needed, as the Lipan do when hunger impels them or when they wish to forestall it with prompt measures.

¶ 52. As to the third, it is undeniable that the establishment

[22] Parilla was sent by Rubí (Bolton, *Texas in the Middle Eighteenth Century*, 104–6).

of the presidio of Bucareli among the Indian friends contributes to the conservation of peace. Some nations, however, break the peace because they consider themselves threatened by the presidio or because it incites their natural war spirit. In such cases the settlers will suffer, as they actually do. Some time they will be the victim of massacres and fury of the enemies. Such a possibility and not remote misfortune will close the hazardous communication which we have today with the settlers of the post of Natchitoches, and not with the province of Louisiana.

¶ 53. Finally, conclusions that the barbarous nations would draw from the abandonment of our weak settlements of the province of Texas are unimportant. The principle of uniting the settlers at the capital and in its contiguous missions is well founded as we would construct for ourselves an establishment which would instill terror in the Indians. With respect to the possibility of foreign colonies being established on the coast, the catastrophe which Governor Don Domingo Cabello announces repeatedly would not eventuate. The increase of troops would not be necessary; he would have them in abundance in the possible formation and advantageous organization of useful militias. In a few years the province of Texas would flourish and put itself into communication, without opposition or with smaller risks, with those of Louisiana, Coahuila, and New Santander with particular benefit to all, and with hopes that an active commerce by sea and land would give them the stimulus which the present system does not permit.

¶ 54. Notwithstanding, I do not think of putting into effect my opinion without seeing the results of the commission conferred upon the emissary Don Nicolas de la Matte; without hearing that of the governor of the province; without assuring myself of the advantages of which I conceive; and without having the royal approbation of his Majesty, unless the hostilities continue and the destruction of the province forces me to take urgently the indicated measures.

¶ 55. In the meantime, I shall wait to see what the governor accomplishes by his plan to have the settlers, at their own expense and labor and without draining the royal treasury, but with the assistance of troops which I have offered him, come in nearer the stockade in the presidio of Bejar and the Villa of San Fernando, there to apply themselves to the raising of abundant crops for their own support, as well as to provide forage for the horses of the presidial company, in stable in dry and wet seasons, and in pasture in the springtime in the field near the post. With these ends achieved, it will be possible to instruct and train the troops and have them always united and in condition to oppose any invasions of enemies, patrol the terrain of the frontier, and undertake other more useful operations. Their training may even enable them to prevent the unfortunate deaths, which the Indians cause in small detachments, of troops established far from their posts for the purpose of cutting hay, looking for stampeded horses, or protecting small groups of settlers, who venture to cross regions of the greatest danger perhaps without arms and always ignorant of their use.[23]

PROVINCE OF COAHUILA

¶56

EIGHT thousand souls in eight villas of Spaniards, four pueblos of Indians, four missions, five presidios, eight establishments, divided into eleven jurisdictions populate the vast territories of the province of San Francisco de Coahuila or New Extramadura.[24] It deserves this title (of province)

---

[23] A.G.I., Guad., 275, No. 267, Chihuahua, September 23, 1778. On Carancaguazes, Croix to Gálvez, No. 268, see above, page 81, footnote 14. On Ripperda's life and difficulties with the settlers, see Morfi, *History of Texas*, Part II, index; see also above, page 33, footnote 98.

[24] On the origin of Coahuila see Vito Alessio Robles, *Francisco de Urdiñola y el norte de la Nueva España* (Mexico, 1931). (Hereinafter cited: Robles *Urdiñola*). The *estado* of Coahuila's population is found in A.G.I., Guad., 267, Croix to Gálvez, No. 208, Chihuahua, June 1, 1778. Regarding Croix's measures and reports of officials concerning Coahuila previous to March, 1779, see A.G.I., Guad., 615, Croix to Gálvez, No. 69, México, July 26, 1777; *ibid.*, No. 75, México, July 26, 1777; *ibid.*, No. 94, Querétaro, August 23, 1777; *ibid.*, No. 108, Durango, October 10, 1777; *ibid.*, No. 124, Hacienda de Patos, November 24, 1777; A.G.I., Guad., 276, Croix to Gálvez, No. 153, Valle de Santa Rosa,

PROVINCE OF COAHUILA

more than Texas, because in less time and with less risk and difficulties, they can establish themselves in pueblos protected and defended by competent and able settlers and stimulate commerce, agriculture, and development of mines.

¶ 57. This province, as a refuge and asylum for the larger part of the Apache of the East, Lipan, and Mescaleros, communicates the contagion of the hostilities from which it suffers to those of New Vizcaya, New Kingdom of Leon, Colony of New Santander, and Texas, and shares in the incursions of the Comanche and the rest of the Indians of the North in the latter province.

¶ 58. The barrier of Coahuila lost, that of Texas could not be sustained, injuries in the other neighboring provinces would be greater, and the Apache would rapidly, without opposition, penetrate as far as San Luis Potosí.

¶ 59. When I took charge of this command the Lipan were ranching on the banks of the Rio Grande del Norte and in the neighborhood of the presidios of Coahuila. They came into the presidios, overbearing and proud, and with hands bloody from victims, vassals of the king, whom they had sacrificed to their fury, they demanded food, presents, and gifts. They not only murdered in the interior of the province, but even at the doors of the presidios, and threatening a general invasion, attacked the presidio of Aguaverde.

¶ 60. My ingress into the province of Coahuila and that of the troop which I quartered on their frontier for aid and security of my reconnaissances calmed the unrest of the Lipan. They immediately gave guarantees, which remorse for their crimes and fear of their punishment extracted. More cowardly than humble, they sought our forgiveness and reconciliation. Exhibiting their natural perfidy, they offered to Captain Don Francisco Martiñez the delivery of two rancherias of their relatives, the Mescaleros, who were close to the presidio of Aguaverde.

February 15, 1778; *ibid.*, No. 189, Chihuahua, April 3, 1778; A.G.I., Guad., 267, Croix to Gálvez, No. 373, Chihuahua, March 29, 1779; see also above, page 26, footnote 64.

¶ 61. In this traitorous action, they proceeded deceitfully and changeably. It was known that the sorrow of seeing the sacrifice of their relatives and the interest of warding off their own sacrifice struggled in their hearts. Although the latter was greater, the two rancherias were not taken completely by surprise because the Lipan did not implement their treacheries in the terms they offered.[25]

¶ 62. In any case, it was a happy beginning of my labors and designs, and even if I was persuaded to meet the Lipan on the frontier to ratify peace, their crimes and cowardice did not give them courage to wait for me on my departure from Coahuila and return from Texas, but taking their families far away, they spied out my marches, dogging my steps.

¶ 63. After the troops had already dispersed and while I was marching from the valley of Santa Rosa to Chihuahua, Indians numbering more than five hundred attacked me. This action was attributed to the daring of the Mescaleros, but it will not be imprudent judgment to believe that Lipan aided them. It is known that the former committed many murders and robberies in vengeance for their injuries, and that the second did not miss the opportunity of using their weapons while excusing their part by blaming it upon their relatives.

¶ 64. However, the presents and invitations of Captain Martiñez to the Lipan, and above all the fear of seeing among their rancherias their enemies, the Norteños, aided by our arms, persuaded them, in spite of the exceptional malice with which they have always proceeded, to volunteer for the war against the Mescaleros.

¶ 65. There was a Lipan of the greatest importance who proposed that we treacherously pretend to have declared war on the Lipan. Then after peace had been made with the Mescaleros and all or part of the nation in the capacity of auxiliaries had been led to celebrate it in an open and exposed spot, they be attacked and exterminated by Spanish and Lipan arms.

¶ 66. Another Lipan, with nine of his followers and three

---

[25] Data on this will be found in the enclosures with A.G.I., Guad., 275, Croix to Gálvez, No. 315, Chihuahua, December 28, 1778.

PROVINCE OF COAHUILA

Spaniards, ran to help recover the horse herd of the presidio of Aguaverde, restored part, captured a Mescalero, and killed another with his own hands.

¶ 67. The same Lipan proposed war in formal agreements against his relatives and the establishment of an extensive rancheria under his control in an organized pueblo at the Ojo de Auga de San Phelipe.

¶ 68. Whether these offers were in good faith or not, it is evident that when the Lipan experienced the forceful attack of the Norteños, at the beginning of the year '79,[26] they were defeated (as never before) in Coahuila and Texas, and that in spite of their fundamental suspicions of our friendship, they lent their support and shed the blood of their relatives.

¶ 69. These evident facts are attributed to fear and interest. They were the consequences of the reciprocal lack of confidence of the Lipan and Mescaleros; the intemperate peace attempted by the latter with the greatest activity and humility in the Valley of Santa Rosa, presidios of New Vizcaya and Chihuahua (then the site of my residence); the Mescaleros' ardent importuning of our support to take vengeance upon the Lipan; the consternation of the Apache of the East and the excellent beginnings of their disunion; the unequivocal proofs of the good faith of the Nations of the North, of the advantages which their friendship offers us and of the importance of our conserving it; and finally, the decline of hostilities in the province of my command. When the Indians of the North assault the Apache, when the Mescaleros meditate vengeance on the Lipan, and when the latter are engaged in safeguarding themselves from three powerful classes of enemies—Spaniards, Norteños, and Mescaleros—who project their impending extermination, they can do much to lessen these hostilities.

¶ 70. It is probable that the forced reduction of one or the other of the two branches of the Apache, Lipan or Mescaleros, would have been achieved, as the assistance of our arms would have decided the fortune of the more fortunate party.

[26] A.G.I., Guad., 270, Croix to Gálvez, No. 337, Chihuahua, January 23, 1779.

¶ 71. To extend peace to the Lipan there were the reasons of their old although unfaithful friendship, of the greater interest which obliged them to conserve ours, and of their own fears which would make them more faithful in our alliance. But that forced us into the position of defending them from all their enemies and consequently drawing upon our possessions of Coahuila attacks of the Nations of the North, which in turn meant the loss of their aid, opportune and advantageous, to subject the Lipan. Thus the unhappy relationship of these Indians having been altered, the Lipan might resort with greater perfidy to use their peace deceitfully and try to reconcile themselves with their relatives, the Mescaleros. The hostilities of the latter excited to unbridled fury, the Lipan could then take opportune advantage, seeing us involved in the new obligation of resisting the just invasion of the Indians of the North.

¶ 72. The Mescaleros, more perfidious, cruel, and barbarous than the Lipan, were not worthy of our honorable alliance. They have made grievous and bloody war on us for many years, although their petitions for peace were submissive and humble. The circumstances of Article 2, Title 1, of the Regulation of the Presidios,[27] which required they be not admitted to peace, are thus seen exactly fulfilled. But the necessity that obliged infringing the cited article in the case of the Lipan, whom I found at peace on the Coahuila frontier, made it more imperative that I condescend to make peace with the Mescaleros.

¶ 73. This was an efficacious means which contributed to stimulating the consternation of both. Although they saw themselves admitted and aided respectively in Coahuila and New Vizcaya, they came to realize that if we declared ourselves for either one of the two parties, the ruin from the vigor of our hostile operations would be irremediable.

¶ 74. Before deciding upon this declaration, I considered it proper to see what the Mescaleros were doing against the Lipan in vengeance for their injuries. They took revenge. The

---

[27] See above, page 16, footnote 22.

result was that they are using us and pretending they are obliged to have our supplies for the continuation of their victories. The Lipan, confused and unhappy, may demand aid to avenge themselves upon the Mescaleros.

¶ 75. The Mescaleros, so motivated, offered and used their arms voluntarily against the Lipan. In order that the latter might not use full force against the Mescaleros, many presents, arguments, and threats of greater evils had to precede if they were to be made amenable to the idea of delivering and sacrificing their relatives. The beginnings of our peace with the Mescaleros were more solid than those with the Lipan. With the latter we had experienced the bad faith with which they had kept peace. The former, after a war of many years, were beginning to enjoy advantageously our friendship, presents, and good trade.

¶ 76. Everything conspired to the end that we declare ourselves for this party (Mescaleros) and with greater reason, because of the ease of hemming in the numerous Lipan in level and known lands. The purpose was not to exterminate them, as I understood that their necessarily weak resistance would not involve this catastrophe, but only to reduce, draw them out, and dislodge them entirely, or in part, from the country from which in a period of more than forty years, and under a protection of their faithless pledges of peace, they have shed streams of innocent blood of the king's vassals. But as the Mescaleros, ruder, more treacherous, bloody, agile, and sagacious by character naturally acquired in the sierras where they are born and live, are dominated by the passion for mule and horseflesh, which the Lipan do not eat, and have a greater knowledge of our territories of Coahuila, New Leon, and New Vizcaya, they are more fearful and venturesome and therefore more difficult of conquest than the Lipan. Yet I was undecided in declaring my intentions and ideas when I received the royal order of February 20, '79.

¶ 77. His sovereign resolutions, wise and pious principles, prevented me from prudently using the troops of my command in the fatigues which the method of warring upon the

Indians demands. These troops have been always used in protecting the frontier, examining its terrains, detaching parties in pursuit of enemies when the latter come in to attack the pueblos or haciendas, or when they flee after theft, to search for them, and surprise them in their rancherias by means of general or particular campaigns. The lack of a competent number of troops, those deficiencies which I noted in the government, and instruction and discipline of the existing troops were the only reasons, therefore, that obliged me to forego the immediate undertaking against the Lipan or Mescaleros.

¶ 78. For the indicated undertaking it was not necessary, nor should it be, to alter the method of making war in these countries. If war were to be attempted against the Apachería of the east, I had as allies the fierce Indians of the North; if against those of the west, the Ute, Moqui, and Gila Pima; if against the Lipan, the above mentioned Indians of the North and Mescaleros; and if against the latter, the Lipan.

¶ 79. With such assistance, I could have promised myself the reduction and subjection in detail of all the Apachería, who have kept these provinces in the most deplorable state. But I needed a larger number of troops to instill courage and the respect of the Indians' allies and to sustain their irresistible operations against the enemy, since in these countries war is made upon the barbarian Indians with the aid of barbarian Indians and not of mission or pueblo Indians, for the reason that these lack the belligerence which recommends the savages. Neither the large number of the Apache, nor the dispersion, rapidity, and silence of their marches could prevent them from falling into the hands of our allies, nor would they find refuge in the rough places of the sierras.

¶ 80. Without this assistance the successes of our troops over the barbarous nations are restricted. With the support of the Tlascaltecans this empire was conquered.[28] The exploration of enemy rancherias in these provinces has always been made with the aid of the mission Indians. With the aid of the Lipan,

---

[28] On the influence of the Tlascaltecans in Coahuila and Texas, see Robles, *Urdiñola*, 388, 169–90.

PROVINCE OF COAHUILA

Brigadier Don Diego Ortiz Parilla attempted to attack the post of the Tavoayaces Norteños; and with the aid of the Seri and Pima of Sonora, general campaigns were carried out in the years of '75 and '76.[29]

¶ 81. These examples favor my principles of conceding alliances to the nations of the North against the eastern Apachería, the Lipan against the Mescaleros, or the latter against the Lipan.

¶ 82. Either one of them would have been very advantageous to the vassals of the king and to the Indian allies and enemies: to the vassals because they were already enjoying or would be nearer to profiting from the benefits of peace; to the Indian allies because they were trying to conserve peace, observing that we were free from obligations and in a better position to punish their attacks; and to the enemies because the extraordinary effort which would have to be the means of their reduction, would be effected without doubt, with the least shedding of human blood.

¶ 83. It appears that they bruited about in the arroyos my proposition against the Lipan, agreed upon in the councils of war. However, in these councils attention was paid to the pious provision, namely, that the Lipan were assured that they, not being able to resist our arms and those of the Indians of the North, should surrender theirs immediately that they suffered the first attacks and that in this case, we would devote ourselves to ward off the inhuman cruelties of the Norteños.

¶ 84. To open the campaign, the general action which was agreed upon in the councils was necessary, and the particular *mariscadas* which are proper for this war should be continued without interruption. There is no doubt that they would cost blood. But how much more will be that which may be shed of the king's vassals and the Indians if no serious efforts are made to decide the fate of these provinces!

¶ 85. I could not make the attacks without that increase of forces which would assure me as far as possible the promised

[29] For a summary of these campaigns see Thomas, *Forgotten Frontiers,* 10–13. Regarding Parilla, see above, page 86, footnote 22.

gains. I observed that the monarchy needed greater forces for objects of more importance and I have fulfilled the obligations of my honor, fidelity, and office by having presented to his Majesty the only means which I considered suitable for the improvement of these provinces; but no consideration was sufficient to assuage the anxieties which agitated my loyal heart.

¶ 86. I had foreseen, and I set forth to your Excellency in my report of March 29, '79,[30] paragraphs 80 to 86, that my projects would be frustrated if I lacked resources at an opportune time. The Nations of the North would lose confidence and take up again their former hostilities; the Apache would lose their fears. With the Lipan and Mescaleros reconciled, a general war would be started, inextinguishable and bloody, and I would see myself forced to reduce my operations to defensive ones which, not providing victories over the enemies, would put the provinces in the most deplorable state.

¶ 87. But as the conjectures of human reasoning are fallible, the sad ones I had were dissipated. I found all the counsel I needed in the pious resolutions of the previously cited royal order of February 20, that conquests, which may be made by kindness, good treatment, and beneficence, though tardy, are consonant with the sovereign wish of the king. Accordingly, it appeared to me that the corresponding means which I had set forth to subject the Apachería of the east would be proper and conducive to the achievement and fulfillment of the royal intentions.

¶ 88. I have made peace with all the Indians which are known as enemies of these provinces with the exception of the Gila Apache. I am even persuaded that these may follow the example of the rest and repeat their former solicitations for peace at Janos, Valley of San Buenaventura, and Paso del Norte. Certainly I am not confident of the good effect of the forced peace, which the Lipan ratified and the Mescaleros made, because of the consternation to which they were reduced and not because of the true sentiments of humanity.

---

[30] See Croix to Gálvez, No. 3, above, page 11, footnote 10.

PROVINCE OF COAHUILA

Also it is experience, wise director of man's actions, that indicated that the peace with the Apache allies would be untrustworthy and that with the Indians of the North would be insubstantial because the former cannot live without robbery and the latter have need of provisions, horses, guns, powder, and balls for their buffalo hunts and for defending themselves from their enemies, the Osage.

¶89. Although the moment was the most propitious for making peace with the Indians, the final proof of his sovereign piety which the king deigned to give them for their own benefit, I was always persuaded that this experience convincingly illustrates the ingratitude of the Indian. The act of making peace would be very useful for revealing the error of it and would give me an opportunity to avail myself of other measures.

¶ 90. The measures which I took in due compliance with the royal order referred to were grounded upon three solid principles: presents; kind treatment and prudence; and just punishment with merit and sufficient forces.

¶ 91. The explanation which I made of these three points to the chiefs of Texas, Coahuila, and New Vizcaya was the same with the difference which the particular objects of their respective provinces demanded. In order not to alter terms and concepts, I shall copy the paragraphs of the report which I directed to the governor of Texas.

¶ 92. "The presents ought to be used so that the Indian, whether those of the North or Lipan (who are all submitting themselves for peace in this province), may receive them with pleasure and at suitable times so that they may not be given cause for conceit or arrogance nor acquire our gifts as if we had been forced to give them. This ought to be understood only with regard to those Indians who are evidencing their voluntary and real subjection and are establishing themselves in formal pueblos, because as to these, it will be necessary to gratify, protect, and guard them as vassals of the king, even if they do not permit in their pueblos the voice of the Holy Gospel which they will hear when the All Powerful illuminates them and dissipates the shadows of paganism. The tokens should also be used with that serious economy which opportunity permits and makes more appreciable and less costly to attract the Indian chiefs or little captains of the Nations of the North, and Lipan, because the persuasion of these can have much more force among their compatriots. Their friendship, if it remains constant, will alarm and restrain both groups, and the more so if we dedicate ourselves with skill and care, so that they may continue to offend each other, and keep guard of their movements to ward off any injury which can be directed at us.

¶ 93. "The second means (prudent treatment) has considerable difficulties in its practice; the treatment is diversified because, the Nations of the North, for example, merit better treatment than the Lipan because of many just and well founded reasons. We must speak the truth to them always; we must not promise them anything that cannot be fulfilled; we must not give them reason to lack confidence in our good faith; barter and decorous treatment by the troop, settlers, and their families must be extended to them; we must not deceive them; we must overlook their slight defects of characteristic badness, the inclination of every Indian arising from his barbarous breeding.

¶ 94. "In truth, it appears just to treat the Lipan likewise, but these Indians for many years have deceived us, enjoying our gifts and devastating at the same time the dominions of the king under the security and pretext of their simulated peace. For these reasons it is necessary that we manage ourselves with greater care until we have proofs (which is impossible) of their good faith. In that case they would be justly worthy of better treatment such as I prescribed for the Nations of the North.

¶ 95. "In a word, for the present your lordship ought to follow your well-understood principles for the Lipan and overlook for them the slight defections, even the gravest ones, which cannot be remedied without exposing the arms of the king to some unworthy actions, etc."

PROVINCE OF COAHUILA

¶ 96. Although to these measures I added other essential ones, consequent upon those of his Majesty, in my first and later orders to the governor, they have not been sufficient to offset the results set forth in paragraphs 86 and 88 of this paper.

¶ 97. In the particular report of the province of Texas, I have stated the matters relative to peace with the Nations of the North. Here it is necessary to refer to the fact that their restlessness has reached the province of Coahuila. Thus having attempted a second irruption on the Lipan rancherias in the month of December of '80, and not encountering their enemies, they directed their attacks against the troop of the presidio of Monclova. They were, however, driven off and put into precipitate flight with five Indians killed. This fortunate outcome I have communicated to your Excellency in letter No. 626 of March 26 last,[31] but if the emissary of Texas, Don Nicolas de la Matte, does not pacify the vengeful spirits of these nations, we shall have these enemies again on the territories of Coahuila.

¶ 98. Their invasions will not be frequent because of the distance from their rancherias, but formidable because of the daring, number of people, and superior arms with which they undertake them, and because the Lipan and Mescaleros, seeing them attacking us, will continue the invasions on all occasions and times of their own, once the bit of their fears and caution is broken.

¶ 99. The Lipan have been forced to abandon the banks of the Rio Grande del Norte and to ranch upon the shoulders of the presidios. This leaves the latter to resist the invasions of the Indians of the North and in doing so they will not be able to remedy the frightful hostilities which the Lipan themselves commit.

¶ 100. Mescalero outbreaks have been less in the last two years than in the year of '78. Since the Mescaleros are provided with supplies in the presidios of New Vizcaya, where they come in peace, their robberies and murders are more fre-

[31] A.G.I., Guad., 272, Croix to Gálvez, No. 626, Arispe, March 26, 1781.

quent in Coahuila. It is believed that they may be reconciled with the Lipan. From all this may be deduced the unfortunate condition of a province which had glimpsed happiness, was beginning to breathe freely from its evils.

¶ 101. Governor Don Juan de Ugalde, zealous, and a lover of the service, has employed in this worthy matter his personal efforts in repeated reconnaissances of the frontier and territories of his command in the campaign which he made against the Mescaleros, aided by some Lipan, and in other sallies, although without results from any particular action. He has been diligent in understanding the sufferings of the province which he commands and the interests and the character of the Indian enemies, in successfully quieting their unrest, and in providing with proper measures the remedy of the province's injuries. He has consulted me frequently in those steps which he considers proper for the benefit of the province, founding them upon many diffuse and important reports, of which I shall send your Excellency copies with the files of papers which are referred to. In view of everything, I consider that it would be just for your Excellency to recommend to his Majesty the distinguished merits and long service of Colonel Don Juan Ugalde, so that he may be pleased to remember him in promotions and confer upon him another appointment corresponding to his rank, which he seeks and has aspired to since the day he took possession of his present post.[32]

¶ 102. When I left for the province of Texas, Ugalde proposed that the Villa of Monclova, where he has his residence, be garrisoned with a strong detachment. I replied to him that I would agree with pleasure to his proposal if he would repeat it after visiting and becoming acquainted with the province.

¶ 103. He made the inspection and broadened his petition, soliciting one hundred men to be kept free to act in the neighborhood of the Villa. He argued the uselessness of the detachment which I had put in Quatro Ciénegas and that of the pre-

---

[32] A.G.I., Guad., 267, Croix to Gálvez, No. 434, Chihuahua, September 23, 1779. For difficulties which arose later between Croix and Ugalde, see above, page 61.

sidios of Monclova, Aguaverde, and Babia. He petitioned for the abandonment of the first two and the detachment referred to; but as the news of the Lipan and Mescaleros and the invasion of the Indians of the North, to which I have made reference, was coming in at that moment, I did not consider it proper to defer to the governor's proposals that reduced themselves to a project of defense, well founded, but incompatible and prejudicial to the objects of the frontier of the North, which demanded all the forces of the province.

¶ 104. Notwithstanding, I put at his disposal a detachment of forty-two men to be placed where it appeared proper to him for the defense of the villa, pueblos, and haciendas along his frontier. But this assistance, greater than that of the dotation of the presidios of Monclova had when it was transferred to the line of the frontier, did not fulfill the desires of the ardent zeal of the governor.

¶ 105. His reports concerning the condition in which the Lipan were as a result of the invasion of the Indians of the North, the attack of the Mescaleros and the rest of the occurrences which are referred to, the necessity of altering the system of our operations and of combining them with those which must be carried out in Texas and New Vizcaya obliged me to direct the governor of Coahuila, in fulfillment of the royal order of February 20, the same advices which I sent to Texas, adding to the first that which I copy in the following paragraphs:

¶ 106. "Regarding the province of the command of your lordship, similar principles must be observed towards the Lipan, the same method of defensive war, and measures proposed for La Vizcaya. I hope that you will tell me at once of the precise assistance which it may need, so that it may go forward, facilitating the work as is possible, as that which is not begun can never be finished.

¶ 107. "As the old Lipan Bocatuerte and his son may be the instruments of the felicity or ruin of the Lipan, So Patule and his companions in New Vizcaya will be with respect to the Mescaleros nation. The Indians of both groups who submit voluntarily to vassalage and pueblo may enjoy just support as well as the punishment which they may merit. Their lack of confidence and aggravations never should be forgotten but should be recalled to memory frequently. We are not to take part in those attacks which they suffer from the Indians of the North; and, finally, we are to learn, from the events of the moment, what will be applicable to future decisions.

¶ 108. "Your lordship can at once distribute, with respect to what is indicated, the troops of your province, as appears best to you. I do not disapprove the abandonment of the presidios of Aguaverde and Monclova, but will defer decision until I have the approbation of the king.

¶ 109. "In the meantime, I permit your lordship, leaving a small garrison in both presidios for the necessary conservation of the post, to retire the company at Monclova to the Villa of San Fernando and that of Aguaverde to wherever it may be useful, counting as forces of your province and under the orders of your lordship the company of San Saba, which must garrison the presidio of its name and that of La Babia. For the present I am separating them from the second division of New Vizcaya because of peace with the Mescaleros."

¶ 110. Governor Don Juan Ugalde proposed, in view of my decisions, that the company of Monclova be transferred to garrison the villa, the capital of the province; that of Aguaverde to San Fernando; that of La Babia be incorporated into that of the Valley of Santa Rosa; that nothing new be done on the Rio Grande; that the useless presidios of Monclova and Aguaverde be put in the custody of officers, a sergeant and twelve men; and that the company of San Saba be not considered then for a better place because of its useless condition.

¶ 111. I approved all at once. I believed the difficulties conquered and the anxieties dissipated, with which the province of Coahuila worried me. With regard to the transference of the presidio of San Buenaventura and the troop of the company, the officers have contributed graciously more than two thousand pesos; those of Carrizal, eight hundred for the building of their church, and all have merited the royal thanks of his

PROVINCE OF COAHUILA

Majesty. It appeared proper to me and very fit that not only the officers and troop of the presidios of Monclova and Aguaverde should make similar voluntary contributions, but also the settlers of the two villas, which they are going to garrison, should do so.

¶ 112. With these objects, I advised the governor, citing him the example of San Buenaventura, that, having made known to the officers and troops the particular benefits which were to be extended them in their new advantageous appointments, and to the settlers the benefits of the most certain defense of their lives and goods, he persuade both with regard to the contributions. I intimated to the governor that I should not demand them, but that if the royal treasury were more free it might be able to support in these provinces expenses other than those which it distributes annually to conserve them.

¶ 113. In his letter of December 28, '79, the governor replied to me that the contributions were unnecessary and that neither the salaries of the officers and troops nor the poverty of the settlers could provide them. For this reason I resolved that the transference of the presidial companies be suspended.

¶ 114. Each day made more visible the uselessness not only of the presidios of Monclova and Aguaverde but that of San Saba and Babia, whose troops consume annually the quantity of 95,561 pesos, without providing defense for the province which they ought to protect. On the other hand, if they were established in better situations, they could defend it from all its enemies. I finally decided upon their total dismantling. I took into consideration that the war with the English will postpone without doubt the royal resolutions of his Majesty that I have asked for concerning the affair. Until receiving them I had thought of conserving the weak presidios and not finishing the quarters of the four above mentioned presidios. There was opposed to this measure the consideration that the small number of troops destined for their custody will not perhaps be sufficient to defend them. Moreover, unable to repair the ruins of the buildings, they will present difficulties attending their relief and transportation of provisions, and lessen the number of troops within the province.

¶ 115. Without the intercession of their governor, the officers and troop of the presidio of La Monclova have obligated themselves to contribute two thousand pesos, and those of Aguaverde, two thousand and six hundred. I am persuaded that this example of generosity may animate the settlers of the villas of Monclova and San Fernando. After they contribute a normal donation, according to their resources, the transference of the two companies and the abandonment of the presidios may be carried out very soon. The same action will be taken in regard to San Saba and Babia.

¶ 116. The bankruptcy of the two quartermasters, which amounted to more than sixteen thousand pesos, has been the reason this San Saba company is in a condition to be suppressed. This I have decided upon. The useful officers and troops will be added to those of Monclova and Babia until an opportune time occurs to reorganize San Saba. That will be when the governor remits me the reports I have asked of him concerning the points that ought to be occupied on the frontier of the Bolsón to impede the invasion of the Indians and dislodge them from the nearby sierras where they are ranching.

¶ 117. In the meantime, I am satisfied that the troops of Coahuila are well distributed in the four principal posts of the province, namely, the presidio of Rio Grande; the Villa of San Fernando, eighteen leagues away; the valley of Santa Rosa, twenty leagues distant; and the villa of Santiago de la Monclova, thirty-five leagues distant from Santa Rosa.

¶ 118. This distribution, proposed to your Excellency in my letter No. 458 of January 23, '80,[33] agrees with the latest solicitations of Governor Don Juan Ugalde. Each post has forces sufficient to resist invasion of any class of enemies. In a very short time all can be united in the center and on the flanks of the territory which they occupy. They will defend without anxiety the pueblos and haciendas of their respective districts.

[33] See above, page 12, footnote 12.

PROVINCE OF COAHUILA

The Indians of the North will encounter resistance, the Mescaleros will withhold their hostilities in the territory of the capital, and the Lipan will see themselves obliged to remain beyond the frontier of our settlements.

¶ 119. These are the only measures that can be taken today in benefit of the province of Coahuila. It is one of the most estimable dominions, which must be sooner or later, in my opinion, the theater of a most useful and advantageous war, but it is necessary to support and develop it.

¶ 120. The establishment of the new bishopric, and the payment of the appropriations for its presidios and those of Texas in the valley of Santa Rosa, will make it flourish in a few years for the reasons extensively set forth in the representation which I have made to his Majesty, and which accompanies the one I made your Excellency in letter No. 507, April 23, '80.[34]

PROVINCE OF NEW MEXICO

¶ 121

THE eight jurisdictions or lieutenantships of which this government is composed, without including that of the pueblo of El Paso, amount to 20,810 persons according to the population list. They recognize as the capital the villa and presidio of Santa Fe. The missions of Ácoma and Zuñi are those which are at the greatest distance, sixty leagues (from the capital).

¶ 122. The Comanche and all the Apache, with the exception of the Navajo and Jicarilla now at peace, attack in this province; the Moqui need today our assistance to avoid perishing from hunger and misery; the numerous and valiant Ute nation remains friendly and aids us happily against the Comanche.

¶ 123. From the pueblo of El Paso there intervenes to the north a desert of more than one hundred leagues to the first establishment of New Mexico. For this reason, and for the reason that this province is advanced beyond the rest of my

---

[34] A.G.I., Guad., 277, Croix to Gálvez, No. 507, Arispe, April 30, 1780.

CROIX'S REPORT OF 1781

command, without other communication with New Vizcaya except by caravans which annually cross the above mentioned desert, it depends for its defenses upon the presidial company at Santa Fe of one hundred and ten units, and upon the strength of its settlers, Indians, and Spaniards.

¶ 124. Its conservation is so important that if we should lose New Mexico a second time,[35] we would have upon Vizcaya, Sonora, and Coahuila all the enemies which now invade that province.

¶ 125. The just view of warding off these possible misfortunes obliged me to hold in Chihuahua, with the attendance of Brigadier D. Pedro Fermín de Mendinueta,[36] who had governed the province more than eleven years, and his successor, Lieutenant Colonel Don Juan Bautista de Anza,[37] the particular councils of war of which I have given an account to your Excellency in letter No. 236, July 27, '78, and which his Majesty approved in his royal order of January 21, '79.[38]

¶ 126. The points agreed upon in the said councils reduced themselves to the arrangement of the militias of El Paso, to the development of this province, an examination of the spot of Robledo, the reunion of the dispersed settlers of the province, the remedy of various disorders, and operations of war.

¶ 127. For the discharge of these objectives, I dispatched to the new governor the necessary instructions. I am leaving for the second part of this report a statement of the results concerning the arrangement of militias of El Paso and development of that pueblo. I shall set forth to your Excellency briefly and methodically the matters which touch the rest of the points.

¶ 128. Having reconnoitered the spot of Robledo, and finding no suitable place to establish the detachment advised in Ar-

[35] The first time was in 1680. See Charles Wilson Hackett, "Revolt of the Pueblo Indians of New Mexico in 1680," *Texas State Historical Association Quarterly*, XV (1911-1912), No. 2.
[36] For data on Mendinueta, see Alfred B. Thomas, "Governor Mendinueta's Proposals for the Defense of New Mexico, 1772-1778," *New Mexico Historical Review*, VI (1931), No. 1.
[37] See above, page 39, footnote 121.
[38] See above, page 39, footnote 121.

PROVINCE OF NEW MEXICO

ticle 23 of the royal instruction inserted in the Regulation of the Presidios, Lieutenant Colonel Don Juan Bautista de Anza agreed with the opinion of his predecessor and proposed to me that the forces destined for Robledo be established in the abandoned pueblo of Socorro.

¶ 129. Of these results, I have given an account to your excellency in letter No. 388 of April 26, '79. Governor Anza, having verified for me by verbal reports the impossibility of establishing the detachment of Robledo, I did not find it convenient to establish it now at Socorro. I based my action upon the fact that the new post was not in keeping with the purposes which the previously cited article 23 of the royal instruction indicates. I held as more useful the measures that the presidial company of Santa Fe conserve its force united, and that the annual expense of the thirty settler-auxiliaries from the pueblo of El Paso, with that which the militia tax fund can support, be devoted to the important defense of the pueblo itself. I also considered that there be maintained in El Paso a detachment of veteran troops which may discharge the duty of escorting the caravan of mule drivers and passengers and resist where possible the contact of the eastern Apache with those of the west.[39] Concerning this matter, I am referring to what I set forth to your Excellency in the second part of this paper.

¶ 130. The point concerning the reunion of the settlers has developed an extensive file of papers. The governor began with efficiency the orders decided upon in the councils. The idea was proposed of establishing the pueblos in good order, walled, close to the fields of labor, and filled with fifty families each. He informed me of the defects of the villa of Santa Fe, and of the necessity of keeping together the company which garrisoned it, and of the possibility of building quarters and rebuilding the villa in its contiguous barrio of Analco. He sought permission from me (which I conceded) to proceed to the execution of the undertakings.

¶ 131. Disgruntled, the settlers came begging me that the

[39] A.G.I., Guad., 267, Croix to Gálvez, No. 388, Chihuahua, April 26, 1779.

measure of their reunion be not continued. I commanded them suspended and advised the governor that he make his reports to me.

¶ 132. In view of them, attending to the fact that the larger part of the settlers were reunited, experiencing the particular benefits in their greater security, arrangement, and defense, and that the governor in a new report, well founded on good and congruous reasons, proposed to me the transference of the presidial company of his command to ten leagues from the Villa of Santa Fe, I decided, agreeing in everything with the opinion of the assessor of this commandancy general, that the reunion of the settlements of New Mexico be carried out in the manner commanded by the governor, Don Juan Bautista de Anza;[40] that the works begun be concluded, and that he should proceed to the transference of the presidio along the banks of the Rio Grande del Norte on the spot which was halfway between the places called Santo Domingo and Cochití.

¶ 133. For this new establishment, the officers and troop of the company have contributed voluntarily 2,175 pesos. I have freed the two thousand pesos which exist in the treasury of Chihuahua for the purpose of building materials for the detachment which was to be established in Robledo. A copy is being made of the file of papers which sets forth the fundamentals of my decisions, to remit it to your Excellency and to ask for the sovereign approval of the king. Likewise, I am doing the same with that which has been brought together relative to the disorders of which an accusation can be made when the assessor may draw it up.[41]

¶ 134. With regard to operations of war, I have given an account to your Excellency in letter No. 462, January 23, '80,

---

[40] Thomas *Forgotten Frontiers*, 379–80, note 59.

[41] Desordenes que se advierten en el Nuevo Mexico y medios ... para mejorar su constitución ... enclosed in A.G.I., 103–4–18, Croix to Gálvez, No. 217 (Confidential), Chihuahua, June 29, 1778, enclosure No. 3. This is without signature and certified to by Antonio Bonilla, Chihuahua, July 22, 1778. This document has been credited to Father Morfi. However, the present editor is not entirely satisfied that Morfi was the author. For similar "desordenes" in New Vizcaya, Coahuila, and Texas, see A.G.I., Guad., 270, Croix to Gálvez, No. 282, Chihuahua, September 23, 1778.

of the fortunate campaign which Governor Juan Bautista de Anza executed against the Comanche in the months of August and September of '79 with a corps of six hundred men, presidial troops, militia, and Pueblo Indian auxiliaries, to which were added two hundred Ute and Jicarilla Apache allies.

¶ 135. Twice they attacked the Comanche; destroyed one hundred and twenty wigwams, killed their great chief called Cuerno Verde, his son, his lieutenant-general, Aguila Bolteada, Pujacante, or priest, and fifty-two other warriors; twenty women and children and thirty-four other individuals were taken prisoner along with five hundred head of stock.[42]

¶ 136. In another representation, No. 476, February 23, '80, remitting copies of documents, I notified your Excellency of the miserable state to which hunger and sickness had reduced the Indians of Moqui.[43] I set forth my measures dictated to reduce them by the Christian means of succoring their necessities, offering them our aid and protection, and not demanding of them anything by violence on the points of religion and vassalage.

¶ 137. To carry out these measures, the governor of New Mexico went to the province of Moqui. He found it destroyed by the rigors of hunger, pestilence, and war. But the chief priests of the nation were inexorable in their purpose of remaining heathen, preserving their customs, and remaining in their desolated pueblos, in spite of the sad references which they made to the fact that, when Father Fr. Francisco Garcés presented himself and was badly received in their towns, he predicted for them the infelicities and miseries they are now suffering.

¶ 138. Notwithstanding, the governor came back with two hundred Moqui, who voluntarily left without opposition of their chiefs, and on allotted land they are now happy in the New Mexican settlements. Unfortunately, forty other families who desired a similar life were murdered by the Navajo Apache.

[42] Thomas, *Forgotten Frontiers,* has this translated, 119–42.
[43] *Ibid.*, 221–45.

¶ 139. After all, the governor, while hoping that the voluntary reduction of the Moqui may continue, intimated that our convenience may force the whole nation to make this choice to prevent the Navajo from seizing them and thus increasing their numbers and our enemies. But having agreed with the opinion of the assessor, Don Pedro Galindo, I directed that the same measures be carried out as practiced for the gentle reconquest of the Moqui; that there should be extended to them the promises made to the reduced Indians. I also indicated that the latter be not disturbed by aggravations, vexations, and injuries, which may oblige them to prefer the infelicities of their people, and flee from the pueblos in which they are settled. I further provided that from the fund for gratification of the presidial company of Santa Fe, from the communities of the pueblos, or from other suitable resources, necessary assistance be sent to enable them to live, so that their own felicity may be the most real and efficacious example for the voluntary reduction of their compatriots. I also determined that to this end, one of the reduced Moqui who may be considered influential and reliable be dispatched to Moqui soon under the pretext of trade. I directed, too, that in order not to see advantages wasted in the future, which the present unhappy condition of the Moqui offer, care be taken not to gather them into a single pueblo, but in many towns distant from the confines of their provinces. These dispositions I hope will merit the superior pleasure of your Excellency and the royal approval of his Majesty when I give an account with copies of the latest developments of this affair.

¶ 140. I have given in letters No. 52, 111, and 389 of March 23 and October 10, '77, and April 26, '79,[44] an account of my first measures for the discovery of a road from Santa Fe to Sonora, and method of operations of war in New Mexico. Under date of March 26 last, letter No. 628, I sent you an extract of the file of papers, with copies of my second dispositions to make effective the discovery, and of the results of the

[44] Harvard College Library, Sparks Mss. 98 (VI), No. 2371, Croix to Gálvez, 387, Chihuahua, April 26, 1779.

PROVINCE OF NEW MEXICO

campaigns executed to aid it with troops from this province and that of New Vizcaya.[45]

¶ 141. In the above cited letter, No. 628, I set forth to your Excellency that the route of the discovery was mistaken, as Anza ought to have reached the presidio of Santa Cruz in Sonora, but came out almost in front of that of Janos, and that it was necessary to repeat the operation in this year. This will be done, if it is possible, with the hope of achieving greater results than those which the campaign detachments produced, which were the death of thirty-one Apache, the apprehension of twenty-five, the freeing of four Christian prisoners, and booty of three hundred and fifteen head of stock.

¶ 142. In New Mexico, a similar discovery of a direct route to the presidio of Monterrey in California failed me when the attempt which the reverend father missionaries, Fray Francisco Atanasio Domínguez and Fray Francisco Velez Escalante, made was frustrated.[46] The execution of the same measures would not be useless respecting a route from Santa Fe to the presidio of Antonio de Bejar, in Texas, and to the Rio Grande, in Coahuila, but nothing of this matter is possible now.[47]

¶ 143. Although incomplete and at a cost of many fatigues, the supply of horses was provided, at the king's expense, for the New Mexican settlers. Of this affair I have given your Excellency an account in letter No. 581, December 23, '80.[48] In the monthly extracts of news of the enemies, I have referred to the matters corresponding to this province.

¶ 144. In these extracts it is seen that the Comanche swept over the province in the year of '78. Its settlers, dispersed, were unable to resist them. The province, at a single blow, saw sacrificed 127 persons dead and captured.

[45] Thomas, *Forgotten Frontiers,* has this translated, 171–221.
[46] A.G.I., Guad., 516, Croix to Gálvez, No. 81, México, July 26, 1777, has a copy of the Domínguez-Escalante diary; the map, however, is missing.
[47] The Bejar-Santa Fé expedition was made later (Bolton, *Texas in the Middle Eighteenth Century,* 122–33).
[48] A.G.I., Guad., 277, Croix to Gálvez, No. 581, Arispe, December 23, 1780.

¶ 145. In line with what was agreed upon in the councils of war, with the reports of Brigadier Don Pedro Fermín de Mendinueta, and with the knowledge which, with these antecedents, Lieutenant Colonel Juan Bautista de Anza immediately acquired of the sufferings of the territory of his command, he made peace with the valiant Ute and Jicarilla Apache. He also took care not to disturb the Navajo, and, leaving for a more opportune time the means of withstanding the attacks which the Apache enemies were committing, he united his forces and employed them with the aid of the Ute in the campaign against the Comanche referred to in paragraph 134.[49]

¶ 146. Others followed this fortunate operation, carried out by the Indian allies and settlers of the province with equal felicity, and with sensible losses on the part of the Comanche. The former, as a result, took courage; the latter swallowed their pride and solicited peace in the pueblo of Taos, but recognizing opposition, transferred their hostilities to the province of Texas.

¶ 147. These established results induced a fortunate reaction so that these Comanche, who are the most valiant and warlike of Indians known on our frontiers, became dismayed by the first unfortunate blows they received and retired from the territory where they found resistance. With what greater reason can we hope that the Lipan Apache, who do not have the asylums and hiding places the Comanche have, will surrender their arms to the first threat of our forces and those of the Nations of the North without giving us reason to shed their blood?

¶ 148. If the Comanche were capable of recognizing their real interests they would never attack in New Mexico; they would be happy and the province would not have the enemies that now incommode it.

¶ 149. The nation is numerous; the country which they live in is wild, and has abundant streams, arroyos, and springs which fertilize it. The species of deer, antelope, and bison

---

[49] See Thomas, *Forgotten Frontiers, passim.*

there are inexhaustible. Thus, without prejudice to the aversion which the Comanche have, as all Indians do, to the cultivation, conservation, and development of possessions which nature providently offers them, they cannot enjoy these things peacefully, but acquire what they need in hostility.

¶ 150. Their possessions are reduced to the horses which they need for their hunts and firearms whose advantages they understand. They can have everything at the hands of the Spaniards. In a few years they would see in their country the procreation of horses in the same abundance as that of deer and buffalo, and then not needing these animals, the acquisition of firearms in barter for hides and herds would be less difficult for them.

¶ 151. The Comanche have on the frontier of their territories enemy nations which impinge upon and fight them frequently. But if they were our friends in New Mexico, they could count upon the support of our arms and we upon theirs.

¶ 152. In this case the Ute, an aggrieved branch but irreconcilable enemy of the Comanche nation, would see themselves forced to live under our protection. The alliances which they are accustomed to make, when it is convenient, with the Jicarilla and Navajo Apache would cause us no fears.

¶ 153. These last, Navajo, deviating nobly from their race, are inclined to work and to recognize a stable domicile, make their woven stuffs from wool, sow and conserve their crops.

¶ 154. The fear of losing their possessions obliges them to keep peace in New Mexico, but when they observe afflictions within the province, they are induced by their relatives, the Gila, to declare war upon us.

¶ 155. To withstand them, no better means has been found than that of availing ourselves of the arms of the Ute. It is sufficient that the latter declare war to make the Navajo desist from war on us. Notwithstanding, in the midst of peace they commit small robberies, are accustomed to mix with the rest of the Apache in their incursions, and cannot live without robbery because of the extreme sterility of the countries in which they dwell.

¶ 156. If only the Comanche, recognizing the advantages which I set forth in paragraphs 148 to 153, were faithful friends in New Mexico, the province would not have to fear the Ute, Navajo, and Apache, as the troop and valorous settlers of the province would be sufficient to punish their hostilities. With the aid of the Comanche they could subject these nations. In this case, with the Ute, Navajo, and Apache remaining in their distant countries where they would have nothing to long for, we would see in our lands the felicitous and desired pacification.

¶ 157. For all these reasons, supported by the councils of war, I advised the governor to try to attract the Comanche to peace, but they have not offered it in good faith. Although perhaps the emissary from Texas, Don Nicolas de la Matte, could succeed in doing away with the memory of their latest injuries and fear of our vengeance because of the injuries which they have inflicted upon us. These achievements are difficult. I shall content myself if the Comanche make less frequent visits to the territories of New Mexico, if the Ute remain faithful to our friendship, and if the Navajo do not take sides openly in the interests of the Apache. In this way the hostilities of the latter can be withstood and punished, and the province will breathe.

¶ 158. Its present condition is neither better nor worse than it was when I took command of all these interior provinces, although I am inclined to the second consideration because a country where hostility does not cease is consequently one which becomes each day more decadent.

¶ 159. So that it may not become more decadent, I can take no measures other than those which I have taken and referred to in this report. Allying ourselves faithfully with the Comanche is difficult and risky. Opening communication and commerce of the province of New Mexico with the rest of the interior provinces is as remote as the projects of reducing, subjecting, or exterminating the Apache.

Tables Showing Financial Condition of New Vizcaya and New Mexico, 1781

CROIX'S REPORT OF 1781

PROVINCE OF NEW VIZCAYA

¶ 160

ALL the branches, congregations, or little bands of this nation (Apache) attack incessantly in New Vizcaya. The settlement farthest from the frontier is not free from their incursions. With more practical knowledge than the natives, the Apache move about over the territory of this province.

¶ 161. Divided into twenty-six alcaldias, or jurisdictions, more than one hundred thousand souls people it—a small number for its vast extension and for the development, labor, and culture of its rural and mineral riches.[50]

¶162. Within a few years from the time of its occupation, its prosperity made it flourish with advantages for all the interior provinces, and even those outside of New Spain, but in the year '48 the war with the Apache began and with it began the decadence of the province's prosperity.

¶ 163. The misfortunes and injuries which, without intermission, it has suffered in the period of more than thirty-two years are the most convincing proof of its opulence. Not only has it sustained itself, but it has increased the royal treasury with large and equitable donations and enriched many vassals of his Majesty who extend its commerce to the metropolis and principal cities of the viceroyalty. Suffering thus from its greatest afflictions it just made the generous donation of more than one hundred thousand pesos, and it is imposing taxes which can render more than seventy thousand annually for the creation and support of its militias.

¶ 164. As soon as I noticed the recommendable circumstances of this province, and its hostilities, I dedicated myself to extending to it means conducive to its felicity. I judge that if

[50] For a description of New Vizcaya about this time, see Pedro Tamaron y Romeral, *Demonstración del vastisimo obispado de la Nueva Vizcaya, 1765*, edited by Vito Alessio Robles (Mexico, 1937). Regarding the contributions mentioned in ¶ 163 below, see A.G.I., Guad., 267, Croix to Gálvez, No. 408, Pueblo de Nombre de Dios, July 23, 1779; *ibid.*, No. 409; *ibid.*, No. 410; A.G.I., Guad., 519, Croix to Gálvez, No. 439, Chihuahua, September 23, 1779.

there had not occurred the misfortune of the sudden death of Commander Inspector Don Joseph Rubio, and my grave sickness, my residence in Chihuahua would have been greater than that which I planned when I came back from the frontiers of Texas and Coahuila.

¶ 165. My first dispositions for the defense of New Vizcaya were those contained in the instruction which I sent to the commander inspector under date of February 24, '77, and which his Majesty deigned to approve in royal order of May 24, of the same year, replying to my letter number two.

¶ 166. I am reducing the instruction to these three objectives of the greatest importance: the protection of the interior country; the continuation of offensive war; and reviews of the troop.

¶ 167. For the first, when I took charge of this command there were a flying company of 145 units garrisoning the Villa of Chihuahua, another of 120 divided into many, and small detachments from Parage de Ancón de Carros on the Rio de Conchos, which is a little less than thirty leagues from the Villa, as far as the Pueblo del Gallo. As this distribution appeared good to me, I commanded the commander inspector to examine only the local situation of the above-mentioned detachments and to have them move closer to the abandoned presidios of Mapimí, El Gallo, Cerrogordo, San Bartolomé, and Conchos, if he should consider that from this measure there would come advantages, namely, that the settlements might receive assistance with greater celerity, and that the troop might benefit by having some relief and rest of which their continuous residence in the desert deprived them, and which contributed to the injury of health, shortage of supplies, loss of uniforms, arms and mountings, and a notable backwardness in instruction and discipline.

¶ 168. As to the second—offensive war—I strengthened the presidios of the frontier line with two more flying companies and the pickets of Dragoons of Spain and Mexico. I made two divisions of these forces. I put in command of them, in the capacity of commanders of the armed forces, captains of presidios oldest in service. I provided that alternately a body of 150 men be dispatched each month over the lands of the enemies, that the remaining troops be employed in garrisoning the posts, examining the frontier, in ambushing, in following with great care the entering trail of the Indians to prevent hostilities and the departing one, with forces and supplies, to recapture from them the stolen goods and punish them on their retreat to their rancherias. Finally, I provided that all the appropriate operations of war of these countries be carried out, both by the troops advanced to the frontier line, and by those destined to protect the interior of the province, so that the Indian enemy will always be ignorant of our movements; the settlements might have more defense ready, the horses would not be made useless in repeated fruitless marches, and the soldier might be employed with discretion in the fatigues of war and in those designed to instruct him in its engagements and obligations.

¶ 169. For the third—troop reviews—I prescribed for the commander inspector methodical rules to bring out clearly in the reviews of inspection the actual condition of the presidial and flying companies for the purpose of finding ways to improve them if they were good, or to correct defects that were discovered.

¶ 170. The commander inspector was not able to hold more than two reviews because of his death. The captain of San Elezario, Don Diego de Borica, has carried on, by virtue of a commission, the reviews of the presidios, and the captain of San Carlos, Don Juan Gutiérrez de la Cueva, those of the flying companies. I have dispatched to your Excellency the first in different mails, and the second have not yet been concluded. But on this matter I refer to the report which I made to your Excellency in letter No. 403 of June 23, '79, and of which I shall speak in the second part of this report.

¶ 171. In the presidios the plan of operations of defensive war was put into operation.[51] Thus on June 1, '77, the fairly large detachment of 150 men set out from Janos. It surprised

[51] Croix to Gálvez, No. 80. See above, page 27, footnote 69.

a rancheria of twenty Apache, killed four, took prisoner six children, and restored a captive and fifteen head of stock. I gave an account of this to your Excellency in letter No. 109, October 10 of the same year.[52] These operations, however, could not be continued because it was necessary to support the operations of my reconnaissance in Coahuila and Texas with troops from New Vizcaya.

¶ 172. My measures for interior protection had no effect because the commander inspector advised of the difficulties in their execution. At the same time occurred the formidable invasion which the Apache made into the territories of Cuencamé, Rio de Nazas, Gallo, and Mapimí, of which I advised your Excellency in letter No. 78 of July 26, '77.[53]

¶ 173. When I came back from Coahuila, I undertook to continue the operations of the defensive war, which were carried out by different routes in the Bolsón de Mapimí. But the bad condition of the horse herds, the worse condition of the flying companies, and the news that the Apache of the west had sought peace in Janos, Valley of San Buenaventura, Paso del Norte, and San Elezario, did not permit it.

¶ 174. By the beginning of the year '78, with information available of the terrains that had been examined, of the condition of the troops of New Vizcaya, and of the causes of its hostilities, I stationed on the frontier of the Bolsón de Mapimí, the First Flying Company, half of the Fourth, a detachment of the Second, and the picket of the Dragoons of Spain, which composed in all 262 men. I distributed them in the abandoned presidios of Conchos, Guajoquilla, Cerrogordo, Gallo, and Mapimí. I provided the rules for exercising these troops in maneuvers of a mixed war of offense and defense.[54] I declared by proclamation the support with which the settlers must assist them for their own greater security.[55] The public which longed for these dispositions received them with inexpressible relief.

[52] A.G.I., Guad., 516, Croix to Gálvez, No. 109, Durango, October 10, 1777.
[53] A.G.I., Guad., 515, Croix to Gálvez, No. 78, México, July 26, 1777.
[54] See above, page 27, footnote 70.
[55] See above, page 27, footnote 71.

PROVINCE OF NEW VIZCAYA

¶ 175. For the safeguarding of the territory of Chihuahua, I took similar measures. I gave the corresponding orders that the presidios keep themselves on the defensive. Having had information that the Apache were considering a second invasion into the jurisdictions near Durango, I covered with detachments of settlers the banks of the Rio Nazas. Of all this I advised your Excellency in letter No. 198, May 1, '78, and his Majesty was pleased to approve it in the royal order of October 30 of the same year.[56]

¶ 176. These measures held off the hostilities. But I could not see the better effects to which they conspired because at that time it was necessary that the detachments of the frontier of the Bolsón be diverted to form escorts for the numerous horse herds that were being gathered for New Mexico, for the light troop recently created, for the transportation of strong boxes from Durango to the treasury of Chihuahua, and for the weekly mails; and to quiet the unrest which was remarked in various pueblos of the Tarahumare. Besides, there was lacking from the detachments more than one hundred units for their completion, vacancies by reason of individuals incapacitated, imprisoned, and sick.

¶ 177. With little difference the same thing happened in Chihuahua. The lack of pastures at the posts which the troops were to occupy necessitated reuniting and establishing them at a distance of twenty to thirty leagues from Chihuahua.

¶ 178. During the month of August, '78, there was completed the recruiting of the larger part of the light troop of recent creation. It was perfectly instructed, disciplined, and provided with all that was necessary for transferring them to their companies and entering upon the fatigues of the service.

¶ 179. To my particular pleasure there was offered an excellent opportunity to test their utility. Because of the results which flowed from the deceitful peace of the Apache of the west, of which I shall speak in its place, I dispatched, at the orders of Captain Don Nicolas Gil, fifty light soldiers so that

[56] A.G.I., Guad., 276, Croix to Gálvez, No. 198, Chihuahua, May 1, 1778.

with them and another forty-eight presidios, flying and dragoons, he could attack the valley of San Buenaventura.

¶ 180. As the time was very appropriate for opening this campaign and this first operation, with respect to the considerable number of the troops, with regard to the concept I had formed of the intelligence, understanding, and spirit of Commander Gil, and the excellent opportunity to have the enemy in view, the most favorable results were possible. I was completely persuaded that if the operation succeeded, future ones would be fortunate. But the Apache disillusioned my hopes, eluding the maneuvers of Captain Gil, and leaving the troops, after a repetition of marches and countermarches, in a useless condition, as I set forth to your Excellency under date of October 23, '78, letter No. 293.[57]

¶ 181. All the troops of New Vizcaya at the beginning of the year '79 were in the same condition. Those of the frontier of the Bolsón had destroyed the horses in their custody on escorts and, on one occasion, in pursuing the enemies; those patrolling between the presidios of Janos and San Elezario, in the operations of Captain Gil; those of El Norte, Principe, San Carlos, and San Saba, in the maneuvers carried out in Coahuila to indispose the Lipan and Mescaleros; and those of Chihuahua, in sustaining other operations, and in the sterile pastures. The two pickets of dragoons destined to garrison Sonora were in the worst situation, and they were in the same condition when they were to escort my next march.

¶ 182. I planned to depart on the eighth of May, '79, and as on the previous march my equipage and papers were traveling along the Sierra Madre, nothing remained except to put foot in the stirrup when God was pleased to prostrate me with the grave sickness which I suffered from May until my arrival at this capital. Thus when I set out from Chihuahua on the last day of September, I was very near the beginning of my convalescence.

¶ 183. Notwithstanding, in the most serious stage of my sickness I attended to the daily dispatch of the grave affairs which

[57] A.G.I., Guad., 270, Croix to Gálvez, No. 293, Chihuahua, October 23, 1778.

supervened from the results of my previous dispositions. I took as far as possible the final hand in the establishment of militias; I left in assembly 175 Provincial Dragoons which today increase the forces of the province without charge upon the treasury; I dictated the general resolutions which the disarrangement of the troops demanded, adverted to in the reviews of inspection in Sonora, New Vizcaya, and Coahuila; and with knowledge of the news occurring in the east regarding the Lipan, Mescaleros, and Nations of the North, I proceeded to the fulfillment of the royal order of February 20,'79.

¶ 184. Thus from the beginning of the year '77, until the end of '79, without losing sight of the affairs of Sonora, Rio Colorado, California, and New Mexico, the first object of my attention was the operations agreed upon in the councils of war against the Apachería of the east. The second was the creation of the militias of New Vizcaya, looked forward to in the royal instructions which govern me, and which I shall consider very necessary for the defense of New Vizcaya and profitable to sustain the undertakings of the east. The third was the reviews of inspection, since putting the troops upon the indispensable footing of good government, management of interests and instruction, assured, as a consequence, the fruit of my desires. The fourth was the defenses of New Vizcaya.

¶ 185. With regard to the first, I have already treated it diffusely in the reports of Texas and Coahuila. I am repeating for the present that I do not see success impossible, and that I did not determine upon the undertaking because I needed a larger number of troops, or because I lacked confidence in the present ones as a result of their unhappy condition, irremediable for many years.

¶ 186. With regard to the second object, it appears to me that the results of the large donations and income from taxes recommend the results—an amount already exceeding twelve thousand pesos; the enlistment of 3,183 men sworn in the obligation of defending the dominions of the king; and the useful service of the pickets, which have been armed.[58]

[58] Croix to Gálvez, No. 65. Footnote 71, page 27, above, deals with plans

CROIX'S REPORT OF 1781

¶ 187. The third also recommends itself because it is not so much the number of troops that makes war as the excellent condition of them.

¶ 188. With regard to the fourth, although I have spoken of my dispositions from paragraph 165 to 176, there are lacking references to other measurcs which belong to this point and which I took in September '79, on the eve of my departure from Chihuahua, and in October from Hacienda de Ensinillas and presidios of San Buenaventura and Janos.

¶ 189. In letter No. 297, October 23, '78, I set forth to your Excellency the reasons which have obliged me to remove the cited presidio of San Buenaventura to the spot called Chavarria, namely, the condition of this region, the possibility of erecting a villa in the shelter of the presidial arms, and the possibility of peopling successively the Villa of Casas Grandes and the abandoned mission of Namquipa.[59] These measures were approved by his Majesty in royal order of April 19, '79. Here I refer to them because, as I stated in paragraph 65 of the General Report No. 3, of March 29, '79, relative to the defenses of the province, they are possible and advantageous as is shown in the paragraph to which I refer.[60]

¶ 190. In another letter, No. 304, November 23, '78, presenting to your Excellency the reasons for my delay in the above province,[61] I set forth that I suffered from the serious drawback of bad faith on the part of the Tarahumare who, now allied with the Apache and now alone, were the agents of many hostilities; that in Mexico an extensive file of papers

---

to form the militias. Footnote 50, page 115, above has data regarding finances, Nos. 408, 409, 410, 439. On condition of the militia, see A.G.I., Guad., 276, Croix to Gálvez, No. 219, Chihuahua, June 29, 1778; A.G.I., Guad., 270, Croix to Gálvez, No. 317, Chihuahua, December 28, 1778; and A.G.I., Guad., 267, Croix to Gálvez, No. 407, Pueblo de Nombre de Dios, July 23, 1779. Regarding the pickets, A.G.I., Guad., 267, Croix to Gálvez, No. 305, Chihuahua, November 30, 1778.

[59] A.G.I., Guad., 270, Croix to Gálvez, No. 297, Chihuahua, October 23, 1778, and ibid., No. 329, Chihuahua, December 28, 1778.

[60] See above, page 11, footnote 10.

[61] A.G.I., Guad., 275, Croix to Gálvez, No. 304, Chihuahua, November 30, 1778.

concerning the matter was delivered to me; and that others were added on my ingress into Chihuahua. The roots of some evils having been illustrated and made clear, if their remedy were postponed the provinces would be lost and the contagion would extend to those which now enjoy the quiet of peace.

¶ 191. I also set forth that I had no other staff from which my determinations emanate for the vast government of these provinces and their new establishments than the secretariat and office of the assessor. The former, equipped with two officials who were unable to discharge all the business, was without funds other than my salaries for the expense which it occasioned, and the office of the assessor had only one amanuensis paid by the assessor.

¶ 192. Notwithstanding, in spite of the lack of greater assistance of this character, which is indispensable for the dispatch of affairs, they have handled all the files of papers arising from the Tarahumare with the exception of the principal one, which is the proof of the Tarahumare infidelity and which is in the possession of the assessor.

¶ 193. In some cases the Tarahumare have been relieved from the vexations which they suffer on their departures from their pueblos to work in mines and haciendas by virtue of the orders of the justices. Accordingly, the issuing of these proclamations has been prohibited and the Indians are permitted to be used only for the construction of buildings on the frontier.

¶ 194. In other files of papers the division of the land among the Indians has been arranged for with greater equity and with just regard for their own benefit and comfort. Certain amounts of money which belong to them from the rent of their lands, have been distributed among them.

¶ 195. In others, rules for good government have been drawn up and commands issued that they be observed in order that the Tarahumare may recognize subjection and docile obedience to their general and justices of the territory, so that they may not leave their pueblos without the permission of their chiefs; and in order to apprehend fugitives.

¶ 196. In one of the files of papers referred to, there has been treated the question of creating a Protector of Indians in each jurisdiction to defend them and protect them in accord with the laws.[62]

¶ 197. In the establishment of militia, the squads of Indian auxiliaries have been put respectively under the orders of the captains of the companies of Spaniards and commandants of the corps, so that upon those who are the most active and warlike[63] has been put a most gentle bridle, which is acceptable and honorable, in order to lead them into the best conduct, to make them useful for the defense of the country, and to make possible the subjection of the rest of the Tarahumare.

¶ 198. Finally, in another file of papers have been determined the just rights of these Indians who have been congregated in missions which the ex-Jesuits administered. This amounts to a considerable sum of pesos which have entered the royal boxes. Restitution has been sought.

¶ 199. Of all I would have given your Excellency an account, but I do not have amanuenses to make the necessary copies. Although prolix extracts could be made from the expedientes, the matters are delicate and time is lacking which is necessary to employ in the office in matters of greater importance.

¶ 200. In letters No. 149, 174, 200, and 293, of February 15, May 1, and October 23, '78, I advised your Excellency of the solicitations for peace made by the Gila at the presidio of Janos, Valley of San Buenaventura, Pueblo del Paso, and San Elezario, and of the capitulations which I advised should be extended to these Indians for celebrating peace.[64] This action was approved in royal order of July 18, of the cited year '78. I also advised of the perfidious proceedings of the barbarians while at the same time pretending friendship, and finally, of

---

[62] On the Protector of the Indians established among the Tlascalan colony near Saltillo, see Morfi, *Viaje*, 155.

[63] For a similar technique in New Mexico, see Thomas, *Forgotten Frontiers*, 222.

[64] A.G.I., Guad., 276, Croix to Gálvez, No. 149, Valle de Santa Rosa, February 15, 1778; *ibid.*, No. 174, Chihuahua, April 3, 1778; *ibid.*, No. 200, Chihuahua, May 1, 1778; and Croix to Gálvez, No. 293. See above, page 120, footnote 57.

the results which obliged refusing their propositions and declaring war upon them. This decision took effect long before I received the royal order of February 20, '79, but these interviews and reports were some of the elements of my anxieties in New Vizcaya. Interlaced with the decision were the measures for the protection of the province, as well as those regarding the campaigns in which, with the aid of our troops, the Lipan Apache and Mescaleros attacked one another reciprocally, as I indicated with documents in letters No. 396, 405, and 518 of June 23, July 29, and May 23, '80.[65]

¶ 201. Before leaving Chihuahua in September, '79, I made my arrangements and formed the idea of the only means that could sustain New Vizcaya, to defend it from hostilities. In this, complying with the latest pious royal resolutions, I ratified the peace with the Mescaleros. As these Indians proposed to me to establish themselves in formal pueblos close to the presidio of El Norte, I sent to its captain and commandant of that division, Lieutenant Colonel Don Manuel Muñoz, the corresponding order conceived in terms similar to those which I communicated to the governors of Texas and Coahuila, adding that which appears in the paragraphs which I am copying:

¶ 202. "Your Grace has indicated to me that the little captains or head men of the Mescaleros nation, Patule, Alonzo and Juan Tuerto, have petitioned me to settle in the abandoned pueblo of San Francisco a short distance from the presidio of El Norte; that they have petitioned for bringing in some of their relatives, the Julimeños, reduced in the mission of Peyotes, belonging to Coahuila, and the Suma who are now in the nearby missions of the pueblo of El Paso, for the purposes of aiding and teaching them to build their houses, grow crops, and perform the rest of the labors of the field; that there be furnished to all the families who reduce themselves to the settlement what is necessary for their support for the first year; that they be protected and defended from all their

[65] A.G.I., Guad., 267, Croix to Gálvez, No. 396, Pueblo de Nombre de Dios, June 23, 1779; No. 405. See above, page 44, footnote 142; A.G.I., Guad., 278, Croix to Gálvez, No. 518, Arispe, May 23, 1780.

enemies; and that your Grace may be the chief to command them.

¶ 203. "They have supported these solicitations with offers to subject themselves to the vassalage of his Majesty, to behave faithfully, to attend our campaigns as auxiliaries, and to make war not only on the rest of the Apache, but upon those of their own congregation who commit hostilities upon the dominions of the king.

¶ 204. "All this your Grace has heard and advised concerning, as I have said. Likewise, I have condescended to the petitions of these Indians, and I have entertained them and made them presents, visiting and presenting them with some baubles which they appreciate; I have distinguished Patule and Juan Tuerto with the title of captains of war, and Alonzo with that of Little Governor of the new pueblo of San Francisco. Finally, I have done the same thing with the Mescalero, Domingo Alegre, dispatching him the title of captain of war of the pueblo of Nuestra Señora de la Buena Esperanza in which he had offered to establish himself with the people of his rancherias, demanding the same agreements as the other Indians, namely, that he provide for one of our men, who understands his idiom and knows how to write, in order that he can report to me directly provided that he suffer any aggravation.

¶ 205. "Thus if results correspond to these favorable antecedents, they will come to understand the great benefits—that we would be able to consider our efforts well directed if we succeed in gathering the ripe fruits which they offer—which will follow not only to this province but to the neighboring ones. The most important consideration is that the thoughts of these Indians comply with what was commanded by his Majesty in Article 13 of the Royal Instruction, inserted in the Regulation of Presidios. Thus it is apparent that among the Mescaleros congregation many nations will be saved (they are those of Alonzo, Patule, and Juan Tuerto) from the nations which put them to flight from their old pueblos of El Norte.

PROVINCE OF NEW VIZCAYA

¶ 206. "By all means your Grace will recognize that I am today alarmed and full of fear of the Apachería of the east, that I am disposed to declare myself in case it is necessary for the party which pleases me more, and to carry out the undertakings with even less equipment and people, which the close union of the Apache demands.

¶ 207. "But by no means am I thinking of sheathing the sword for the other operations of war that are purely defensive, because thus I am complying religiously with the sovereign intentions of his Majesty which your Grace will see in the attached copy of the royal order of February 20, last, the observance of which makes possible my previous dispositions without losing sight of the objectives to which up to now they have been directed.

¶ 208. "It is thus because of the peace of the Lipan and Mescaleros, the disunion of these congregations, the fear which they have of the Indians of the North, and the friendship which we are conserving with the latter, that a field is opened to undertake decisive war or to reduce our operations to the defense of the dominions of the king, achieving, perhaps, without a greater exertion, the destruction or ruin of our enemies. This second means is what I desired and must carry out, etc."

¶ 209. These advices I illustrated with others pertaining and relative to the objects and constitution of the province. In a separate order I asked for a report from Lieutenant Colonel Don Manuel Muñoz concerning the circumstances of various spots of the frontier close to the settlements, in order to erect upon them the cordon of those settlements, a plan which he had already proposed to me to remedy the hostilities and achieve the success of this project. This matter I have had presented to your Excellency in letter No. 458, January 23, '80.[66]

¶ 210. In October, '79, already on the march for Sonora, I dispatched from the Hacienda de Encinillas the instructions and orders conducive to the establishment of the new cordon of military settlements which begins with the abandoned Mis-

---

[66] For No. 458, ¶ 96 and 109, see above, page 12, footnote 12, and for Croix to Gálvez, No. 396, see above, page 125, footnote 65.

sion of Namiquipa, a little less than fifty leagues east of Chihuahua, and which is to conclude in the province of Coahuila, covering all the frontier of New Vizcaya. It is understood that its posts and forces are to be distributed in four divisions under the command of their respective commandants, as I set forth to your Excellency in letter No. 519, May 23, '80, and as the documents I sent with it explain.[67] Various quantities of pesos have been freed from the militia funds with the provision of opportune repayment for the building of settlements and expenses of the Mescaleros at peace.[68]

¶ 211. In the month of October, too, I reached the presidio of San Buenaventura where I saw myself forced to take various economizing measures because of having found it without any progress in its works, crops, and settlements. Although a considerable part of the funds destined for these ends had been consumed, it was without assistance from the Tarahumare, contrary to the provision by proclamation.[69] These, displeased, had gone back to their domiciles because they were not satisfied with the just and equitable daily wages which were offered them. I observed in a word that nothing has been done about the instructions which I gave for the good order and arrangement of this establishment. Finally, from Janos I intimated all of my dispositions to the governor of the province, so that he might see to their punctual fulfillment.

¶ 212. On the thirteenth of November, '79, I entered this capital. With my letter of May 23, '80, No. 520, I dispatched to your Excellency an extract of the news that had occurred and measures dictated from the day on which the Mescaleros Apache ratified the peace, and a table of the military settlements corresponding to the division of the command of Lieutenant Colonel Don Manuel Muñoz.[70] I also indicated the notable variations of the Mescaleros from the time of treating with them concerning the fulfillment of their offer of peace;

---

[67] A.G.I., Guad., 278, Croix to Gálvez, No. 519, Arispe, May 23, 1780.
[68] *Ibid.*, No. 523, Arispe, May 23, 1780.
[69] *Ibid.*, No. 537, Arispe, June 23, 1780.
[70] *Ibid.*, No. 520. See above, page 47, footnote 153.

the insistence with which they demanded our fulfillment; the remote hopes that they will congregate and establish themselves in pueblos; the fears that they may be reconciled with the Lipan, and that they may follow the same example of the latter's infidelity to their peace.

¶ 213. Notwithstanding, it is necessary to confess, according to the reports of Lieutenant Colonel Don Manuel Muños, that the Mescaleros have alternated their actions, good and bad. Among the first, particularly notable, is the attack, as auxiliaries of a detachment which Muñoz himself commanded, on a rancheria of Gila, capturing one, wounding another, and seizing their horses and whatever they had, proceeding in the engagement with fidelity and spirit. Further good is their continuous offer to aid us in making war against the above mentioned Gila, and the death they just brought about of the little captain of the same nation, Juan Tuerto, who always has been the cause of many sad outrages which New Vizcaya and Coahuila have experienced. Among the unfortunate aspects of the Mescaleros peace is noted the fact that they have not taken root, although the building of the new pueblo of San Francisco has been concluded for them and in it more than eighty individuals have congregated. They prefer the vagrant life. They have not seemed able to build an adobe, or to apply themselves to work in the fields, which has been done for them by our field workers, or to incline their sons to these labors. Besides there are well-founded suspicions of their having committed various murders and robberies in different parts of the province. It is established that they have carried on similar hostilities in the territories of Coahuila. But nothing of this ought to be wondered at in a nation in which each Indian is master of his actions without fear of punishment and without looking for other rewards than those he secures at the point of his arrows. Notwithstanding, the little captain, Domingo Alegre, and other Mescaleros of his band, are proceeding, as it appears, in good faith. They are giving us some confidence that the hopes and expenses that they have had expended upon them up to the present are not fruitless.

¶ 214. Concerning all the affairs touching these Indians and the new establishments of the command of Lieutenant Colonel Don Manuel Muñoz, I am awaiting a complete report from this officer, which I shall remit to your Excellency, and in the meanwhile I am guiding myself by the news of his reports. I state now that in the current year the settlements referred to are completed; that in some, settlers have been congregating; that regular crops of wheat, corn, frijol, and barley were raised last year and during the present one. These will be very abundant because of the extensive sowing that has been done, and accordingly, the present condition of their crop will make it possible to reimburse a considerable part of the expenses put forth.

¶ 215. In the division of the command of Captain Don Domingo Díaz similar progress has not been achieved. But already the troops are occupying the posts as far as that of Pelayo, next to the Real de Mapimí, in which the settlements must be erected. Work is begun on their buildings at the direction of various officers, under the inspection of Captain Don Juan Gutiérrez de la Cueva.

¶ 216. For the establishment of the third and fourth divisions, the territories of the frontier are being reconnoitered in detail.

¶ 217. Besides these measures, I have recently taken one according to which the troops of New Vizcaya may make mixed war of offense and defense in accord with the instruction which I gave to the deceased commander inspector and which is cited in paragraph 165.

¶ 218. Alternately each month from the presidios of Janos and San Elezario will set forth a detachment of 130, more or less, according to the possibility, to surprise, incommode, and dislodge the Gila Apache who are ranching on both sides of the sierras of the frontier. The remaining troops of this division will be employed in the rest of the maneuvers of defense. Those under the command of Lieutenant Colonel Don Manuel Muñoz will be exercised in similar operations with the aid of Mescalero allies. Those under the command of Díaz will examine with frequency the Bolsón de Mapimí. All, taking care

PROVINCE OF NEW VIZCAYA

to defend the territory of their respective frontiers, will combine their movements while provincial pickets of forty men and another of fifty, established in El Parage and Cerrogordo, will protect the highway from Rio de Nazas to Chihuahua and escort monthly the mule teams which come and go.

¶ 219. These are the only means that I can avail myself of at present for defending the province of New Vizcaya from the invasions of the Apache of the west, and castigating the Mescaleros that do not keep the promised peace, persuading myself that when the cordon of settlements is completed, the defense will be less hazardous.

¶ 220. In the year '77 the province of New Vizcaya suffered many hostilities. In that of '78 they were lessened. One is able to note that from the thirteenth of March of the same year, which was that of my ingress into the Villa of Chihuahua, until July, '79, the robberies and murders which were suffered in that territory were very few. But in August and September there was no day without misfortune. Violences have continued with frequency in all the province in the last year, '80. Its condition, as a consequence, is worse than when I took command of it.

¶ 221. Although its frontiers are covered with a numerous army, it can never conquer its enemies without aid of Coahuila, New Mexico, and Sonora. It may drive them out and breathe freely from hostilities, but the neighboring provinces will be lost because the enemies will attack them. If I assist those provinces, dismembering the forces of New Vizcaya, its afflictions will return.

¶ 222. The province would not have so many afflictions if an intendant, skillful, disinterested, zealous, and loyal, might arrange the political and economic government of the pueblos, and if intendants of the missions might have what they need so that the Indians may be happy.

¶ 223. This intendancy established, the province of New Vizcaya does not need a military governor. The command of this great area could be divided among various chiefs as I shall propose in the sixth part of this report. There will serve, by way of supporting this thought and the care which New Vizcaya has always merited from me, paragraphs 19 and 29 of the instruction which the viceroy sent me under date of March 20, '77, which I am copying:[71]

¶ 224. "I have thought more than once that the office of commander inspector, having been indispensable for the establishment of the new line, can, established, be prejudicial. This is not because of the character and function of the inspector, which are suitable to withstand abuses, but because of that of the commander. The governors in their respective provinces ought to answer for the safeguarding of them with dependence and direction directly upon this government. None ought to be a captain of a presidio. *Chihuahua needs an independent governor who could ask other alterations of the present system of the frontier or give it the corresponding safeguarding which its extensive area permits.* Today in the midst of the new office of your lordship, you are attending to many of the injuries I desired to forestall. It has appeared to me that this reference cannot be useless so that your lordship may not be unaware of anything preceding.

¶ 225. "I am studying the forces of war which are in New Vizcaya, a province which merits primary attention because of its richness and the particular circumstance of its abundant minerals. These are in general those whose working is impossible because water impedes it. There is a great deal. The risk to which those are exposed who benefit by them, and the destruction which the haciendas have suffered from the continuous hostilities of the barbarians, has made working the minerals more impossible in recent years."

PROVINCE OF SONORA

¶ 226

MANY times I have offered to your Excellency the particular report of the province of Sonora that I was holding back until I might have complete the necessary supporting documents. But as it is not possible to report upon

[71] See above, page 22, footnote 46.

PROVINCE OF SONORA

them for some days, the time for fulfilling my promise has arrived.

¶ 227. I shall not delay myself in a dissertation upon the country that your Excellency has seen and knows, and whose appreciable characteristics merit your worthy appreciation and powerful protection. But I shall speak, guiding myself by the reports of the population lists of settlements. The number of its inhabitants consists of 87,644 of both sexes and all ages distributed as the following table explains:[72]

JURISDICTIONS	MEN	WOMEN	BOYS	GIRLS	TOTAL		
Real del Rosario	1546	1868	1217	996	5627		
San Juan Baptista de Maloya	629	568	283	270	1750		
San Joseph de Copala	2725	2274	1657	1477	8371	[sic]	8133
San Miguel de Culiacán	3234	3254	2055	1947	10490		
Sinaloa	2471	2531	2144	2032	9178		
El Fuerte	2376	2172	897	696	6151	[sic]	6141
Cosalá	1184	1055	685	595	3519		
Alamos	2055	2005	2107	1670	7837		
Ostimuri	3477	3564	3058	3131	13680	[sic]	13230
Sonora	6231	6052	4495	4280	21041	[sic]	21058
TOTAL					87644	[sic]	86963

¶ 228. I desired nothing more when I reached Mexico than news of the condition of Sonora. I had it complete because the recently appointed governor intendant, Don Pedro Corvalán, and Lieutenant Colonel D. Juan Bautista de Anza, were in that capital and with them there had entered a few days later Colonel Don Francisco Crespo, who was just ending his service in that government.

¶ 229. The reports from the Minister of the Royal Treasury and from these two officers were accounts of such a character as to indicate that the province was suffering the greatest hostilities and that it needed quickly remedies and assistance.

¶ 230. As Anza had already concluded the matters which brought him to Mexico and was returning to Sonora, I conferred upon him the command of the armed forces, which belonged to him because of his rank. Desiring certainty, I advised him before setting out that he should set forth the means

[72] Croix drew up a later census of Sonora, A.G.I., Guad., 284, Croix to Gálvez, No. 921, Arispe, June 2, 1783.

conducive to the well-being of the province and the discharge of his command.

¶ 231. He did so, proposing that the four presidios of Pimería Alta be reënforced with the company of Buenavista, the Flying Company of Terrenate, and sixty-five Opata. With this force he could make the monthly campaigns against the Apache and attend to all the objects of defense and offense.

¶ 232. All this appeared proper to me. I not only conceded him the Opata, but a greater increase, that of sixty-two men from the Third Company of the Flying Corps of New Vizcaya, leaving him free to use them according to his zeal, judgment, and experience of the country and of war. Of these dispositions I have given an account to your Excellency in letter No. 3. His Majesty approved them in royal order of May 24, '77.

¶ 233. As soon as Anza set out, I received the first papers from the viceroyalty. I verified from them the information that I had acquired of the sad condition in Sonora. Without detaining myself in its discussion, I reminded your Excellency in paragraphs 27 to 35 of my letter No. 38 of April 25, '77,[73] that the Gila Apache were attacking from the presidio of Santa Gertrudis del Altar in Pimería Alta as far as the neighborhood of the Real del la Trinidad in Lower Pimería; that the Seri and Pima and, as a consequence, the Tiburones and the heathen Papago, were acting with bad faith; and that these affairs and the transference of the presidios and new establishments to the Colorado and Gila rivers were the principal ones which gave rise to anxieties in the province.

¶ 234. When Anza entered Sonora on May 7, '77, he found the troops in the most deplorable condition because of lack of arms, horses, and clothing; forty Seri and twenty-three Pima rebelling, allied with Apache, were attacking frequently the highway from Orcasitas to La Ciénega. The Apache were running over the province with impunity and the Seri and Pima were making local aggressions to enable the rest of their nation to abandon Pitic. But although Anza took notice of the unrest of these Indians, he did not have serious fears and be-

[73] See above, page 22, footnote 48.

PROVINCE OF SONORA

lieved information propagated among the Indians themselves that the forces of the provinces were to be increased would make them cautious and keep them in subjection.

¶ 235. For these reasons and, for the fact that the number of troops which he had at his command was 502 men, he distributed over the Apache frontier 396 to be employed in monthly compaigns, leaving him with 106 for the protection of the interior of the province. Of everything I advised your Excellency in letters No. 72 and No. 76 of July 26, '77.[74]

¶ 236. But in June of the same year, the Seri revolted because their little governor, Crisanto, murdered an Indian of his own nation. This was a frivolous pretext which established the suspected infidelity of the murderer to whom the uprising was attributed. They had no reasons other than their natural warlikeness, their propensity for unrest, desire for liberty, and their inclination to engage in robbery and treason.

¶ 237. Anza was afraid that these rebellious movements would extend to the Pimas Altos and Bajos. He called in the troops from the interior of the province, offered pardon to the Seri, prepared himself to war on them, and dispatching me news by extraordinary mail, asked my advice and assistance.

¶ 238. His letters I received in Querétaro with others in which he advised me of the damages committed by the Apache in a pueblo of Pimería Alta and Rancho of Ocuca, near the presidio of Altar. Finally, he reported the bitter complaints of the Opata because of unfortunate treatment by the father missionaries and because the military chiefs were neglecting and abusing them.

¶ 239. Recognizing the critical situation of Sonora, and the well-founded fears of Don Juan Bautista de Anza, I immediately had 120 militia sent him to reënforce the presidial companies. I petitioned the viceroy for volunteers in Guadalajara under the command of Don Pedro de Fages. The viceroy gave them to him and I increased the powers of Anza to act according to events and as his zeal and understanding

---

[74] Croix to Gálvez, No. 72. See above, page 26, footnote 65, and page 26, footnote 67.

dictated to him. Of this I gave an account in letters No. 90 and 94 of August 23, '77.[75]

¶ 240. These arrangements his Majesty deigned to approve in a royal order of December 13, following, and in another of the thirtieth of the same month and year. Those which I made benefiting the Opata nation, and to which I shall refer in their place, received similar benign deference.

¶ 241. Until Anza could receive my instructions, he took measures to protect with detachments the spots most exposed to attack of the enemies; he armed the settlers, utilized their assistance and that of the Indian allies, and continued his dispositions to attack the Seri in Cerro Prieto if they did not accept the pardon conceded.

¶ 242. He remarked that these Indians, although robbing, did not commit murder. Their declared rebellion, however, and the news which he had from various officers and justices of the province, persuaded him to fear a general uprising of the nations reduced, including even the Opata.

¶ 243. This just lack of confidence, incessant Apache hostilities, the uselessness of the presidios, the unfortunate condition of their garrisons, the terror of the settlers, and the small number of troops kept Anza under the greatest apprehension.

¶ 244. Having reminded me of all this, he proposed in spite of lack of forces to make an entrance into the Tiburon Island where the Seri were sheltered, using for the purpose the mail packet of California at Guiamas. But I advised him to proceed with the greatest discretion and care in operations against those Indians, especially in attacking them on the Island, because if the blow miscarried, or victory fell to the enemy, more serious troubles would result than those which were being experienced.

¶ 245. He also advised me that he had arrested various Pimas Altos of the pueblos of Pitiquí and Caborca. I indicated to him that if this measure were not carried out with prudence

[75] Croix to Gálvez, No. 90. See above, page 27, footnote 75; A.G.I., Guad., 515, No. 94, Querétaro, August 23, 1777; *ibid.*, No. 91, Querétaro, August 23, 1777; A.G.I., Guad., 516, Croix to Gálvez, No. 92, Querétaro, August 23, 1777.

PROVINCE OF SONORA

and success, it could be the reason for the nation to declare itself openly.

¶ 246. With regard to the fear of the Opata, I had him see that measures taken with them ought to be very well considered and prudent; that in these countries one talks and thinks with agility, attempting to divine from the slightest indication the ideas and movements of the Indian friends and allies; that the Opata were worthy of being looked after as their well-established fidelity demanded; and that for no reason should he permit these Indians to be treated with a lack of confidence.

¶ 247. Regarding the uselessness of the presidios, I left it to his free will to maintain them or move them from their local situations, even if he put upon them the just responsibilities of a measure whose advantages my knowledge would not be able then to embrace.

¶ 248. With regard to the bad condition of the troop, I stated to him that I was seeking prompt reviews of inspection, charging him that in the meantime he should take care to remedy the condition as far as possible. Finally, I indicated to him that while the troops that he had at his command appeared sufficient to defend Sonora, I offered him a larger increase of militia.

¶ 249. In letters No. 106 and 123, October 10 and November 24, '77, I gave an account to your Excellency of these developments, and in the royal order of March 2, '78, his Majesty approved my decisions.[76]

¶ 250. Their effects were so fortunate, as I set forth to your Excellency in letter No. 140 of December 9 of the above year, that the Seri sought pardon for their crimes. The Pimas Altos gave proofs of their fidelity in two campaigns which they made against the Seri and Apache, and the unfounded suspicions against the Opata dissolved. No unrest was noticed among the Pimas Bajos, or among any other reduced and pacified nations.

¶ 251. At once I gave thanks to Anza concerning the skillful-

---

[76] See above, page 31, footnote 92.

ness of his measures. I advised him to treat well the Seri who surrendered, the fulfillment of which will be put in a treaty with them. This will also be the means of having them recognize the new benefits and of subjecting them to the better government of a rational and Christian life, without causing greater expense to the royal exchequer.

¶ 252. I also advised him that he animate the Pimas Altos to continue their campaigns and reward them according to custom with three pesos for each head of an enemy captured or killed; that he resort to all means conducive to the felicity of the Opata; and that with the militias, newly increased, the presidios of Pimería Alta will be reënforced to make war upon the Apache. But the Seri did not permit this last measure because they continued their hostilities.

¶ 253. The deceased captain, Don Miguel de Urrea, had already had a remarkable engagement with these Indians. In the small detachment of the Real de San Marcial, and in those of the Piato of Bisanig, the Indians encountered valorous resistance. The Pimas Altos and Bajos destroyed three rancherias. Lieutenant Colonel Don Juan Bautista de Anza with the aid of these allied Indians, the Opata and Yaqui, reënforced the troops of his command and executed three campaigns at Cerro Prieto. The first had no particular results; in the second, he had two engagements with one hundred and seventy Seri; and in the third, he attacked thirty-two rancherias, put the occupants to flight, and killed twelve individuals.

¶ 254. These campaigns, whose successes were spoken of in the province with little decorum toward the commander, I referred to your Excellency in the extracts of February 15 and April 3, '78, numbers 152 and 176, with news of the important hostilities of the Apache according to reports Anza gave me.[77] To him, in view of everything, I dispatched instructions contained in the order of the February 13, which I am copying.

¶ 255. "The letters of your Grace, numbers 53, 56, 58, 59, and

[77] A.G.I., Guad., 276, Croix to Gálvez, No. 152, Valle de Santa Rosa, February 15, 1778; *Ibid.*, No. 176, Chihuahua, April 3, 1778.

PROVINCE OF SONORA

65, which I have received on the same day, informed me of the hostilities committed by the Seri and Apache and of the operations of our troops and of the measures taken by your Grace for the defense of this province.

¶ 256. "I am persuaded that the forces which today garrison it are irresistible to the Seri and that they will not delay long in surrendering themselves, if the good faith of the Pima continues, the felicity of their campaigns, the ones which must be made without intermission at Cerro Prieto, and the vigilance and activity in pursuing the enemy whenever they attack, so that they may never escape without punishment.

¶ 257. "If all actions were as successful as those of Lieutenant Don Miguel de Urrea and the detachment of San Marcial, we would see these provinces quieted in short time. I shall recommend to the king the merit of Urrea, and I shall attend to the corporal of the detachment of San Marcial, as well as the soldiers and settlers who may have distinguished themselves in both actions, provided that your Grace remits me the corresponding information of names and services.

¶ 258. "The news which you communicate to me concerning the Apache is not agreeable in any manner. I see that they commit their hostilities with impunity, and that commonly they come out victoriously. The troop of Santa Cruz defended the horse herd and killed and wounded some Apache, but fled from the rocky sierra without having succeeded in obtaining any other success. I notice that the captain of that presidio did not take consequent measures to move against the Apache with the seventeen Opata in the Vado of Las Travillas, a short distance from Santa Cruz; perhaps he did not have troops at hand to pursue the enemy.

¶ 259. "Your Grace will already have in the province the company of Catalonian Fusiliers, and in place of the militias, the increase in each presidio of a standard bearer, sergeant, and sixteen men of the light troop. I believe that with these reenforcements there are enough troops so that your Grace may operate with comfort while I am making my journey there.

¶ 260. "The detachments of San Marcial, Pitic, and Santa Rosalía are established with much skill, and it appears to me proper that your Grace may reënforce the latter. I approve of the support which you have sent to the pueblos of Coguiarachic and Fronteras, but I am advising you that the safest rule is to make certain that the number of the detached parties is of respectable strength and easy to bring together, because otherwise they offer a weak defense.

¶ 261. "Your Grace will take much care to conserve the good faith of the Pima. Offer them in my name remuneration for their fidelity and services, and persuade them to continue their campaign against the Seri.

¶ 262. "I trust a great deal the loyal Opata. Your Grace may esteem them and encourage them with the assurance that the king loves them and desires their happiness.

¶ 263. "The Yaqui are excellent for everything, and without them it will be more difficult to disembowel from this rich country the immense treasures which it contains. It is a numerous Indian group and most docile to suggestion; if its good will can be procured, I prefer this nation to everything else that can be hoped for from the rest.

¶ 264. "The frequent campaigns at Cerro Prieto under the rules which were made at the time of the Expedition[78] will be very advantageous; it is well that your Grace may arrange to make them.

¶ 265. "The operations against the Seri ought not to impede those against the Apache. Your Grace may send every month a large detachment for campaigns into the rancherias of these Indians, alternating the captains of the presidios and flying company in both duties. The personal attendance of your Grace in the province should never fail to look after La Ciéneguilla, the pueblos and presidios, where it is convenient, as he who is commander in chief is responsible for everything and can govern but badly when absent from the territory.[79]

[78] This refers to the Elizondo expedition. See Bancroft, *History of the North Mexican States and Texas*, I, 694–702; also Priestley, *op. cit.*, Chap. VI.
[79] A.G.I., Guad., 276, Croix to Gálvez, No. 156, Valle de Santa Rosa, February 15, 1778.

PROVINCE OF SONORA

¶ 266. "Finally, your Grace may discount the common gossip, work well, and fear nothing, as I do not know how to alter conceptions with ease, and that which your Grace merits with me is distinguished."[80]

¶ 267. As the attendance of Lieutenant Colonel Don Juan Bautista de Anza was necessary at the councils of war which I held in Chihuahua, and at the conclusion of which he was to serve the government of New Mexico, and I to fix my residence in Sonora (all of which I believed would be done in a few months), I arranged that Anza deliver the military command of the province to the captain of the oldest presidios, Don Pedro de Tueros, and that he give him complete instructions for his government. This was done. Tueros took over command of the province in March, '78, and Don Juan Bautista de Anza entered Chihuahua on May 13 of the same year.

¶ 268. It is apparent that this officer, during the time he held the command of the Commandancy of Arms of Sonora, discharged his obligations with creditable zeal, skill, efficiency, and felicity, as he failed in nothing.

¶ 269. His personal exertions on campaigns; his well-taken measures to prevent the feared uprising of the Pima, to dissipate the complaints of the Opata, to avail himself of the resources of these nations, of the Yaqui, and of the settlers, to make more respectable and fruitful their maneuvers of war against the Seri, who surrendered even before Anza left the province—these and various other reasons recommend him, no less than his reports do, as well as his well-founded petitions concerning the transference of presidios and establishments on the Rio Colorado and Gila, and other affairs which I shall treat where they belong.

¶ 270. He could not remedy the incursions of the Apache, nor arrange for the monthly campaigns which he proposed to me in Mexico, for that was not possible under the anxieties which he experienced from the day he took military command, with

---

[80] Anza suffered from criticism by the religious of the province, arising apparently from his spirited defense of the Opata against the impositions of the religious. See above, page 27, footnote 75.

small forces in poor condition, of the province menaced by a general rebellion.

¶ 271. Sonora had a better appearance when Captain Don Pedro de Tueros took command of his office, as on April 22, '78, the Seri began to surrender themselves and to congregate in El Pitic, subjecting themselves in everything to my will and dispositions under the absolute capitulations of attending church in the morning, and in the afternoon being instructed in Christian doctrine; of obeying and respecting their father ministers; of sustaining and clothing themselves by their own efforts, like the rest of the Indians in the mission; of delivering the horses, mules, and *álgas* stolen at the time of their rebellion; and of not carrying arms without permission of the commander of the fort.

¶ 272. Of this happy news I gave an account to your Excellency in letter of June 29, '78, No. 221, adding that the Tiburones were seeking our reconciliation, and that because the Seri families who had surrendered reached El Pitic nude and hungry, the governor intendant, Don Pedro Corvalán, provided them with supplies until the time arrived to harvest their crops.[81]

¶ 273. The congregation of the Seri was slow and difficult, and was brought about by force of diligence and care.[82] In the beginning they complied with the capitulations, giving proofs of humility and good faith, but soon they delayed by altering their procedure. Then Tueros himself was obliged to propose to me, under date of December 2, '78, the expatriation of these Indians, assuring me that they would never behave themselves.

¶ 274. One of them named Biquinete never wished to go down to Pitic; he remained in El Cerro with the other rebels. He did whatever he could to disturb the ones who surrendered, to indispose the soul of the Tepocas and Tiburones, and to per-

[81] A.G.I., Guad., 276, Croix to Gálvez, No. 221, Chihuahua, June 29, 1778; *ibid.,* No. 223, Chihuahua, June 29, 1778.
[82] *Ibid.,* No. 222, Chihuahua, June 22, 1778.

suade all into hostility, but nothing in particular occurred after the day on which the Seri began to surrender.

¶ 275. Tueros, unembarrassed by the war of these Indians, or by the fear which he had of the Piato or Pimas Altos, thought of devoting his attentions to the Apache frontier by beginning the monthly campaigns.

¶ 276. The first was carried out in May, '78, by the captain of the presidio of Tupson, Don Pedro de Allande, with seventy-nine leather coats, militia, and Opata and Pima auxiliaries. He had instructions from Tueros to pursue and dislodge the enemies he found on the frontier. He was prohibited from searching for them in their lands in order not to expose our territories, as going away any distance left the province entirely defenseless since the remaining troops were utilized to care for the horse herds, serve as garrison detachments, and transport supplies.

¶ 277. Allande examined parts of the frontier of the province and found various trails of the Apache who were setting out for their lands. He did not follow them in order not to violate the orders of his commander. He retired without having secured any success. Notwithstanding, Tueros assured me that he had had the satisfaction of having put fear into the barbarians by the mere fact that our troops had examined the frontier.

¶ 278. The second campaign was made in July of the same year, '78, by the Flying Captain, Don Luís del Castillo, who attacked a small rancheria close to the presidio of Fronteras, but the enemies escaped, leaving behind five horses, three burros, and three head of cattle.

¶ 279. Results from these operations were not appreciable. They could not be continued because of the difficulties Tueros encountered in taking troops from the detachments; because of the necessary reunion of those being reviewed by Adjutant Inspector Don Roque de Medina; and because troops were needed to supply the presidios with provisions and protect the horse herds. The latter, in spite of these precautionary measures, were carried off frequently by the Apache.

¶ 280. In the year '77 they committed many murders and robberies so much more felt because of increased hostilities of the Seri. In '78 the latter ceased, but those of the Apache were greater and increased in '79.

¶ 281. Lieutenant Colonel Don Juan Bautista de Anza was not able to hold back the attacks in the time of his command; under Tueros occurred the unfortunate engagement between a party of thirty-four presidials of Santa Cruz and sixty Apache on an open, level plain. There the latter killed in the retreating rear guard Captain Don Francisco Ygnacio de Trespalacios and nineteen soldiers and settlers. There also occurred the unfortunate murder at Apache hands of eight men from the same presidio, who were carrying to San Bernardino the mail sacks of the monthly correspondence. There were too-frequent robberies of allotments of horse herds, attacks on the mule provision trains, on the presidios, and repeated Apache incursions into the interior of the province.

¶ 282. Tueros never dared to lose sight of the serious cares which the Seri gave him. He reënforced the unfortunate presidios of Santa Cruz with the disengaged company of volunteers. He attempted various fruitless sallies against the enemies. Finally, after repeating to me the difficulties which impeded the execution and good results of the best operations, namely, the bad condition of the troops, their distribution in the many detachments that he and his predecessor, Anza had established, custodies of posts and horse herds, transports of goods and effects, useless and prejudicial situation of the presidios of the frontier, he acknowledged he found no means for remedying the sufferings of the province.

¶ 283. For this reason, and since I was unable to begin my march because of my serious sickness, I dispatched immediately Military Governor Don Jacobo Ugarte y Loyola, who had remained in Chihuahua until after the councils of war were concluded, to accompany me on the reconnaissance of the Sonoran frontier. I advised Tueros to inform his chief of the condition of the territory and deliver to him the orders,

PROVINCE OF SONORA

instructions, and the rest of the papers relative to the command of the arms of the province.

¶ 284. When Tueros took charge, the hostilities of the Seri had already ceased, but he worked diligently to attract them to El Pitic. This duty obliged him to remain in San Miguel de Orcasitas and prevented his personal assistance on the Apache frontier. He had two encounters with these Indians on the road of La Ciéneguilla where he was defending the monthly caravan of mules which he was escorting with seventeen men. He defended them, putting to flight the enemy, who carried off fifty-six mules and killed a soldier and a mule driver. Finally, Tueros, having acted with the equally broad powers which Anza had, did not abuse them and did what he could in the discharge of his command with credit to his valor, knowledge, and experiences.

¶ 285. On July 31, '79, Brigadier Don Jacobo Ugarte y Loyola took the military command of Sonora. But as I entered this capital on November 13, he had hardly time to instruct himself of the unhappy state in which he found the province.

¶ 286. I thought of remedying conditions on my ingress, basing a well-founded hope of the success of this plan upon the influence that my presence, authority, powers, and active measures would have in overcoming the obstacles. But I confess outright that in the personal command of the province, I have had no better success than the commander, Anza, and Tueros had.

¶ 287. Commander Anza put down the rebelling Seri, but left Sonora submerged in Apache hostilities; Tueros could not remedy conditions or change the restlessness of the unquiet souls of the Seri. I found in the province the same enemies that in all times have devastated it, and I found no line of presidios or troops to defend it.

¶ 288. Consequently, although in a sally arranged by the military governor, the death of the Indian Boquinete, a little chieftain of the Seri, was attained, the latter tribe, in company with the Tiburones, revolted in the pueblo of Guaimas. They have committed other murders and robberies in the jurisdictions of

Sonora and Ostimuri. They are continuing to disband their establishment of El Pitic; the expense that the royal treasury suffered in support of these ungrateful and treacherous Indians has not been redeemed.

¶ 289. The Apache, in large and small groups, have crossed the province with impunity, committing many murders and robberies. They have attacked pueblos, presidios, horse herds, and mule trains, and, among other misfortunes they have caused are those of the Pueblo of Teopari, jurisdiction of the mission of Saguaripa situated on the slopes of the Real de la Trinidad. Thus, in these invasions made by the enemies, they have caused the death of fifty persons, carried off twenty-eight captives, burned the houses, and profaned the church, sacred receptacles, and ornaments. At the presidio of Fronteras fourteen soldiers were killed in one day. Attacks are experienced frequently in the neighborhood of this capital.

¶ 290. To remedy such sad events it was necessary that the presidios of Sonora be placed on the most useful line for their reciprocal defense and that of the province. But when I went through the presidio of San Bernardino, I recognized that from that spot it could neither give nor receive assistance from the presidio of Janos. This contact, always difficult, was closed entirely to impede the ingress of the Apaches into New Vizcaya and Sonora. The presidial company itself, reënforced with another flying company, was hardly discharging its obligation to defend the post and the horse herd, or furnishing escort for the mule train for their provisions. The valleys of Cuchutá and Teuricahi were unprotected. The pueblo of Fronteras, and consequently that of Coguiarachic, were about to suffer the same misfortune. The building of the presidio of San Bernardino was just beginning; the works were menaced with ruin and the funds consumed.

¶ 291. All these well-established reasons, set forth extensively in paragraphs 45 to 60 of my letter No. 458, January 23, '80, obliged me to decide upon the prompt transference of the above presidio to bring the defense of the province nearer, to make less impossible the operations of the troop, and to de-

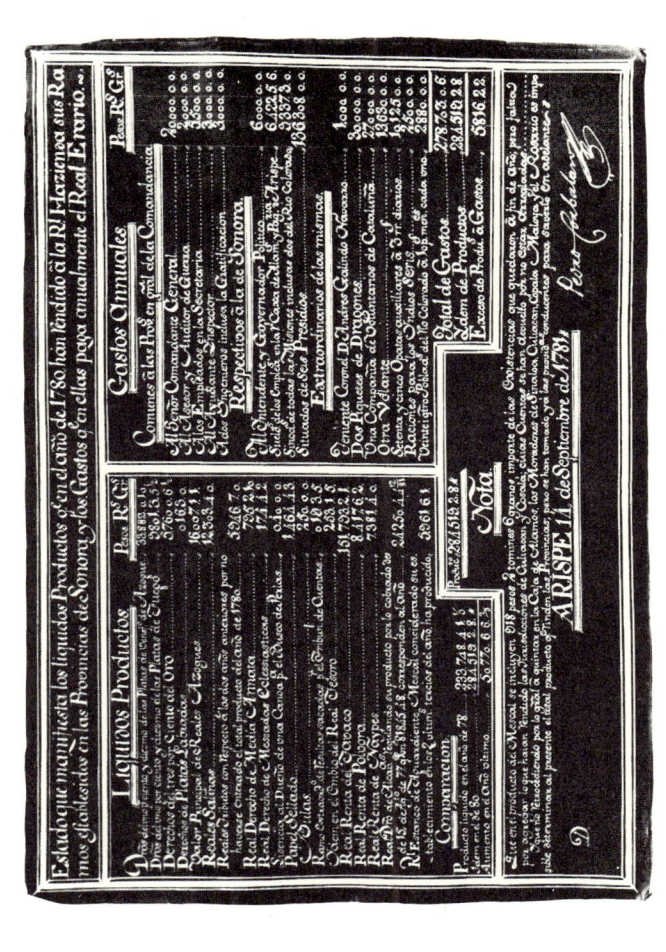

Table Showing Increase in Income from Sonora, 1778–1780

PROVINCE OF SONORA

velop the beautiful valley of Fronteras in the last stages of ruin.[83]

¶ 292. As I personally had begun to recognize the just complaints and representations of Lieutenant Colonel Don Juan Bautista de Anza and Captain Don Pedro de Tueros concerning the grave injuries which the establishments of the line of presidios had caused, and, as in view of what I set forth to your Excellency under date of August 23, '77[84]—that the removal or continuance of these presidios should be left to the free will of Anza—his Majesty deigning to approve in a royal order of December 30, it appeared convenient to me that without loss of time, the most intensive reconnaissances be carried out along the frontier to determine with accuracy this matter of the greatest importance.

¶ 293. I earnestly desired to carry out this reconnaissance in person, but as the slow, weakening convalescence from my sickness and other attentions of the service did not permit it, I commissioned the military governor of the province, Don Jacobo Ugarte y Loyola, sending to him in this capital under date of April 15, '80, the order which I copy:[85]

¶ 294. "In articles 2, 3, 4, 5, of the royal instruction inserted in the Regulation of Presidios, his Majesty deigned to decide upon the transference of those of Santa Gertrudis del Altar, Tubac, Terrenate, and Fronteras to the new line proposed by the most excellent señor, the Marqués de Rubí, and in article 29 of the same instruction, the abandonment of those of San Miguel de Orcasitas and San Carlos de Buenavista.

¶ 295. "Corresponding to the fulfillment of these sovereign resolutions, the deceased commander inspector, Don Hugo O'Conor, carried out the requisite investigations. From these resulted the change in the direction of the frontier line. The presidio of Fronteras will be transferred to the valley of San Bernardino; that of Terrenate to the abandoned pueblo of

---
[83] See above, page 12, footnote 12.
[84] A.G.I., Guad., 515, Croix to Gálvez, No. 93, Querétaro, August 23, 1777.
[85] Croix to Ugarte, Arispe, April 15, 1780, enclosed with Harvard College Library, Sparks Mss. 98 (VII), No. 2795, Croix to Gálvez, No. 704, Arispe, November 30, 1781.

Santa Cruz; and that of Tubac to Tupson; while that of Altar will remain in its position; and the abandonment of Orcasitas and Buenavista will be suspended.

¶ 296. "Concerning these measures and the succeeding ones, that were discussed to improve them and assure the defense of the province, the above mentioned commander inspector and the governor, Don Francisco Antonio Crespo, set forth their opinions. But nothing could be done because the unrest of the Seri and the hostilities of the Apache did not permit it.

¶ 297. "Both these outbreaks obliged Lieutenant Colonel Don Juan Bautista de Anza, the Commander of the Arms of this province, to represent to me the necessity of returning the presidios (which had already been transferred) to their original terrains. Acceding to his petition, I decided that he should proceed as he was with present matters and with the just responsibility to which immediately their considerations forced him.

¶ 298. "I gave an account of them to his Majesty and although in the royal order of December 30, '77, he deigned to approve my determinations, it has not been possible to carry them out yet, but having conferred on your lordship the commission of the reconnaissance of the frontiers, I hope that your results may be the happy fulfillment of the sovereign resolution of the king.

¶ 299. "To assist this fulfillment, it is necessary that your lordship make the most scrupulous and extensive examination not only of the terrains which the presidios of the province actually occupy, but also of those which they covered previously; those which the royal instructions provide for the new line; and those which can be advantageous for continuing the line to a point where it can unite with the new establishments of the Rio Colorado and the communication opened with northern California. The importance and seriousness of the ends to which the royal resolutions are drawn demand the indicated indispensable reconnaissances.

¶ 300. "Your lordship may take, at your orders, Engineer Don Gerónimo de la Rocha to aid you. Your lordship ought to begin your commission at the presidio of Fronteras. As soon as you take into consideration the situation, resources, and advantages of the cited presidio, your lordship will continue your march along the direct highway or a short cut to the spot at which the Rio de San Pedro begins to run without stopping, and from there examine the arroyos of Cuachuca, Las Nutrias, and Terrenate to their sources.

¶ 301. "Afterwards your lordship will direct yourself along the banks of the San Pedro to the point where it unites with the Gila, and coming back to the presidio of San Agustín de Tupson, your lordship will reconnoiter the old site of Tubac, returning to that of Terrenate.

¶ 302. "Having concluded this examination, your lordship can go to El Pitic through the presidio of Santa Gertrudis del Altar, reconnoitering in this recess the valley of Arive, Busanic, Saric, Tubutama, and the rest of the missions along this route. You shall remit me a corresponding plan or sketch which Engineer Don Gerónimo de la Rocha will draw up, a clear report, well circumstanced with distances, sierras, passes, canyons, rivers, springs, and arroyos which conserve water all the year, and those which lack it in the dry season; details of the Rio de San Pedro; number and names of fordable places in the waterways; resources of the land on their banks; and the possibility or impossibility of fertilizing that land.

¶ 303. "According to this prolix dissertation upon the country, your lordship will set forth to me what suggests itself and appears to you concerning the spots that ought to be on the line that really is that of the frontier for the defense of the province, remembering the fact that in the shadow of the presidios respectable settlements are to be established, which in time may not need the assistance of troops.

¶ 304. "In the same report, or separately, your lordship will tell me your opinion concerning the erection of the presidio, which the Opata have sought. Finally, whatever your lordship may learn about the territories of the frontier, I hope to find in your reports all that may be desired and may be conducive to the benefit of the province in fulfillment of the royal resolutions of his Majesty, and the arrangement of my future measures.

¶ 305. "Near the arroyo of Las Nutrias your lordship will find transferred the presidio of Santa Cruz. Captain Don Joseph Vildósola will be there with orders to erect barracks for the temporary lodging of the troop until your lordship may advise me whether it will be proper to establish the presidio there.

¶ 306. "Likewise the above mentioned captain, as well as the captain of San Agustín del Tupson, Don Pedro de Allande, will accompany your lordship if you consider it necessary. Your lordship can confide to them the reconnaissances that you may consider proper, for although I have detailed all that must be carried out with the presence of Engineer Don Gerónimo de la Rocha, I am leaving to your lordship the freedom of making the reconnaissances yourself or through officers who merit your estimation for the quickest conclusion of the important commands which I am giving to the accredited zeal of your lordship."

¶ 307. With this order I directed that the reports of Commander Inspector Don Hugo O'Conor, Colonel Francisco Crespo, Adjutant Inspector Don Antonio Bonilla, and Father Fray Juan Díaz, who accompanied Don Juan Bautista de Anza on the discovery of the road of Monterrey, be delivered to Ugarte so that he might have in view these documents.[86] They were sent to Engineer Rocha and he will return them to me when the commission is finished.

¶ 308. To the Engineer I sent another order following that of the governor.[87] I advised him to send his reports to me separately. He received from my secretary a general map of the provinces, a copy of the Regulation of the Presidios, and various instructive papers.

¶ 309. On the above mentioned day of April 15, '80, Briga-

---

[86] See below, pages 33, 35, footnotes 97, 102, 103, 104.
[87] Croix to Rocha, Arispe, April 16, 1780, and Croix to Rocha, April 15, 1780, with Croix to Gálvez, No. 704. See above, page 147, footnote 85.

PROVINCE OF SONORA

dier Don Jacobo Ugarte y Loyola set out from this capital and concluded the reconnaissances on the sixteenth of July following.

¶ 310. His reports essentially agreed with those of Engineer Rocha, and from them is deduced the fact that when he entered this province, there was no line of presidios.[88] The defects of that of San Bernardino I have already spoken about. That of Santa Cruz was distant more than forty leagues from San Bernardino; its provisions were brought from great distances over roads with great risk; the road from this presidio to San Bernardino has become impassable to regular parties of troops, as one party of ten men detailed to take mail bags had perished at the hands of the Apaches. Likewise did thirty others and their captain, Don Francisco Tovar, suffer the same fate in the year '76. The company of Santa Cruz of regular dotation was unable to defend the post. Reënforced with volunteers composed of eight men, it was suffering daily attacks of the enemies. It was never able to prevent the ingress of these into the interior of the province; and already the troops were becoming possessed with the terror of panic. The presidio of San Agustín del Tupson, farther beyond the line, received and extended untimely and weak support to Santa Cruz, distant thirty-five leagues. It (Tupson) was not counting upon help from Santa Gertrudis del Altar, established to the rear at a distance of more than sixty leagues. Thus the four presidios of the Apache frontier were on the line: San Bernardino and Santa Cruz, without communication with each other; San Agustín established in a corner of the province serving solely to protect its two neighboring missions and as a stopping place for the Rio Colorado; Santa Gertrudis del Altar in its old terrain, at a considerable distance from the frontier. Consequently this cordon of posts, considered as unconnected parts, embraces more than 136 leagues.

¶ 311. I repeat thus that in Sonora there is no line of presidios and insist that it does not have troops either. I shall set forth

[88] Ugarte to Croix, Presidio del Pitic, August 14, 1780, and Rocha to Croix, Arispe, October 31, 1780, with Croix to Gálvez, No. 704. See above, page 147, footnote 85. Rocha's diary is enclosed.

in brief statements the condition in which I found them and the condition in which they exist today.

¶ 312. They did not have firearms, as when I entered the province the guns and pistols of the new armament were just arriving. With the exception of the company of Tupson, which is well trained, and Altar, which is moderately so, the rest were ignorant of the use of these arms.

¶ 313. The forces of the presidios of San Bernardino and the first half of the flying company were divided between that post and Fronteras, with horses and without supplies. Santa Cruz and the second half of the flying company were incomplete, their horse herds in a worse condition, and there was a greater scarcity of provisions. Tupson lacked nothing, but it alone could not defend the province. Thus this company, and those of Altar, Orcasitas, and Buenavista, were not sufficiently distributed in large and small detachments to discharge with poor horses the duties of their respective posts, that is, the formation of incessant escorts and the holding back of the hostilities of the domestic enemies, the Seri, Tiburones, and the revolting Pima.

¶ 314. The company of volunteers composed, as I have already said, of eighty men was at half its strength because of desertions, deaths, invalids, and soldiers on leave. The two pickets of dragoons arrived with me at this capital in a condition useless for duty.

¶ 315. All the above troops and the seventy-five Opata that were increased in '77 compose the total of 730 men including officers, but this number was really imaginary, as one could hardly count upon troops who were largely without instruction, direction, arms, horses and supplies, and were divided among many posts and hardly able to defend themselves.

¶ 316. It appears that everything could have been remedied with the uniting of forces in one or two advantageous posts of the interior, such as El Pitic and San Joseph de Pimas, to oppose the hostilities of the rebellious Seri, and in two others in Pimería Alta, like the presidios of Santa Cruz and Fronteras, to hold back and punish the Apache. The suggested union contained the possibility of instructing the troops, the least difficult collection, transportation, and custody of remounts, the provision of supplies, and consequently the most useful maneuvers of war. However, I can only state to your Excellency that in the last year no crops have been raised in Sonora; that in the presidios of Santa Cruz and Fronteras the troops and families have perished from hunger; that the same thing occurred in the larger part of the pueblos of the province; and that to provide this capital with the little which its very recent population needs, it has been necessary to carry supplies from various distant jurisdictions with much anxiety that they perhaps will not be sufficient to remedy the scarcity that may be suffered. This did away with the project which, although I know its advantages, I shall consider as problematical until the means and measures can be realized which I am setting forth in the corresponding paragraphs in the second part of this report.

¶ 317. Nothing has remained undone to give effect to my desire and that of Governor Intendant Don Pedro Corvalán to remedy the lack of supplies which today afflicts the province. I have sometimes refused orders for the purchase of remounts, considering this a useless expenditure because the duty of guarding the horse herd with horses and without supplies cannot be rendered. The risk that the horses will be carried off by the enemies is increased. In this case the obligations of the companies will be enlarged. Finally, I have advised repeatedly that the time should be taken advantage of to instruct the presidial and flying corps.

¶ 318. In order to put the company of volunteers in a state of service, it was necessary to complete it with good European recruits and provide it with arms and clothing. None of these resources could be provided in the province. I saw myself forced to dispatch to Mexico in January, '80, Lieutenant Colonel Don Pedro de Fages, captain of the above company. Having completed the recruiting, he has just returned to the province, but the mule trains which are bringing arms and clothing have not yet arrived.

¶ 319. The two pickets of dragoons were reviewed in the month of January, '80. They were put upon the footing of the arrangement commanded in the royal order of May 20, 79. I indited the following short and clear instruction of which I sent copies to your Excellency in letter No. 479[89] of February 23, '80, with the documents of the reviews. Although I advised in the above mentioned instructions that one of the pickets ought to be employed in reënforcing the garrison of the presidio of Fronteras, and the other in the duties of the service of this capital, both alternating in their activities, it has been necessary to keep the pickets in my sight to cut wood, and to escort monies, supplies, and effects, in order to free them from their debts. I have achieved this with regard to the pickets of Spain, but not that of Mexico, whose bankruptcy reaches now to more than thirteen thousand pesos. This menacing quantity would have once rendered useless this picket, throwing it into a condition to be dissolved, if I had not taken necessary and efficient measures so that it can serve and cover its obligations at the lowest cost in time and money.

¶ 320. I have availed myself of everything possible to put the troops of Sonora in a condition to defend the province, but insuperable obstacles have supervened.

¶ 321. I have already spoken of those which I have succeeded in overcoming to improve the useless condition of the company of volunteers and which the pickets and dragoons were approaching. The former will have a remedy in El Pitic to which I have allotted it, and the latter will march to the frontier of the Apache as soon as they have supplies with which to support themselves without apprehension.[90]

¶ 322. The presidial company of San Bernardino would have perished from hunger in that sterile valley exhausted of everything. The presidio of the valley of Fronteras exhausted in all respects, was being desolated, suffering the greatest needs. Santa Cruz, transferred to the spot of Las Nutrias, has experienced similar lack of necessities and now maintains itself

---

[89] A.G.I., Guad., 278, Croix to Gálvez, No. 479, Arispe, February 23, 1780.
[90] A.G.I., Guad., 228, Croix to Gálvez, No. 224, Chihuahua, June 29, 1778.

PROVINCE OF SONORA

in scarcity. Tupson has reunited its detached forces, but out of these and those of Santa Cruz, Altar, Orcasitas, and Buenavista are composed the escorts of the families and remounts for California and the new establishments on the Rio Colorado.[91]

¶ 323. The indispensable assistance for the success of these expeditions is the reconnaissance which the military governor, Don Jacobo Ugarte y Loyola, made of the frontier, and the campaign carried out against the Apache by Captain Don Joseph Antonio de Vildósola. These have been the essential labors which the troops of this province were able to carry on during the entire year of '80. But it reduced them to the most useless condition, and consequently the province to the most deplorable state, each day causing greater difficulties for its remedy.

¶ 324. There could be the better location of the presidios, the establishments of the Rio Colorado and Gila rivers, the formation of militia, and the erection of some new settlements. Upon these points I am going to set forth my measures and ideas.

¶ 325. The Opata Indians having been disgusted by the unhappy treatment of their father ministers and of the military chiefs, as I noted in paragraph 238, the excellent action taken by Anza toward them and the dispositions which I took from Querétaro, quieted their unrest.[92] These amounted to declaring the enjoyment of the salary which was not being paid to the general of the Opata nation, Don Juan Manuel Varela; conferring upon him the government of the pueblos of Baserác and his followers under the immediate orders of the governor intendant; seeing that the Opata were employed with discretion and prudence in the fatigues of war; and seeing that the Father Provincial of Xalisco impressed upon the religious ministers the necessity for good treatment of these Indians.

¶ 326. The result of these measures was the petition of the Opata general that a presidio of his nation be erected in the

[91] A.G.I., Guad., 277, Croix to Gálvez, No. 505, Arispe, April 20, 1780.
[92] See above, page 27, footnote 75.

pueblo of Baserác, or in Babispe. Although the establishment appeared good to me, I suspended my decision until arrival in Sonora, as I explained in letter No. 157 of February, '78.[93] His Majesty deigned to approve it in the royal order of July 18 of the same year.

¶ 327. I was positively desirous of clearing up this matter, and as my grave sickness impeded me, it appeared suitable to entrust it to the military governor, Don Jacobo Ugarte y Loyola, and to the political governor, Don Pedro Corvalán, dispatching them under date of July 12, '79, with the orders which I am copying.

¶ 328. "When Lieutenant Colonel Don Juan Bautista de Anza was commander of the armed forces of this province, the Reverend Father Fray Angel Antonio Nuñez, minister of Baserác, in the name of the general of the Opata, Don Juan Manuel Varela, proposed the erection of a presidio in the pueblo of Baserác, or in that of Babispe, garrisoned with Indians of his nation. Having made a similar proposal to the military commander, he was of the opinion that in place of the presidio, a flying company be substituted of the same Indians, establishing it in Bacoachi to reconnoiter the Sonora and Oposura rivers.

¶ 329. "Of this matter I gave an account to his Majesty and suspended my measures, to take them on my ingress into the province. However, as these cannot be taken with the promptness which I desire, and the breakdown of my health does not permit it, although I am now quite active and in a real state of convalescence, it is therefore necessary to take advantage of time to avoid postponing the most urgent resolutions and interests of the royal service.

¶ 330. "With this view and those which I am communicating to your lordship in a secret official order of this date, I am advising in the paper of general resolutions the reorganization of the Opata explorers serving now in the presidios and the seventy-five permitted under the increase. But attending to

[93] A.G.I., Guad., 276, Croix to Gálvez, No. 157, Valle de Santa Rosa, February 15, 1778.

PROVINCE OF SONORA

the fact that this nation, by its well-known valor and constant fidelity, is the only one which we can use in this province for war, I am trying to employ part of it in war and take care of the rest of these faithful and deserving Indians. In this way his Majesty may distinguish them with the trust that he has deigned to give me to watch over them in particular.

¶ 331. "For the success of the first stated purpose, I agree that the proposed creation of the presidio of the Opata will be proper. But as I do not know these territories, I am doubtful as to which is the most advantageous site to select for the defense of the province. It is necessary that your lordship make the election, after being accompanied by the most intelligent and experienced officers of the country. You may reconnoiter for yourself the proposed spots of Baserác, Babispe, and Bacoachi.

¶ 332. "Having found the most adequate place, without any inconvenient or grave difficulty that may be opposed to the establishment, your lordship will send me the corresponding reports. Also I remember that the new presidio or flying company must be supplied with the number of Opata considered necessary, including in it the corporals or officers of the same nation, but without increasing the expense which the seventy-five Indians actually employed in the service may occasion.

¶ 333. "Besides your lordship must propose to me two veteran subaltern officers so that the one of the highest rank may be entrusted with the command and government of the Opata company and the other with the management of interests. This resolution will not produce new expense to the royal treasury either, because having added the people of the flying company, which was at the command of the deceased captain, Don Luís del Castillo, to those of the presidios of San Bernardino and Santa Cruz, two surplus subaltern officers will be left to replace these named and transferred from the presidios for the new one of the Opata.

¶ 334. "The execution of the measures for the erection of this presidio and for the formation and rules of the company belong to your lordship as military governor, as soon as I decide upon them in view of your reports and those respecting the settlements and support of the Opata who belong to the governor intendant.

¶ 335. "There has been an oversight in that the petition of Father Muñez in the name of General Varela and some documents relative to the affair have not been remitted with the papers from the archive which arrived with my equipage at the pueblo of Arizpe. As I must make your lordship some other observations concerning the petition and the documents, I shall dispatch it by extraordinary mail in a few days.

¶ 336. "In the meanwhile I am stating under this date to the governor-intendant that if it does not inconvenience him he can go either alone or in company with your lordship and by whatever means, with a necessary escort, to reconnoiter the three pueblos of Baserác, Babispe, and Guachinera. His arrangements having been made, or measures taken for them, he can also examine the pueblos themselves of the Opata Nation to the end that the vexations from which they are suffering may be remedied.

¶ 337. "I am communicating everything to your lordship for your punctual observation in matters which concern you, advising you that because the governor intendant has perfect knowledge, experience, and instruction in the affairs of this province, your lordship may agree with him so that the two arms, military and political, aiding each other, may see the achievement of the happy ends to which my measures conspire."

¶ 338. [MARGINAL NOTE: Copy of the order given to the Political Governor.] "The new footing upon which I have arranged that the presidial companies of this province be placed is the same as that detailed for all those which are garrisoning the rest of the frontier of my command. It is differentiated from what was provided for in the articles of Title 2 of the Regulation of Presidios only in the larger number of troops approved by his Majesty, each company of which must be composed one half of soldiers from leather and light soldiers,

PROVINCE OF SONORA

and one half from dragoons, and in the general reorganization of Indian explorers.

¶ 339. "This I have decided upon because commonly Indians serve uselessly and with ill humor and carelessness; there are few fit for war, and some under suspicion of infidelity; their desertions are repeated; they leave the pueblos with few laborers for the field; they do not procreate; the castes are used up and the population diminishes.

¶ 340. "The reorganization, then, of the explorers not only avoids these injuries but provides a better defense and conservation of the country because Indians reunited in their pueblos can defend themselves from the enemies without neglecting attention to agriculture. We shall always have them as assistance in exploration on the formal campaigns for which they volunteer, rewarding them without burden to the royal treasury at the cost of the products of the communities, and when they do not suffice, at the cost of the gratification of the companies of the presidios.

¶ 341. "I understand that the best and most fruitful results of these resolutions must be achieved in the province of Sonora because it conserves in its bosom, although now diminished, the very faithful Opata nation. It appears to me we shall be able both to use them for war and to hold back the martial ardor of the other nations which always has been unfortunate for us.

¶ 342. "I reserved these points and other important ones to confer upon with your lordship at our desired meeting. As the breakdown of my health is postponing that, it will be necessary to put them into effect at once to advance what may be possible until divine piety deigns to concede me health and until I can go to that province, if the particular improvement which I am at present experiencing continues.

¶ 343. "I have provided in the general resolutions for the reorganization of the explorers of these presidios and of the seventy-five Opata, increased with the approval of the king when Lieutenant Colonel Don Juan Bautista de Anza was commander of the armed forces, and I have attempted to utilize some of these Indians in war and look after the useful conservation of the rest.

¶ 344. "Their general, Don Juan Manuel Varela, through the reverend father minister of doctrine, Fray Angel Nuñez, sought the erection of a presidio of his nation in Baserác or Babispe. Afterwards he agreed with the idea which Lieutenant Colonel Don Juan Bautista de Anza proposed concerning establishing, in place of the presidio, a flying company of Opata in Bacoachi to reconnoiter the rivers of Sonora and Oposura, although he was always inclined to the one in Babispe. This petition of Father Nuñez, supported with the proposition that the Opata should pay tributes and *diezmos,* adding various others was directed toward the development of the territory which includes the pueblos mentioned, of whose fertility, beauty, and richness he makes a pleasing picture.

¶ 345. "As the king deigned to approve the expense of the increase of the seventy-five Opata, I have considered that perhaps the erection of the presidio will be convenient. But as I do not know those territories, I am doubtful as to which is the most advantageous spot to select for the defense of the province and think of leaving it to the choice of the military governor, Don Jacobo Ugarte y Loyola after he has in company with intelligent officers acquainted with the country, reconnoitered the spots proposed by the Opata General, and by Lieutenant Colonel Anza.

¶ 346. "After the most appropriate spot, without any inconvenient or serious difficulty opposing the establishment, has been found, I shall arrange to man the presidio or flying company with Opata considered necessary without increasing the expenses which the seventy-five Indians of this nation actually employed in the service occasion. But there must be placed over them, besides their own corporals or officers for the command in war, two other veteran officers. He of the higher rank may be charged with the command of the company and the other with the management of the interests. This measure will not place a new burden upon the royal treasury, for by adding the flying company of the deceased captain, Don Luís del Cas-

PROVINCE OF SONORA

tillo, to those of the presidios of Fronteras and Santa Cruz, two subaltern officers will be left over to replace those to be named and taken from the presidios for the new one of the Opata.

¶ 347. "The execution of these measures belongs to the military governor. To your lordship belong those regarding the settlement and support of the pueblos of Opata, which I am persuaded can be achieved by the skillful and prudent measures which your lordship proposed to me in your report of August of the last past year.

¶ 348. "In this understanding, if your lordship considers it not inconvenient, you can go either alone or in company of Señor Loyola, and by all means with the necessary escort, to reconnoiter the three pueblos of Baserác, Babispe, and Guachinera. Your arrangements decided upon, you may examine also the rest of the pueblos of the Opata so that the vexations from which they suffer may be remedied and attended to in detail. In this matter I was expressly commanded by the king, since these Indians merit help because of their valor and fidelity."

¶ 349. The governor intendant gave himself with pleasure to the fulfillment of my orders, which he could not effect at once for lack of escorts. Since then, his residence in this capital has been necessary. But in his letter of August 31, '79, he stated to me that notwithstanding he had not examined the spots proposed for the establishment of the Opata presidio, he was of the opinion it should be erected in Bacoachi in order to enjoy the riches of its gold placers, reputed better and more permanent than those of La Ciéneguilla, and in order to establish in the shelter of the presidial arms a numerous population which would in a short time protect the Rio de Sonora and would at once produce prodigious sums.

¶ 350. The military governor entered this province through the pueblos of the Opata. Having made the general reconnaissance of the frontier, he reported to me under date of August 14, '80, that the new presidio would be very useful and advantageous and that it ought to be located in the beautiful, fertile, and spacious valley of Babispe: first, because of its admirable resources for all kinds of crops, herds of animals, and the establishment of many pueblos since the river watering the valley, known there as the Grande and elsewhere as the San Antonio or Hiaqui, is the largest of all this province; second, because the presidio placed in Babispe covers as far as possible the largest part of the territory which the settlements of the Opata occupy; third, because this presidio will lessen the distance between Janos and Fronteras, leaving hardly more than thirty leagues from one to the other; fourth, because the three presidios, aiding one another, can defend the point of entrance of the Apache into this province and into that of New Vizcaya, and dislodge them with frequency from the sierras of Teras, Espuelas, Embudos, and various others which are opposite the valley.

¶ 351. Finally, he stated that although the little valley of Bacoachi is appropriate for a good settlement, it is protected by the nearby presidio of Fronteras which it has almost in front of it; that if the presidio of the Opata were established in this spot, it would be withdrawn into the country without forming a line with the rest, without communication with that of Janos; and that such a settlement in Bacoachi was not comparable with one in the more useful and advantageous valley that Babispe would offer.

¶ 352. As I had traveled by road from Janos to Sonora in the opposite direction followed by the military governor, I noted at once the solid foundations of his report.[94] I just finished confirming them with the opinion of Lieutenant General Marqués de Rubí and with the diary of the deceased commander inspector, Don Hugo O'Conor.[95] The first followed the same road I followed, and the second crossed over to the presidio of Fronteras through the pueblos of the Opata.

¶ 353. The route which the Marqués de Rubí followed, according to the dairy of Engineer Don Nicolas de La Fora, was the following:[96]

[94] Diary of Mascaró. See above, page 44, footnote 144.
[95] See below, page 163, footnote 97.
[96] Bolton, *Guide*, 210.

PRÓVINCE OF SONORA

ROUTE	LEAGUES	DIRECTIONS
Palotada	3	North by Northwest
San Francisco	11	Idem
Valley of San Luís	15	Idem
Valley of San Bernardino	15	West
Cóaguionac	12	South by Southwest
Fronteras	8	East
	64	

¶ 354. [MARGINAL NOTE: *Idem*: that of the second.] And that which Brigadier Don Hugo O'Conor made was as appears in his diary.[97] The data are set forth as follows:

ROUTE	LEAGUES	DIRECTION
Mezquite	3	Southwest
Peñuelas	11	Idem
Cuesta de Carretas	6	Idem
Pueblo de Babispe	3	Idem
Milpillas	4	North
Chiltipin	6	Northwest
Tesquín	3	Idem
Cavilán	3	Idem
Potrero	8	West
Fronteras	5	Idem
	52	

¶ 355. The difference of twelve leagues by the shorter road, which Brigadier Don Hugo O'Conor marched, establishes the

---

[97] For a copy of O'Conor's diary see Bolton, *Guide*, 103, item No. 2. The inspiration for O'Conor's report on the presidios came from a letter to Bucareli from Father Juan Diaz who urged the need of altering the presidios to assure the Gila-Colorado route to California. Diaz had accompanied Garcés to the Gila in 1774 (Bucareli to Arriaga, Ceballos, *Bucareli*, I, 271–73). Bucareli then asked O'Conor to investigate the matter during his inspection of the Sonoran presidios in 1775. O'Conor commanded Bonilla to report on the location of the presidios, which the latter did on August 14, 1774 (see below, page 168, footnote 102). O'Conor, having finished his inspection of the frontier as far as Janos by August 29, remitted his diary and recommendations for the removal of the presidios of Orcasitas and Buenaventura to the Gila-Colorado frontier (A.G.N., Provincias Internas, Tomo 88, 38–47, O'Conor to Bucareli, No. 449, Presidio of Janos, August 29, 1775); this is translated in part herein, ¶ 413–17. O'Conor, however, was directed by Bucareli to suspend the transfer until Anza had reported on his 1775 expedition. See below, page 218, footnote 135.

fact that the direction of the line of presidios from Janos ought to be continued through the pueblo of Babispe, and not through the valley of San Bernardino. The direction of his route demonstrates clearly what the frontier covers. Sonora has its beginnings in the pueblo of Babispe. The dividing point of the jurisdiction of this province is the crest of the Sierra de Carretas, through which with more frequency the Apache enter to attack both governments.

¶ 356. Lieutenant General Marqués de Rubí says in chapter or paragraph 8 of his *Dictámen*[98] that all the length of the road which he traveled from Janos to Fronteras was exposed to the most serious blows of the Gila Apache. He refers to the names of many of the sierras, passes, canyons, and openings which can be seen along the road itself. He assures that they are known habitations of the barbarians; that through them they can enter to attack as far as the interior of Sonora, the neighborhood of Chihuahua, the intermediate missions of Baserác and Babispe, and the valley of Basuchil. The distance between Janos and Fronteras is the most feared of all our line. It is at the same time the most inadequately guarded and the one which always has been most responsible for the present decadence of Sonora and New Vizcaya.

¶ 357. These propositions laid down, he gave his opinion that the presidios of Janos and Fronteras can support one another. Yet without proposing the obvious measure of establishing, with forces from both, a post to divide the distance, it ought to be nearer to Fronteras than Janos, the proper place to be sought in the valley of San Bernardino.

¶ 358. There is no doubt that the road from one to the other presidio is of the greatest risk and that the Apache are ranching in the sierras, passes, canyons, and openings, as the Marqués de Rubí stated. But it is also certain that in crossing from Janos to San Bernardino along the frontier or along the only necessary and passable short-cut, which is the one I followed, one goes through El Aguage de la Palotada. There are on the left El Caliente, El Aguage del Perro, La Sierra de Carretas,

[98] See above, page 16, footnote 21.

PROVINCE OF SONORA

En Medio, San Francisco, San Luís, Cuchuverachic, Pituayacachic, and many others. One enters through La Cañada de Guadalupe into the valley of San Bernardino, leaving behind this sierra, the slopes opposite—Fronteras, La Tinaja, Cóaguionac, El Potrero, La Purica, Las Espuelas, Embudos, Teras, Pertica—and an infinite number of other sierras where the Apache ranch with more room.

¶ 359. As a consequence, even if it were possible to have in Janos and San Bernardino forces three times as great as their present allotment, and if they were to examine incessantly the terrains of their frontier, they could never come upon the trails of the Indians nor be able to impede the ingress into New Vizcaya of the Indians who dwell seasonally in El Ojo Caliente, El Perro, Carretas, and Sierra de Enmedio, or the ingress into Sonora of those Indians who are ranching in the spots mentioned in the above paragraph.

¶ 360. I cannot comprehend what the proper location for the establishment of a post to divide the distance between Janos and San Bernardino should be. Between the two places there is not another permanent water hole except La Palotada, which is but three leagues from Janos. But even if the difficulty our parties have in examining the frontier were overcome, they could never discover the trails of Apache who dwell in the sierras near the settlements.

¶ 361. It would not come out thus if the halfway post were established in the Opata pueblos at Babispe, and the presidio of San Bernardino in the valley of Fronteras were maintained.

¶ 362. This valley, that of Babispe, and the presidio of Janos, form a scalene triangle in this manner: Janos faces east-west with the valley of Fronteras sixty leagues in length. It has on the southwest, at a little more than twenty-three leagues, Babispe; and at another twenty-nine leagues northwest is the valley of Fronteras.

¶ 363. Thus with a post or presidio established in Babispe, the line continues without stopping from the corresponding ones to Sonora, leaving opposite the sierras, passes, and openings through which the Gila Apache enter La Vizcaya and this province. The three presidios might aid one another mutually with undeniable advantages, and the fruitless expenses of the transference and retrocession of San Bernardino would be avoided.

¶ 364. For all these reasons the opinion of the military governor, Don Jacobo Ugarte,[99] concerning the establishment of the proposed presidio of the Opata in the valley of Babispe and not in that of Bacoachi (where I have been) appears well founded to me. Although the riches of the latter's placers are certain, I do not believe they ought to be preferred to the general defense of the two provinces of New Vizcaya and Sonora which the continuation of the best line of presidios provides through the pueblos of the Opata. In order for the placers of Bacoachi to be enjoyed, there is no inconvenience in having them defended by a detachment from the presidio of Fronteras, less than twenty leagues distant, or by the garrison of a picket of dragoons under the protection of which the settlement can be encouraged, as the political governor, Don Pedro Corvalán, correctly proposes. I hope that it may be done if the divine piety concedes this year less calamities than the last.

¶ 365. The lack of supplies has suspended my dispositions for the establishment of the new presidio of the Opata, but the selection has been made of the best Indians who are to garrison it. There has been conferred upon the veteran officer who is to command them the undertaking that the largest crops be raised in the pueblos of the Opata. The Indians have dedicated themselves with such diligence and willingness to the fulfillment of my orders that I am now thinking of seeing the presidio located by the next harvest of the corn crop, and of using the Opata in pursuing and punishing the Apache with the mutual aid of the armed forces of Janos and Fronteras.

¶ 366. In any event, I still consider the new presidio of the Opata as a proper point in the cordon of presidios of Sonora. I am going to consider the continuation of this line.

¶ 367. Lieutenant General Marqués de Rubí detailed this

[99] See above, page 151, footnote 88.

matter in paragraphs 5 to 9 of his *Dictámen*.[100] He proposed that the presidio of Altar be moved back to a spot close to the coast of the Gulf of California to impede the intrusion of the Papago and Piato, who live in the northwest, and their evil alliance with the Seri.

¶ 368. He proposed also that the presidio of Tubac be brought close to Altar by moving it in or giving up terrain towards the west, so that the distance between these two presidios should not exceed forty leagues, to assure their communication, to cut off trails, and impede entrances and departures of the enemies.

¶ 369. He says that the Papago, the Piato, and the Apache of the Gila are near Tubac. The establishment of a detachment from the two companies of Altar and Tubac halfway to oppose the entrances which the first make over the rough land appeared proper to him. Accordingly he demands that the captain of Tubac examine as frequently as possible the intervening distance between his two posts from right and left to curtail the incursions of the Apache into the interior of the province.

¶ 370. He continues describing the situation of the presidio of Terrenate. With a view to protecting the spots where the enemies make ingress, he proposes that this presidio be established on the Rio de San Pedro or in the arroyos of Guachuca, las Nutrias, etc. He demands that the spot of the new establishment be sought closer to the presidio of Fronteras than to Tubac and face north-south to the sierra of Chiricagui so that the sierra of Magallanes and Mavava are on its flank.

¶ 371. Finally, concerning the transference of the presidio of Fronteras to the valley of San Bernardino, he opined what I have already stated in paragraphs 356 and 357 of this report. But the Marqués de Rubí points out in many of those paragraphs his opinion and, especially in the fifth and sixth, the necessity of reconnaissances of lands before deciding upon the removal of the presidios.

¶ 372. Articles 2, 3, 4, 5, and 6 of the royal instruction, in-

[100] See above, page 16, footnote 21.

serted into the Regulation of the year of '72,[101] provide the same repeatedly, detailing the line of Sonora, to accord with what was proposed by Lieutenant General Marqués de Rubí. The royal instruction added in the second article that attempts be made to establish the presidio of Altar in terrain not too difficult for detachments to go over and to examine the districts to the right and left. The sixth article provides that the sites which the transferred presidios vacate should be occupied by their settlers, to whom should be added other Spanish settlers and Opata Indians, with the lands and waters divided among them. These should be armed under the condition that they be maintained, equipped, and deployed to defend their respective districts and aid the detachments of troops.

¶ 373. In the year 1774, Adjutant Inspector Don Antonio Bonilla was commissioned by Brigadier Don Hugo O'Conor to establish the line of Sonora.

¶ 374. This officer entered the province through the presidios of San Carlos de Buenavista. His commission concluded, he retired through Janos to Chihuahua where he made to his chief the corresponding reports composed of seventy-seven paragraphs.[102]

¶ 375. In the first to the thirteenth, he referred extensively to the unfortunate condition to which the Seri and Pima were reducing Sonora, and the excellent effects of the military expedition against these Indians; to the quiet and peace in which he found them; and to the fact that no hostilities were being suffered in the interior of the province between the presidio of San Carlos de Buenavista and that of Santa Gertrudis del Altar. But at the same time he indicated that, the arms of the expedition not having been able to reach the frontier of the Apache, these barbarians kept the province desolated and exposed to new uprisings of the subjected nations.

¶ 376. From paragraph thirteen to seventeen, he speaks of the idea he formed of the presidios of Buenavista, Orcasitas,

[101] See above, page 16, footnote 22.
[102] A.G.N., Provincias Internas, Tomo 88, 10–33, Bonilla to O'Conor, Chihuahua, August 14, 1774.

and Santa Gertrudis, and of the tranquillity which the interior of the country was enjoying. He gives the reasons that obliged him to alter his opinions concerning the better fortune of Sonora when he was on his march from Altar to Tubac. He observed the roughness and character of the terrain, which Lieutenant General Marqués de Rubí sets forth in the sixth paragraph of his opinion. Although the latter had already indicated the spot for the transference of the presidio of Altar because it had appeared to him to conform to the provisions of the second article of the royal instruction he considered it very necessary to proceed to execute the most prolix reconnaissances. With this view he went to examine the banks of the Rio de Terrenate, or San Pedro.

¶ 377. He contracted paragraphs seventeen to twenty-four to refer to the favorable features of this river, demonstrating that it protects all of Pimería Alta, and that it is the real Apache frontier. Yet, in spite of this sound judgment, he proposed to detail the new line of presidios in arrangement with the articles of the royal instruction and suspend the transferences until he had made his reconnaissances known to the superior government. He did this, electing for the location of the presidio of Altar the little valley of Escomác between the pueblos of Caborca and Bisanig; for the presidio of Tubac, the valley of El Arivác, forty-one leagues distant from Escomác; for the presidio of Terrenate, the arroyo of Las Nutrias, forty-two leagues from Arivác; for the presidio of Fronteras, the valley of San Bernardino, thirty-four leagues distant from Las Nutrias.

¶ 378. In paragraphs twenty-four and twenty-five, he states the mistake which Rubí suffered from in arranging for the removal of the presidios of Terrenate and Fronteras and asks opportunely of his chief to command them suspended, setting forth that the pueblo which the second was leaving ought to be protected by the organization and development of its settlers before taking out the presidial forces.

¶ 379. In paragraphs twenty-six to forty-three, he sets forth the good and bad qualities of the troops of Sonora; the defects he adverted to in the reviews. He lays down the operations of the ad interim detail of service which he formed to defend the province. He makes a résumé of its preceding reports. He states the idea that the Apache have of it, and the fear that the Seri and Pima may revolt again, and he offers to indicate the best possible means to make the war defensive and offensive, laying down as the principal fundamental of these operations the useful establishment of the presidios on the line of the frontier.

¶ 380. He treats this from paragraph forty-three to fifty-six in the terms which I am copying because it is the essential point. With this illustration I desire to establish the care and tact with which I am dictating my measures in the most serious matter of altering the present situations of the Sonoran presidios:

¶ 381. He speaks thus: "The prolix examination which I made of the Rio de Terrenate, or San Pedro, and the news of the fortunate discovery made by Captain Don Juan Bautista de Anza of a route overland to northern California, obliged me to form the well-founded idea that today the line of presidios which the royal instruction prescribes for Sonora is not so advantageous as it was in the year of '67.

¶ 382. "I had not seen all the frontier when I selected the valley of El Escomác for the presidio of Santa Gertrudis del Altar, and thus it appeared to me that I had found the real, useful spot for its new location. But that has the defect of being separated considerably from the line, and this fact will force the presidio of Tubac to be moved from the line. Thus Tubac and Terrenate may be situated in spots little advantageous, weak and scanty in the indispensable resources for the support of troops and the horse herd, such as pasture, water, and wood. Finally, the settlers are to be abandoned or withdrawn from these two presidios and missions nearby.

¶ 383. "The presidio of Altar was erected to control the Pimas Altos. In its present situation it is opposite La Papaguería, as the map shows. Transferred to Escomác, it is withdrawn only eight or nine leagues and is placed among the three pueblos of Piato recently pacified. They may look upon this innovation with the fear that it is directed to surprise and exterminate them. Because of their delinquencies and natural fear they are capable of imagining the greatest fantasies. During these years they are beginning to suffer in the neighborhood of Altar the incursions of the Apache, so that if this presidio went to Escomác, its settlers, La Ciéneguilla, and the nearby missions would remain unprotected and the door would open to the Apache to make himself owner of the territory which he has not hitherto invaded and possibly to end all of Pimería Alta, while perhaps the Piato, impressed by their fears, may abandon their pueblos and flee to the hills.

¶ 384. "The distance is more than forty-one leagues from the valley of Escomác to that of Arivác, where the presidios of Tubac is to be located. The detachment of Altar which must examine the terrain to the right ought to direct itself precisely either through the missions of San Antonio de Oauitva as far as El Búsanic, or in the direction of Alamo Muerto, Puerto del Carrizal, Sierra del Humo, as far as the hill of La Horca. Their terrain is not passable and is extremely dangerous because of roughness, and lack of water will make useless the fatigues of the troops.

¶ 385. "The valley of Arivác is distant from Tubac eight leagues towards the west; from Altar, forty-one; in a direct line through El Búsanic and its missions, forty-three; and from Terrenate, established in Las Nutrias, forty-two.

¶ 386. "The supporting detachments of Tubac and Terrenate will be risked more than those of Altar, both because of the roughness of the road and because of the ease with which the Indians enter from the sierras of Guachuca, San Cayetano, and Santa Rita into the cordillera of those which shelter the entire road. They will repeatedly and successfully sally out upon our detachments in many places and passes similar to that of San Antonio, where they only now twice attacked the detachment which was enroute from Terrenate to Tubac, killing some of our people, and stealing their horses and luggage. The settlers of Tubac and the mission of Tumacacori are in the most unprotected condition and will, without support, emigrate as soon as the presidio is moved to Arivác.

¶ 387. "This valley is large, but swampy and unhealthy. It has no more water than that of La Ciéneguilla, which dampens everything. The horse herds will enjoy good pastures, but the soldiers no health, and the only good which this transmigration will produce will be that the rich mines of silver called Longoreña, La Duri, and others will be worked. But in Sonora where minerals are plentiful, people and the spirit to work the mines are lacking.

¶ 388. "The spot which they call Las Nutrias is fertile, although scarce in wood. It is distant from Terrenate about two short leagues. It does not appear best that the king should spend four thousand pesos in this useless transference, especially when the presidio of Fronteras, established in the valley of San Bernardino, is not more than thirty leagues distant from Terrenate.

¶ 389. "The line drawn from the coast of the South Sea between the presidio of Altar and the abandoned mission of Sonoitac to the debouchment of the Rio de Guadalupe into that of the Rio del Norte and the Gulf of Mexico was proposed with solid reasons by the most excellent Señor Marqués de Rubí. I am not opposing its recognized usefulness. Thus with the addition of a presidio on the Sonoran frontier, all would be well placed and the province defended successfully without its being necessary to restrict the new locations of Altar, Tubac, and Terrenate to the spots of El Escomác, Arivác, and Nutrias, the only suitable ones in forty leagues that must separate these presidios. But today we find ourselves with the recent occurrence, not foreseen in the year '67, of the discovery of the route by land to Monterrey. As Captain Don Juan Bautista de Anza and one of the religious missionaries who accompanied him surmise, not only is the route short, but in the greatest part fertile, pleasing, settled by numerous heathen. I understand that this new discovery may oblige us to alter the line proposed, drawing it from the junctions of the

Colorado and Gila rivers as far as the debouchments of the Guadalupe into the Sea of the North.

¶ 390. "I already see that for this reason it will be imperative that we repeat the corresponding prolix examinations of the country, suspending meanwhile the changing of the presidios of Sonora with the view of not risking expenses which their transference will occasion. But if, after the terrain has been reconnoitered, the direction of the line from the junctions of Guadalupe and Norte rivers is resolved upon, as I believe it certainly will be, the line will go straight to the junction of the San Pedro and Gila.

¶ 391. "This is in my opinion the real frontier which we must cover in Sonora to defend it from all its enemies. Thus it supposes that there is established a new presidio at the junction of the Colorado and Gila to sustain the missions of the heathen who may wish to be reduced, and to open communication with those of Monterrey. I propose that another presidio be placed at the junction of the rivers of San Pedro and Gila, as this spot, being the beginning of the Apache frontier, will impede the entrance of these Indians, defending the missions of Tupson and San Xavier del Bac. I also propose that Tubac be transferred to the Valley of Los Santos Angeles Custodios (El Quiburi), Terrenate to the valley of San Pedro, and Fronteras to San Bernardino.

¶ 392. "I do not know the distance between the junctions of the rivers Colorado and Gila, and the Gila and San Pedro, but it will be the greatest distance between any of the five presidios. The second presidio I am proposing will be twenty-six leagues distant from Tubac; this from Terrenate, twenty-two; and Terrenate from Fronteras, thirty-one. The frontier of the Apache will be protected along its short extension of sixty-nine [seventy-nine?] leagues with all the resources considered advantageous for the new establishment of the presidio. Another second line which the settlers of the transferred presidios promise with undeniable advantages will assure the certain defense of the territory, provided that they are organized in the terms which the documents of my review manifest. While we are making certain of the good faith of the nations which have surrendered, the continuance of the presidio of Santa Gertrudis del Altar in its present site to garrison the interior of the country appears convenient to me. Also half of that garrison should be detached with a subaltern to remain at San Miguel de Orcasitas where the respective disputes of the Piato, Papago, Seri, and Pima can be attended to. To this matter the large number of residents of San Miguel and Santa Gertrudis can very well contribute.

¶ 393. "It is to be deduced from what has been set forth that to defend the province of Sonora the six presidios are needed which today garrison it. The first of these will be to the left of the line as the new discovery demands; the four which follow are the same which the royal instructions provide for. Considering the continuance of Santa Gertrudis del Altar with its force divided between its duty there and San Miguel de Orcasitas until the perfect pacification of the surrendered Indians is achieved, it appears to me that from my propositions the royal treasury comes out benefited and the country safeguarded. Thus, to prevent the enemies from the northwest from coming in to attack the province, which is the object to which, according to the second article of the royal instruction, the presidio of Altar is destined, I consider sufficient half of its garrison. Meanwhile, the spiritual conquest aided by the arms of the new presidio at the junction of the rivers Colorado and Gila, the reduction to missions of the Papago and the rest of the heathen who live in the lands situated to the northwest may be achieved."

¶ 394. Up to this point Bonilla speaks concerning the line of presidios. I am restricting the rest of the paragraphs of his report to the operations of war, defensive and offensive.

¶ 395. At the end of the year '74, its governor, Colonel Don Francisco Crespo, reconnoitered the frontier of Sonora and reported on the results to Brigadier Don Hugo O'Conor as follows:[103]

[103] O'Conor asked Governor Crespo to comment on Bonilla's report wherein he reënforced the ideas here included by Croix, although in other parts of his reports the governor was very critical of Bonilla. A.G.N., Provincias Internas,

PROVINCE OF SONORA

¶ 396. "I consider the junction of the rivers of San Pedro and Gila (looking only at the Apache enemies) as the final point of the frontier. Although on the other side of the Gila there are some Apache, they cannot enter the province because they are opposed to the Gila, Pima, and Papago. Besides, even if there was not this block, it is not possible for them to enter because the extensive land they would have to cross is so scarce in water that at certain times it is impassable, even for the natives themselves. Supposing this, I believe that attention ought only to be directed from the said junction to San Bernardino, or Coaguionoc, whose distance through Santa Cruz in my understanding, will not exceed seventy or eighty leagues, all passable without the necessity of crossing any sierra. Accordingly, locating the three presidios in San Bernardino, or Coaguionac, Santa Cruz, and the junction of the rivers, or their neighborhoods, this line will be protected as is provided for in the royal regulation. Moreover, the cordon is best arranged in this way to continue it, provided that the establishments in the direction of Monterrey are decided upon.

¶ 397. "The three indicated spots have the advantage of being points which, if not absolutely necessary, are the ones most utilized by the enemies for entering and departing, especially if they have herds and if they find themselves very close to their principal points of reunion. These advantages can facilitate the retrieval of stolen property which they have and their frequent punishment."

¶ 398. This is the substance of the report of the governor, who sent a copy to the viceroy of New Spain. This superior chief received another report at the beginning of the year of '75 from Father Fray Juan Díaz, of the College of Santa Cruz de Querétaro, who had accompanied Lieutenant Colonel Don Juan Bautista de Anza on the discovery of the road to Monterrey.[104]

Tomo 88, 142–61, Crespo to Bonilla, San Miguel, January 16, 1775. See also H. E. Bolton, *Anza's California Expeditions,* V (Berkeley, 1930), 238–48 regarding Crespo's report to Bucareli on the route to California.

[104] The entire Díaz-Garcés report is translated in Bolton, *Anza's California Expeditions,* V, 276-90.

¶ 399. This religious indicates that this report or representation is made in the name of Father Francisco Garcés with regard to the second expedition of Anza to occupy the port of San Francisco in California. He indicates the great usefulness of this establishment, the relationship which it has with the Rio Colorado and Gila, and the relationship of these with the line of presidios of Sonora. He enlarges upon the reasons which obliged him to set forth his opinion concerning the final point, although he confessed with ingeniousness that it is foreign to his sacred ministry.

¶ 400. As a consequence he shows that the troops of Sonora cannot contain the hostilities of the Apache and that the province is in a deplorable condition. He continues his report concerning the establishment of the line in the following terms:

¶ 401. "To avoid the grave injuries that Sonora suffers and to facilitate the new foundations without increasing the armed forces, it is necessary to alter the order of the new regulation in the establishment of presidios. I have already seen the difficulty of the undertaking, but the convenience offered is patent. I consider, thus, it would be extremely opportune to suppress at once the presidios of San Miguel and Buenavista. However, in the latter a detachment of ten men could be left to control the Pima of the pueblos of Suaqui; another of fifteen men in El Pitic to avoid the disorders of the Seri Indians and to reduce them to the method of life which they must observe; another fifteen men in the presidio of Altar to control the Piato of Caborca and to keep in mind the Papago country of the west because of some untoward event which may occur there. Each one of these detachments commanded by a subaltern of good conduct, I consider quite sufficient for discharging its particular duty provided that it does not have on hand the care of horse herds, for if this particular duty were added more than those assigned would be necessary.

¶ 402. "With regard to the cordon, or line of presidios, I consider San Bernardino in a very good spot (although it has some inconveniences). It has the same number that the regulation assigns for the company of Fronteras, namely, the dotation of one hundred men from which it can provide ten for Buenavista, and another ten for the pueblo of El Pitic. It will then have eighty to protect the pueblos of its neighborhood and pursue the Apache enemy. Regarding the presidio of Terrenate, ordered located in Las Nutrias, it appears to me it would be very useful to transfer it to the advantageous spot of Santa Cruz, distant from San Bernardino some thirty-five leagues to the west in territory also very good for communication, if I have been well informed. Having allowed it the same dotation of one hundred men, it can place five men in El Pitic, fifteen in Altar, and retain eighty to attend principally to the Apache. The presidio of Tubac, commanded located in El Arivác, would be very suitable at the junction of the San Pedro River with the arroyo of Santa Teresa, distant from Santa Cruz some forty leagues to the northwest, also in very good land for communication. If it were allowed the dotation of ninety men with the corresponding officers, it would be able to protect the mission of the Rio Gila, by extending to them the corresponding garrison, and attend to the punishment and harrying of the enemies. The presidio of Altar is ordered transferred to the post of El Escomác, between the pueblos of Caborca and Bisanig, to punish the Apache to the northwest. It has never been verified that the Apache have lived to the northwest of Caborca, nor within a very great distance. Accordingly, I consider it would be extremely important to establish this presidio with the dotation of fifty men (or, if it appears suitable to your Excellency, to add some troops), with the dotation of sixty on the Rio Colorado some thirty leagues to the northeast of its confluence with the Gila to support the new missions that it is intended to establish on the river.

¶ 403. "This is, most excellent señor, the collocation which I conceive the most important for the purposes which I have already set forth, without increasing especial costs, but always in the understanding that at the present it is indispensable to attend to the urgent necessity that we are experiencing. I consider it very advantageous to add at least the number of one hundred men so that, aided by the existing detachment, they can bridle the pride of the Apache, drive him out of the land, and put fear into him, if more cannot be achieved.

¶ 404. "The advantages which I consider can result from this decision are the following: First, there will be an increase and extension of our Catholic Faith in all those nations so worthy of this singular benefit, because of the reasons which I have intimated, and this without especial expense for the royal treasury. Second, the enemy can be castigated with greater facility because the presidios are nearer to their lands, for less encumbered, presidial companies can with greater promptness make many *entradas* and have greater results. Third, the number of the horse herds being less, and the quartermasters and presidios being fewer, so many people will not find themselves employed in the garrisons and necessary escorts, and many can be employed in the persecution of the enemy. Fourth, with the presidios established in the spots proposed, all the missions and Spanish settlers are within their cordon or line. This would not follow if they were located where the new regulation commands. Thus, in this case the settlers of Tubac, the pueblos of Tumacacori, Calavazas, San Xavier, Tupson and those which can be established all along the Rio Gila and Colorado are exposed. Fifth, the missions having been founded under the protection of these presidios, all the Papago country on the Rio Gila will be surrounded by Christianized pueblos. For this reason they are closest to the Catechism. Thus there is less danger that they may attempt some revolt because they will not have the refuge of the roving Indians which up until now has served them as an alternative and asylum for their evil activities. Finally, I consider extremely useful this decision for making more certain the road to Monterrey, which without doubt it is necessary to utilize either through the Pima Gila or through the proposed cordon of presidios."

¶ 405. This report and that of the governor, Don Francisco Crespo, were remitted by the viceroy to Brigadier Don Hugo O'Conor, who set forth his opinion concerning the line of pre-

Croix's Capital: Arizpe, Sonora

sidios of Sonora under date of the twenty-ninth of the same month and year. I copy it verbatim as follows:[105]

¶ 406. "The manner of achieving successful progress in defensive war against the Apache who attack the province of Sonora consists, first, in situating the presidios usefully, and second, in distributing with method the troops to garrison them.

¶ 407. "The prolix examination which I made of all its frontier and the news of the discovery made by Lieutenant Colonel Don Juan Bautista de Anza of an overland road to northern California made me understand the usefulness which will result from the new transference of the presidios to terrains which I shall describe in their place.

¶ 408. "That of Santa Gertrudis del Altar was erected to withstand the Pimas Altos. In its present location, it fronts on the Papago country, as is shown on the map which the captain of engineers, Don Nicolas de Lafora, made. Having been transferred to the spot called Escomác, in fulfillment of the second article of the royal instruction for the new location of presidios, or the neighborhood of the mission of Caborca, it is withdrawn only eight or nine leagues. It is placed between the three recently pacified pueblos which can look upon this innovation with the fear that it is directed to surprise them in order to exterminate them, because their natural fear and lack of confidence are capable of instilling them with the most unfortunate fears. I am for the present of the opinion that nothing should be done at the moment to establish this presidio, and that the location of the rest in Sonora having been made on the spots that I shall propose in their place, Altar be transferred to the mission of Caborca, or the site called Escomác, as the second article of the royal instruction provides.

¶ 409. "There are more than forty-two leagues between the valley of Escomác, or mission of Caborca, to Arivác where the presidio of Tubac is to be situated in accordance with the third article of the royal instruction. The detachment of Altar that is

[105] O'Conor to Bucareli, No. 449, Janos, August 29, 1775. See above, page 163, footnote 97.

to examine the terrain to the right must go either through the mission of San Antonio de Oquitoa as far as El Búsanic, or along the straight road to Alamo Muerto, Puerto del Carrizal, Sierra del Humo, as far as El Cerro de la Horca, whose places, impassable because of the roughness of the sierras and lack of water, will make useless the fatigues of the troop.

¶ 410. "The valley of Arivác is distant from the presidio of Tubac seven leagues towards the west; from Altar, thirty-eight on the direct road along the Rio del Búsanic, and from its missions, forty; from Terrenate, established in Las Nutrias, forty-two.

¶ 411. "The reciprocal assistance which Tubac and Terrenate can give will be less useful than that from Altar, because of the roughness of the road, as well as the ease with which the enemy can enter by way of the sierras of Guachuca, San Cayetano, and Santa Rita, along the cordillera which overshadows the entire trail. They will, with advantage, repeatedly attack our troops from the many hiding places and passes which the sierras provide.

¶ 412. "The valley is large with considerable pasture, but without any water except in the marshes which in time of drouth hardly provides the necessary amount to satisfy thirst, a condition which makes it impossible to locate the presidio of Tubac there.

¶ 413. "The place they call Las Nutrias, indicated by the fourth article of the royal instruction for the settlement of the presidio of Terrenate, is fertile, although scarce in wood and water, and is distant from Terrenate but two leagues. This useless transference does not seem very necessary, especially if we stop to consider that the presidio of Fronteras is established in the valley of San Bernardino separated from Terrenate not more than thirty-five leagues.

¶ 414. "The most excellent señor, Marqués de Rubí, with good reasons, proposed to draw the line from the coast of the South Sea to that of the North and Mexican Gulf between the presidio of Altar and the abandoned mission of Sonoitac. Its utility is recognized, and in my opinion this difficult idea ought

PROVINCE OF SONORA

to be put into execution without any change other than that of advancing the presidios of Terrenate and Tubac to keep them on the line with San Bernardino and the rest of Vizcaya. This would be entirely achieved by situating the first in Santa Cruz, and the second in Toixon; a detachment of twenty-five men from the flying company could be placed in Sonoitac, and the presidio of Altar in Escomác. With this measure entire fulfillment is given to the royal instruction. Besides Sonora is safeguarded, and without the need of increasing the expenses of the royal treasury other than those which it actually causes. Its new presidios would enjoy all the conveniences that they can desire, such as making their short sallies along open roads, without fear that the enemy may surprise them. They will have behind them all Pimería Alta; the sierras of Guachuca, El Babocomeri, San Cayetano, Santa Rita; and the missions of San Xavier del Bac, and consequently all those close to the presidios of Altar, Tubac, and Terrenate. They will also be protected at Pimería Baja by transferring the presidio of Fronteras to San Bernardino where it is at present awaiting orders I have sent its captain, Don Gabriel de Vildósola, for this purpose.

¶ 415. "The spot of Santa Cruz, destined for the location of the presidio of Terrenate, besides having abundant pastures, waters, and woods, is at an average distance of thirty-three leagues west of San Bernardino. Toixon, indicated for Tubac presidio, is thirty-five leagues in the same direction from Santa Cruz with similar resources. The mission of Sonoitac is twenty-five leagues; the same from there to Escomác, where, according to the second article of the royal instruction, the presidio of Santa Gertrudis del Altar ought to be placed.

¶ 416. "This is in my opinion the real frontier which we must protect in Sonora from all its enemies. Thus supposing that perhaps two new presidios were established, one on the Rio Gila and the other on the Colorado, to support the heathen missions whom it is desired to reduce and open the communication with those of Monterrey, I propose that the useless presidios of San Miguel de Orcasitas and Buenavista be transferred to the above mentioned spots. With regard to these two places, the flying company of Sonora can be utilized to maintain control exercised by the two presidios in their present locations. With this well-taken measure, not only does one save the king annually 38,260 pesos, which would be the cost of the two new presidios, but also protects the communication with Monterrey and the fathers from being attacked by the barbarians who live in those regions. Besides, with a subaltern officer and twenty men from the flying company in each one of the pueblos in which the presidios are today, the recently pacified Seri will be kept more under control than they are now because of the shameful inaction of the companies. Their individuals are employed only in taking care of the horse herd, carrying mail, providing escort, caring for cattle, and in keeping eleven men in Pitic to observe the movements of the Seri.

¶ 417. "It is to be deduced from what has been stated that to defend the province of Sonora, six presidios and the flying companies are needed. The first four are for the formation of the line. The strength of the flying company is to be divided between San Miguel de Orcasitas and Buenavista, until there is secured the complete eradication of the defeated Indians. Two are to be on the Gila and Colorado rivers as the above noted discovery of the Monterrey road demands. It appears to me that from my propositions concerning the direction of the line, benefit results to the royal treasury, and the country is safeguarded. The presidio of Santa Gertrudis del Altar is devoted to the purpose of preventing the enemies from the northwest from entering to attack the province, which is its objective, according to the second article of the royal instructions. I consider its garrison sufficient until, with the aid of the presidial arms which are to be transferred to the Gila and Colorado rivers, the spiritual conquest and reduction to mission of the Papago and the rest of the heathen Indians who live in the sierras situated in the above route to the northwest are achieved."

¶ 418. I have copied the essential paragraphs of the reports of Brigadier Don Hugo O'Conor, Governor Don Francisco Crespo, Adjutant Inspector Don Antonio Bonilla, and Father Juan Díaz, for greater clarity, because as I have already stated, the useful location of the presidios of this province is one of the most important matters.

¶ 419. All agreed that Fronteras ought to be situated in the valley of San Bernardino, and that the line be continued through the Rio de San Pedro to assure the defense of Sonora, the new establishments on the Colorado and Gila rivers, and the communication with California. Also they agreed in selecting the spot of Santa Cruz for the presidio of Terrenate, as the valley of Quiburi, which Bonilla proposed, is distant three short leagues from Santa Cruz. Finally, they were of the same opinion concerning the occupation of the junctions of the rivers of San Pedro and Gila, and of those of the latter and the Colorado, with the difference that Crespo and Father Díaz proposed the increase of one hundred men and Bonilla, one hundred and fifty-two Opata.

¶ 420. The viceroy agreed with the proposals of Commander Inspector Don Hugo O'Conor, advising him under date of October 18, '75,[106] that the presidios be transferred to the spots which he had investigated, suspending the removal of those of San Miguel de Orcasitas and San Carlos de Buenavista until seeing the results of the second journey which Lieutenant Colonel Don Juan Bautista de Anza made to California to occupy the port of San Francisco.

¶ 421. Everything merited the sovereign approval of his Majesty in royal orders of September 6, '75, and February 14, '76. When I took charge of these provinces there were the presidios of Fronteras in San Bernardino, Terrenate in Santa Cruz, Tubac in Tupson, and the rest in their old locations. But the residents of the three presidios which were removed were at the door of ruin, either because many families had been transferred with the troop to the new locations, or because there were no facilities to put into effect what was provided for in the sixth article of the royal instruction concerning the building up and defense of the settlers. Although, for these

[106] See above, page 163, footnote 97.

reasons, the measure of garrisoning with detachments the pueblos of Fronteras, Tubac, and Terrenate was taken, it was at a time when the injuries could not be remedied. For at the moment when the removal of the presidio of Fronteras was made to San Bernardino, one saw the abandonment of the two nearby pueblos of Cuchuta and Teuricachi; Terrenate suffered the same fate, and Tubac is now depopulating itself.

¶ 422. I have already referred in paragraphs 243, 247, and 282 of this report to the forceful petitions of Don Juan Bautista de Anza and Don Pedro de Tueros to provide for the return of the presidios to the spots they left. I have spoken also of the exact reasons that moved me to arrange for the abandonment of the posts of San Bernardino, the establishment of its company in Fronteras, and my measures for the establishment of the Opata in Babispe. I now come to the matter of stating the results of the general examination of this frontier made by Brigadier Don Jacobo Ugarte y Loyola and Lieutenant of Engineers, D. Gerónimo de la Rocha; the concepts that I owe to the reports of these officers, after comparing them with the former ones,[107] with the opinion of the Marqués de Rubí, and with the articles of the royal instruction; the resolutions that I have taken and those which I am thinking of taking at a proper time to establish in Sonora the real line of presidios.

¶ 423. Brigadier Loyola, presupposing the importance of the erection of the presidios of the Opata in Babispe and the useful return of that of San Bernardino to Fronteras, states in his report concerning the line the following:[108]

¶ 424. "The second presidio ought to be located in Las Nutrias where the company of the suppressed presidio of Santa Cruz is actually encamped. The reasons which support the preference of this site, I set forth to your lordship in my report of May 7, last, adding solely that this spot is distant from that of Fronteras along the road of Magallanes, twenty-five to twenty-six leagues, and via that of El Ojo del Gato from twenty-eight to twenty-nine leagues.

[107] That is O'Conor, Crespo, Bonilla, and Diaz.
[108] Ugarte to Croix. See above, page 151, footnote 88.

PROVINCE OF SONORA

¶ 425. "On the spacious and suitable mesa of La Mesa of Buenavista, I consider proper that the third presidio be located. This is situated on the banks of the Rio de San Antonio with all the resources for a good settlement and is distant from the depopulated Hacienda of Buenavista a league and a half; thirty-five from the presidio of Altar; twenty-six from Tupson; and twenty-five from the site of Las Nutrias. The location of a presidio on this site will animate the people, and in time the advantageous spots of Santa María Sonaca, San Antonio, Rancho del Torreon, Valley of San Lázaro, Hacienda de Santa Bárbara, Rancho de San Luís de Buenavista, and Pueblos Cuevabi, can be settled. All are sites at a fair distance from the proposed presidio. If done, it will serve the province with greatest usefulness for the growing of crops and the raising of herds of cattle. Besides that, the missions and pueblos of Calavazas, Tumacacori, and Tubac, which form the line from Buenavista to Tupson, are also protected, and the dwellers can coöperate with the troops of the presidios to their mutual defense.

¶ 426. "The three presidios of which I have spoken up to now I consider proper for the formation of a new line that really may be the frontier for the defense of the province without losing sight of the fact that under their protection there can be established respectable settlements which in time may not need the support of troops. But since your Excellency has been pleased to advise me to set forth my opinion concerning those which can be advantageous to the continuation of the line, until it is joined with the new establishments of the Rio Colorado, and until the communication with northern California is opened, I ought to say in obedience to this superior order that for these purposes I consider the present presidio of Tupson very necessary and advantageous.

¶ 427. "Although this presidio, which is in a corner of the province, can serve slightly in defense of the frontier line, excepting its support of the missions of San Xavier del Bac and Tupson, which are close to it, it is nevertheless most suitable to continue the above mentioned line, directing it in this case through the Casas Grandes de Montezuma whence the religious and others who cross the Rio Colorado have traveled and are going to travel. In its site or neighborhood can be established a good presidio. I am not able to speak of this site or of the subsequent ones with the certainty with which I have spoken of the previous ones, because I have not reconnoitered them.

¶ 428. "What is certain is that I am not of the opinion that the line should be directed along the banks of the Rio de San Pedro or Terrenate, nor should there be located any presidios at the junction of this river with that of the Gila. The presidio that is placed here will be very much advanced and distant from the interior country; it could extend no defense to the province; to sustain it would necessitate a numerous dotation; and it would be necessary to transport from Tupson everything it needed because that country offers no suitable spot for crops, much less for the establishment of new settlements under its protection in the future.

¶ 429. "And although in the valley of Santa Teresa which is about a league and half distant from this site, some crops can be raised, they will always be so small that they will not ward off the scarcity of supplies for the presidios, nor attract people to settle in a region that offers them so little in resources and supplies.

¶ 430. "The same thing I consider ought to be said of the Rio de San Pedro or Terrenate. It is no less unsuitable for continuing the line of the frontier because, although on its banks are found various sites where it appears presidios can be located, such as El Quiburi, Tres Alamos, Zequias Hondos, and others, this line would always be very prejudicial. First, because these spots offer resources for only small settlements that never can be maintained without the support of troops.

¶ 431. Second, because it would be necessary to establish them with notable distance from one another, unless the number is increased, which would occasion considerable expense to the treasury.

¶ 432. "Third, because the presidios would be advanced to a

PROVINCE OF SONORA

great distance from which they could not aid one another or attend, in case of invasion, to the support of the frontier pueblos. The province thus would remain unprotected, and the interior pueblos without defense.

¶ 433. "Finally, it would be indispensable (as I have said of the junctions of the rivers) that a numerous dotation be established, or they would be useless for making war on the enemy, defending only the skulls of the presidios.

¶ 434. "The line I have detailed has none of the above mentioned drawbacks but, on the contrary, has the greatest advantages and resources. With it the interior pueblos remain more protected against what may possibly occur; the settlers, Indian allies, and soldiers can with more facility mutually aid one another; with the presidios located at a regular distance from one another, journeys are less exposed; respectable settlements can be established under their protection. Besides not necessitating in time the support of troops, they will serve the province usefully, cultivating the fertile lands which up until now are depopulated. Finally, contact will be had by the shortest and most suitable road with the above mentioned new establishments according to reports I have."

¶ 435. Here Brigadier Don Jacobo Ugarte y Loyola concludes his proposals concerning the line of presidios of Sonora, indicating that those of Altar, Orcasitas, and Buenavista ought to remain with their present forces until a transference overseas of the Seri frees the province from the attacks of these Indians.

¶ 436. Although Engineer Don Gerónimo de la Rocha indicated the same opinion as Brigadier Loyola, I shall copy what is most essential of his report.[109]

¶ 437. "Since the presidios are to be advanced into the country of the enemy, they will be taken away from the settlements that they were to protect and shelter. Embracing as a consequence the greatest part of the advanced terrain, the result is necessarily that the circumference of the line is greater than

[109] *Ibid.*, Rocha to Croix.

that the presidios were to form and occupy, and the distance they were to be located from one another more extensive. To the difficulty with which the small garrisons can impede the entrance of the enemy through the large open or exposed places on their flanks, there is added that of being unable to employ all the force in this precise and fundamental object. For, since there are no supplies in the new locations to support the troops and their families, it has been and is still necessary for the latter to go where the settlements that grow supplies are located and utilize large bodies to conduct and escort them. Thus, the troop can engage in no other service nor be employed in that of defense or offense. This fact is responsible, in my opinion, for the ease and frequency with which the enemies have repeated their attacks. Finding free the entrance over the open terrain between the neighboring presidios, they introduce themselves accordingly into the interior of the country. They cause injuries without encountering resistance because the settlements are not sufficient to defend themselves and are without the protection of the troop, of whom they are deprived because of its having been advanced.

¶ 438. "When the number of troops may be sufficient for garrisoning the province in order to attend to this injury, it appears indispensable that they should have no other duty or purpose than that of defending it, impeding the entrance of the enemies, pursuing them and castigating them, making upon them active and incessant war, and attacking them wherever possible in their own rancherias and lands, as Article 10 of the regulation provides. Thus if a large part of the force is employed, as has happened up to now, in looking for and escorting remounts and supplies, it will cause perforce a failure in that primary object of their existence, and the time will never come when this object can be fulfilled as the state of the province demands. Unless presidios are located in terrains capable of producing crops for their provision and consumption, at the same time that there is being encouraged, in them and in their shelter, agriculture and the raising of herds, this idea is impossible. I pass from this point to indicate the spots which

PROVINCE OF SONORA

I have found with these resources and which appear to me sufficient to form the new line.

¶ 439. "In my former reports of April 29 and 25 of the present month, I had presented to your lordship the unsatisfactory location of the presidio of Fronteras, which is the first of the line, and the advantages which are to be achieved by building it in the site of Badeguachi, distant only a league to the south of its actual location. Referring to those reports, I have nothing to add concerning this establishment. The same is true of Santa Cruz de Terrenate, the second, which, having been transferred to the plain of Las Nutrias, as I have likewise informed your lordship, will reduce to twenty-five leagues the distance of about fifty which it actually has from its neighbor, Fronteras. It will facilitate the communication of both and the uniting of its forces for the defense and offense. Together they will protect the spots and cañadas most frequented by the enemies. In the shelter of both presidios, with the benefit of fertile, extensive lands and abundant waters of their neighborhoods, two good settlements can be formed which may provide them with what is necessary and support their arms in case of necessity. Under the protection of the first, the rebirth of the destroyed settlements of Cuchuta, Terricachi, and Real de Nacosari may even be hoped for. Those of Cuquiarachic, Bucuachi, San Joseph de Chinapa, La Hacienda de Bacanuchi, Cumpas, and others farther within may be improved. Finally, the defense and protection of the two presidios may be achieved, and the gold placers of Bucuachi, Canannea, and various others may be worked with liberty and constancy. Today they give only constant proofs of their prodigious richness because the risk and fear which the attacks of the enemy have instilled do not permit searching for and exploiting their riches.

¶ 440. "I have also informed your lordship that the present location of the presidio of Tupson is very good. It enjoys whatever resources can be hoped for in a good settlement to encourage in its shade and defense those which are in its neighborhood. Because of these reasons, then, I think it cannot and ought not to be removed. But there is left open the extensive distance of forty-five leagues which intervene to its neighboring one, established in the plain of Las Nutrias. As it is not possible for the forces of both to impede the enemy who make many and very frequent sallies and retreats in the intermediate terrain, I consider the location of another presidio in the center, or half-way between the two, necessary to block the enemy. Not having encountered or reconnoitered any other spot more suitable for locating it than the Estancia of Buenavista, it appears to me that here its early erection would be very appropriate, because, besides having excellent resources for a medium sized settlement and for many ranches and haciendas, it divides equally the distance from Las Nutrias to Tupson, leaving twenty-six leagues from the latter and twenty-one to the former. It also has the advantage of protecting the passes of La Plomosa, Chihuahuilla, Divisadoros, and San Antonio; defending the pueblos of Calabazas and Tumacacori, facilitating the return to their old site of those destroyed, namely, Guevavi, Sonóita, and Santa María Suanca; and covering with herds the beautiful valleys, ruined haciendas, and ranchos of Buenavista, San Luís, Ranchito, Santa Barbara, and San Lázaro. Finally, it offers also the best communication of the line and the union of its forces with those of its two neighbors, and, if it were necessary, with those of the presidio of Altar, which, though situated outside the line, is but a distance of thirty-five leagues to the southeast.

¶ 441. "I have already indicated to your lordship that on the banks of the Rio de San Pedro I have found no site fit for establishing a presidio, nor even for founding a settlement; and that the same is true at its junction with the Gila. For this reason I cannot indicate that it will be appropriate for the new erection resolved upon by the piety of his Majesty. To be able to do so with understanding and certainty, I consider it indispensable to make a new and detailed reconnaissance of the banks of the Gila as far as its junction with the Colorado, for besides the examination of those terrains, it will give information for selecting what may be the most advantageous site. It will conduce also to give preference to the one which unites to these resources that of aiding better the contact and union of its forces with those destined to protect and garrison the new pueblos of the Colorado.

¶ 442. "With the line formed in the spots which are to be proposed, the present presidio of Fronteras will remain in Badeguachi at thirty degrees, fifty-seven minutes, and fifty-two seconds latitude. It is free from the inundations which those valleys have suffered, is in a location entirely cleared of obstacles, with sufficient land for a good settlement at the point where the valleys of Fronteras, Cuquiarachia, and Cuchuta unite along the road of the Potrero Pass, which serves to unite the pueblo of Babispe with the Vizcaya line. It will have, at a distance of one league to the north, the pueblo of Fronteras; two leagues to the west, Cuquirachia; three leagues to the south, the abandoned settlement of Cuchuta; and about eight hundred varas to the west, the Rio de Fronteras. Since this has no ford for more than half a league it is very important for protecting and safeguarding from the enemy along that front. Besides, there being along the river a high hill on which a small watch tower has been established, the extension of the three valleys may be observed. Their agricultural lands can be developed and the placers of Bacuachi stimulated. Frequent sallies can be made from the Sierra Purica to the slopes of Mavavi to impede the entrance of the enemy. For this purpose it would be very suitable to establish a detachment in the depopulated pueblo of Cuchuta from which, three leagues south, is Turisachi; three to the southwest, a quarter to the south is the Turicachi Pass; five to the west, Mavavi; and four to the east is Teras. These spots are the points at which our enemies enter.

¶ 443. "The presidio of Santa Cruz, transferred to the plain of Las Nutrias at thirty-one degrees, twenty-four minutes, and ten seconds latitude, twenty-five leagues west northwest from Fronteras along the road called Magallenes, will be situated in an open and fertile terrain. It will have the valleys of Guachuca two leagues to the northwest; the headwaters of

San Pedro and its cultivated fields two and a half to the east; the pueblo or old presidio of Terrenate two to the west northwest; La Avra, formed between the old Cannanea and the corner of El Burro, where the enemies enter and flee with the larger part of their stolen goods, eight to the south. It will be easy to cut the enemy off if, before leaving for the attack, advice were had from the settlements, which can well provide the warning as they are only twenty-five leagues away. Finally, in case of making campaigns to hunt and attack them in their own rancherias, the point will be more important for the union of the troops, because of the ease both of quartering and of provisioning them, as well as being closer to the sierra where the enemies are ranching. They can accordingly be located more promptly.

¶ 444. "The new and third presidio established in La Estancia de Buenavista will be at thirty-one degrees, forty minutes, and twenty-five seconds latitude on a large mesa, along the base of which flows the Rio de Santa María. It has its origin in the Ojo de San Antonio, and although it is not very large, it never loses its water even in the dry season. It has a beautiful and rich valley in which at a league to the south was the abandoned hacienda of Buenavista, which was extremely abundant in fruits and herds. Three leagues to the west and a fourth to the northwest is the ruined pueblo of Guevavi. Four to the northwest is the sierra of La Chihuahuilla, second in riches and known minerals. This presidio will be distant twenty-one leagues to the northwest and fourth to the west from Las Nutrias. It will be in the best position to protect the passes of La Plomosa, Chihuahuilla, Divisadoros, and San Antonio; to defend the pueblos of Calabazas and Tumacacori; and to stimulate the repeopling of the ruined pueblo of Sonóita, and of the beautiful valleys of Buenavista, St. Luís, Ranchito, Santa Barbara, San Lázaro, Santa María Suanca, Torreon, San Antonio, and others farther within the province. It should be noted that although the site of Guevavi divides better the distance between Las Nutrias and Tupson, I select preferably La Estancia because it has more abundant pastures and is closer to Altar.

PROVINCE OF SONORA

¶ 445. "The fourth and final one, which is the presidio of San Agustín del Tupson, is at thirty-two degrees, thirty-one minutes, and thirty seconds latitude. It is in a terrain quite free from obstacles, very abundant with water and cultivable lands, with pastures surrounded by two irrigation ditches, where the horse herd is well safeguarded with a small garrison. It defends and sustains the missions and pueblos of Tupson and San Xavier del Bac, which under its shelter have enjoyed a well-known growth. It would decline entirely if the garrison were lacking. Finally, it is the precise point which, along the Rio Gila, opens and facilitates the communication of this province with the Colorado and the province of California. It has the spot of Tres Alamos at a distance of seventeen leagues to the east; the pass of Zevadilla, nine to the east northeast; that of La Mololoa, four to the north and a quarter to the northeast; El Aquitune, sixteen to the northeast; the sierra of Tupson, three to the west; Ojo Grande, source of its waters, a quarter of a league to the south. Twenty-six leagues to the southeast is the presidio of Las Nutrias. The junction of the rivers San Pedro and Gila is another twenty-nine to the north.

¶ 446. "The junction of the San Pedro and Gila rivers at thirty-two degrees and twenty-one minutes latitude is in a closed canyon, which the rough sierras form, called Aribaipa. Because the flow of the Gila is copious and the current shallow, the immediate terrains are flooded in all directions. These terrains as far as the eye reached and as far as they could be reconnoitered are very broken. If in the new reconnaissance which must be made of the banks of the Gila there is found far to the west a suitable site on which to establish the presidio commanded erected by his Majesty, it will be at too great a distance from its neighbor, Tupson. Perhaps if it is impossible to establish communication along the road which is called El Aquitune, on which one now crosses to the Colorado, because there is no permanent water, it will be necessary to open a route through the *cañadas* of El Oro and La Virgen del Consuelo, or even through that of San Simón, to come out on the Rio de San Pedro and valley of Santa Teresa, from which to continue along the banks of the Gila to the new establishment. In this case, to protect this greatly extended line, I believe indispensable the formation of a new post with a strong detachment in the valley of Santa Teresa, which, although it lacks the best resources, is the most suitable of those which I have reconnoitered in those lands.

¶ 447. "The location of the presidio of Santa Gertrudis del Altar is at thirty-five degrees, three minutes and twenty-five seconds latitude, in a terrain quite unobstructed, but scarce in pastures and water, especially during the dry season when the river becomes shallow. But the troops and settlers have never lacked necessities, on some occasions searching for and bringing them quite some distance, as happened when I went to reconnoiter it. It has various irrigated lands which abound in products because of the great fertility of that soil. To the west southwest is the mission of Caborca with its pueblos on the site of El Pitiqui, and Bisanic; the sierra of Santa Teresa is twelve leagues to the northeast; the Cerro del Banuri, a league and a half northwest, quarter to the north; the pass of El Chanate a league and a half to the northwest, quarter to the west; the sierra of Ojo de Agua three to the south southwest; the Cerro del Carnero one to the southwest, quarter to the south; and the pass of Santa Ana is another to the west southwest. Although this presidio is within the province and outside the line of the frontier, I consider it indispensable to contain and punish the uprisings of the Seri and Tiburones, and keep open the road of the Real de la Ciéneguilla, as well as to maintain in due respect and obedience the Pimas Altos and the rest of the nations in the pueblos of its surroundings, whose fidelity is very suspicious. It would not be surprising if they revolted should the bridle of force that obliges them to remain quiet fail—a condition of deceit and appearance rather than of reality and truth.

¶ 448. "The presidio of El Pitic is at twenty-nine degrees, eleven minutes latitude, in a very spacious location, abundant with lands and waters, although exposed to floods. It suffered from floods to such an extent in the year of 1770 that it was necessary for the presidio to take refuge on the Cerro de la Campana. This risk would be avoided by placing it in the spot where the Seri at present have their huts. The presidio of Santa Gertrudis del Altar is distant more than sixty leagues to the north northwest; the Cerro del Tonuco, a quarter to the west; the Colorado, two to the northwest, a quarter to the north; Los Pozos of San Joseph, ten to the northwest; Santa Teresa, three to the west, a quarter to the southwest; Palos Blancos, two to the south southwest; and the Campana, a very little to the north. Their forces combined or united with those of Altar can be employed in punishing the Seri who rebelled, and the Tiburones, their friends and allies, whose attack I consider will not cease while they subsist in the pueblos called reduced, because according to what I have been able to observe, they are only so in appearance. They keep up contact and trade with those who attack us and it will not be strange if they serve them as faithful spies so that our enemies may attack us without risk. To avoid these known evils that each day will be greater because the number is being increased by those who desert and return to the Sierra, I find no means more proper than that of transplanting them all at quite long distances and to places where there is not left to them even the hope of returning to their country or soil."

¶ 449. In the year 1596 there was created in the Villa of Sinaloa the company which today garrisons the presidio of Santa Gertrudis del Altar. With the support of its small forces, reductions and conquests were extended to the provinces of Ostimuri and Sonora. Afterwards in the capacity of flying troops, it was situated in Bayoreca, Buenavista, San Miguel, Santa Ana, Caborca, and other different locations according to the state of the Indians, the Mayo, Fuerteños, Yaqui, Seri, and Pimas Altos and Bajos, until in the year 1757 it fixed its establishment in the spot of Altar. There it had fifty-one units with no other purpose than that of defending the province from the attacks of the Seri and Pima, and restraining the Papago.

¶ 450. These were the duties of the presidio of Santa Gertrudis del Altar when Lieutenant General Marqués de Rubí visited and reviewed it. As a consequence his proposition of transferring it to the neighborhood of the coast to embarrass the introduction and retreat of the Papago and Piato who live to the northwest, and the contact of these Indians with the Seri then in revolt, was well founded.

¶ 451. These reasons no longer existed when Brigadier Don Hugo O'Conor and Adjutant Inspector Don Antonio Bonilla entered Sonora, since, as a result of the Military Expedition the Seri were kept congregated in El Pitic; the Piato in their three pueblos of Bisanig, Caborca, and Pitique; and the cowardly Papago were committing no injury. They maintain the greatest subordination toward the captain of the presidio, Don Bernardo de Urrea; but the Apache had come in as far as the neighborhood of the Real de la Ciéneguilla. They began to know this terrain and that of the presidios. It was rightly suspected that, allied with some Piato who dwelt in small numbers at El Cerro, they would not long delay in making greater incursions upon all the territories which, after the military expedition, were to be populated with settlers, herds, and crops attracted by the riches of Ciéneguilla.

¶ 452. Without doubt for these reasons, although O'Conor and Bonilla selected the valley of Escomác for the transference of the presidio of Altar, they set forth the uselessness of the measure and the injuries which it could occasion.

¶ 453. O'Conor and Bonilla, remembering the detachment which Lieutenant General Marqués de Rubí proposed for a point midway between the presidios of Altar and Tubac, undertook to locate it, first, in the abandoned mission of San Marcelo at Sonoitac; and secondly, in the depopulated one of Búsanic.

¶ 454. Father Fray Juan Díaz gave as his opinion that, with Altar left garrisoned with fifteen men, the presidial company should be transferred to the Rio Colorado, giving it a dotation of sixty units. Although I have no documented information of the opinion of Governor Don Francisco Crespo concerning this matter, I am persuaded that he held the same opinion con-

PROVINCE OF SONORA

cerning the garrison of fifteen men in Altar. Finally, the military governor, Don Jacobo Ugarte y Loyola, and Engineer Don Gerónimo de la Rocha proposed the maintenance of this presidio in its old terrain which it occupies today.

¶ 455. After serious reflection upon all the opinions, I have found the most powerful and congruent reasons in those of Loyola and Rocha, first, because even if the Apache frontier were garrisoned with the necessary forces, those of the presidio of Santa Gertrudis del Altar will never be sufficient for greater opposition to the attacks of these Indians and defense of the Real de la Ciéneguilla whose riches, if they have been prodigious in their gold placers, do not offer less opulence in the unusual veins of silver which are just being discovered; second, because the troop keeps the Piato and Papago respectful; third, because while the Seri, Tepocas, and Tiburones remain, the forces of the company of Altar are very necessary for maneuvering with those of Orcasitas and Buenavista in order to withstand the hostilities of these Indians; fourth, because, since there is no spot other than the valley of Escomác for the transference of the presidio of Altar, it appears to me useless because of the short distance of nine leagues which intervenes between one and the other spots, because of the expense which it occasions, because Escomác is not fit for settlement, and because the injuries, well stated by Don Hugo O'Conor and Don Antonio Bonilla, would be incurred at once in any rebellion of the Piato if they saw within the pueblo presidial forces.

¶ 456. Consequently I consider proper the continuance of the presidio of Altar with the dotation of sixty-four units, to which I have reduced it, because I have had taken out of this company seven men for the detachment which garrisons the two settlements of Spaniards and Yuma Indians established on the Rio Colorado.[110]

¶ 457. The presidio of Santa Rosa de Coro de Guachi, known by the name of Fronteras, was erected at the end of the last century. It was quite useless until the year 1728, because of

[110] See above, page 155, footnote 91.

the reason which Brigadier Don Pedro de Rivera set forth in paragraph 13 of the first part, and 16 of the second part, of his general report,[111] but it was the one which defended the province from the hostilities of the Apache until the year 1742, when Terrenate was established.[112]

¶ 458. When the viceroy Duque de la Conquista was governing New Spain,[113] there was under consideration the transference of the presidio to Cóaguionac or the valley of San Bernardino, afterwards to Terrenate, and to various other places. Finally, its removal was considered unnecessary and dangerous.

¶ 459. Its transference to San Bernardino was given effect, in consequence of the opinion of Lieutenant General Marqués de Rubí and of the reports and reconnaissances of Don Hugo O'Conor, Don Francisco Crespo, and Don Antonio Bonilla. But I have arranged that the presidio of Santa Rosa de Coro de Guachi be returned to its old terrain of Fronteras, because, as I have stated in paragraph 290 of this paper and in paragraphs 46 and 56 of the representation which I presented to your Excellency under date of January 23, '80, No. 458,[114] it served in the valley of San Bernardino only to increase the number of the king's vassals who might be victims of the cruelty of the Apache, to fatten the latter's robberies among the horse herds and mule trains bringing provisions, to keep the troop eternally employed in weak maneuvers for their own defense, to accelerate the ruin of the valley of Fronteras, to open the door wide to the Indians for their daring hostilities in the interior of the province, and to occasion to the royal treasury the annual expense of more than thirty-four thousand pesos, which the salaries for the presidial company and for the flying company which reënforced its garrison, amounted to.

[111] See above, page 84, footnote 18.
[112] For some data on the defense of the province between 1735–1745 see Donald Rowland (ed.), "The Sonora Frontier of New Spain, 1735–1745," *New Spain and the Anglo-American West*, I, 147–64.
[113] That is, Pedro de Castro Figueroa y Salazár, viceroy from 1740–1741.
[114] See above, page 12, footnote 12.

PROVINCE OF SONORA

¶ 460. The worst is that after twenty months, counted from the day on which I arranged for the return of this presidio until today, the injuries which sprang from its transference have not been remedied, because injuries which flow from misfortune or mistaken commands are difficult to remedy in these countries. If one succeeds it is at the expense of time and care not to make new mistakes.

¶ 461. I consider that there is no mistake in the establishment of the Opata presidio in Babispe. This in truth is apparent in the miserable condition of this nation, particularly that part which has shared the general terror that the Apache have inspired; in the small number of Indians existing in that pueblo, and in those of Baserac and Guachinera; in their scarce crops; in the loss of sheep and horse herds; and in the industry based on the various products woven from crops of the land which are sold and highly valued. These reasons established the necessity for the support of forces to conserve a nation that voluntarily sought the Catechism and embraced with pleasure religion and vassalage, and that has always given proofs of its fidelity. It is certain that among some of our people there exist reasons which make them suspicious, but according to my concept it ought to be understood that this evil is not only uncommon, but rare, among the Opata. This is usual among the nations who blame the triumphs of the Apache for their own robberies and evils. These inclinations are characteristic of all castes of Indians; I do not know whether because of influence of climate or because of their profound ignorance of the true principles of rational and Christian life.

¶ 462. Be that as it may, even this reason supports the usefulness of the establishment of the presidio in Babispe. Thus it will serve as a bridle and punishment of the evil and delinquent; it will defend the Opata pueblos; it will make them flourish in a few years, and the nation, recognizing these benefits, will continue faithful and subordinate, contributing with particular advantages to the defense of this province and to that of New Vizcaya, and aiding reciprocally the two neighboring presidios of Janos and Fronteras.

¶ 463. The latter presidio, established at the distance of twenty-nine leagues from Babispe, which in turn is placed at thirty-three from Janos, has already made known the ease with which events that occur may be communicated in the small district of fifty-two leagues of frontier; the forces of the three presidios can be united and the combination of their operations, that necessarily must be fruitful and fearful to the Apache, assured.

¶464. In the shelter of the presidio of Fronteras, its settlement and that of Cuquiarachi will again be encouraged. One may be able to see the repeopling of Cuchuta and Teuricachi. The troop will not be under the necessity of searching outside for their supplies and perhaps will have an excess. Thus, with the government's taking measures for the union, or assembly, of the largest forces in this presidio, from it frequent sallies or monthly campaigns may be carried out to incommode the Apache, dislodge them from their rancherias in the nearby sierras, and punish and harass them in the ones farthest from our line.

¶ 465. I am presupposing, well located on the line, the presidio of Santa Rosa de Coro de Guachi, occupying its old location. In any event the plain contiguous to Badeguachi offers the best resources for its material construction. I have arranged it already, counting on about ten thousand pesos for the expenses for crops and encouragement of settlers. Eight thousand pesos have been offered by Captain Don Joseph Antonio de Vildósola, as I set forth to your Excellency in letter No. 517, of April 23, '80.[115] The remaining amount the officers and troops of the presidio are contributing voluntarily.

¶ 466. The presidio of Santa Cruz, known by the names of San Felipe de García Real, San Felipe de Jesús de Guevavi, and Terrenate, was founded in the year 1742 upon the advice of Governor D. Agustín de Vildósola.[116] In 1749 it was considered removing it to the valley of El Quiburi on the Rio de San Pedro.

[115] A.G.I., Guad., 277, Croix to Gálvez, No. 517, Arispe, April 23, 1780.
[116] He had urged it in 1735 as a militia *Sargento Mayor*. See Rowland, "The Sonora Frontier of New Spain," *loc. cit.*, 155.

¶ 467. I have already stated that this river, according to the common agreement of Brigadier Don Hugo O'Conor, Governor Don Francisco Crespo, Adjutant Inspector Don Antonio Bonilla, and Father Fray Juan Díaz, is the real frontier which the presidios of Sonora ought to protect in order to oppose the Apache, continue the line to the Rio Colorado, and open safe communication between this province and California. But as these new establishments were considered distant in the year '67, Lieutenant General Marqués de Rubí skillfully directed his attention to the business of improving the location of the presidio of Terrenate, placing it closer to the sierras of Chircagui, Magallanes, and Mavavi, and transferring its neighbor, Fronteras, to San Bernardino.

¶ 468. In consequence of this opinion and in fulfillment of what was provided for in Article 4 of the royal instruction,[117] Don Antonio Bonilla selected the arroyo of Las Nutrias for the new location of the presidio of Terrenate. But considering that the advantage of advancing it two leagues to the frontier was not fulfilling the purposes of its transmigration and was incurring useless expenses which perhaps it would be necessary to assume if the direction of the line were altered because of the discovery of the road to California, he proposed that the presidios be transferred to the headwaters of the Rio de San Pedro, a little more than seven leagues distant from Terrenate and thirty-one from San Bernardino.

¶ 469. Brigadier Don Hugo O'Conor subscribed substantially to this opinion. Although he arranged for the transference of the presidio, which was done, from the arroyo of Las Nutrias, he determined upon its abandonment and upon the occupation of the spot of Santa Cruz situated along the banks of the Rio de San Pedro at a distance of twenty-five leagues from Terrenate and forty-one from San Bernardino. This measure was in accord with the opinion of Governor Don Francisco Crespo, and P. Fray Juan Díaz.

¶ 470. According to the opinions of all, not only did the above

[117] This is the Regulation of September 10, 1772. See above, page 16, footnote 22.

mentioned river have the circumstances mentioned of being the real frontier that ought to be protected, but also the important considerations that on its banks were possible the erection of settlements. But the military governor, Don Jacobo Ugarte y Loyola, and Lieutenant of Engineers, Don Gerónimo de la Rocha, have held in their reports everything to the contrary. In truth the first two reports ought to prevail, having the majority of votes. These were made by the two chiefs of superior rank, a captain who viewed and examined the lands, delegated by the Commander Inspector Don Hugo O'Conor, and an informed religious, who was interested in the success of the establishments on the Colorado and Gila rivers.

¶ 471. It clearly appears to your Excellency that these were influenced by the reports which the Archbishop Viceroy Don Juan Antonio de Vizarrón made in the years 1735 and 1737 because of the revolt of the Pericua and Guaivera tribes in California.[118] In consequence of this a royal cedula was dispatched under date of November 13, 1744, directed to the viceroy Conde de Fuenclara, and in view of an extensive report which the Father Provincial of the ex-Jesuits, Cristoval de Escabar y Llamas, sent to his Majesty, the cited royal cedula was repeated to the Conde de Revilla Gigedo on December 4, 1747.[119]

¶ 472. I have in my possession the original file of papers which I asked for in Mexico. It was brought together in fulfillment of the royal cedulas referred to. Although it is incomplete it has served, and is serving, me greatly in assuring my decisions and measures by offering a comparison of the reports. accounts, and opinions which were given to the government in the years of '40 and '51 with those which have been given concerning the same material in the years from 1774 to the past year of 1780.

[118] Bancroft, *North Mexican States and Texas*, I, 458–59. See also Fernando Ocaranza, *Crónicas y relaciones del occidente de México*, Tomo I (Mexico, 1937), 269–73 (Biblioteca Histórica Méxicana de Obras Inéditas No. 5).

[119] Bancroft, *North Mexican States and Texas*, I, 465, summarizes Escobar's report and gives citation to it (p. 466, n. 61) and to the two royal cedulas of November 13, 1744, and December 4, 1747.

PROVINCE OF SONORA

¶ 473. So it appears in the cited file of papers, with regard to the features of the Rio de San Pedro according to the report of Captain of the Presidio of Fronteras, Don Francisco Tagle y Bustamante,[120] that the valley of the Pimas Sobaipuris is fertile in lands, waters, and pastures, but scarce in wood; that the river begins in the plains of Terrenate; that in places it is shallow; that it unites with the Gila at a distance of more than one hundred leagues; and that in the year 1746 it had along its banks the settlements or rancherias of Indians called Babispe, Quiburi, Optuabo, Escuevac, Baicata, and Bascomarize, to whom the father missionary of Santa María de Suanca administered.

¶ 474. According to another report which Governor Don Agustín de Vildósola made in the previously cited year of 1746, reference is made to the fact that the Sobaipuri had their rancherias under the name of pueblos in the arroyo of Cuachuca, the headwaters of the Rio de San Pedro, and in various spots close to its banks called Quiburi, Tres Alamos, Naideni, Bacoachi, Santa Cruz, and La Azequia Grande; that the father missionary of Santa María de Suanca was visiting them; that to this mission the Sobaipuri took their sons to receive the holy baptism; that the Indians were workers, reaping in abundance maize, frijol, and the rest of the crops; and that, inclined to war, they made campaigns against the Apache.

¶ 475. Appearing in the file of papers is an instructive and extensive opinion of the Auditor of War, Marqués de Altamira, given in the year 1751. This minister says that the presidio of Terrenate could leave its incommodious terrain in the *cañada* of San Mateo and advance twenty leagues to the north, establishing itself in the valley of El Quiburi to protect the frontier and new mission of the Las Cruzes, and serve as a step to the new discoveries, but that in this case the division of the lands among the soldiers and settlers ought to be carried out for the best establishment of the presidio and for its permanence.[121]

[120] Bustamante y Tagle later served in New Mexico, Bolton, *Athanaze de Mézières*, I, 48.
[121] Bolton, *Guide*, 453, gives the location of Altamira's report in Chihuahua. See Chapman, *op. cit.*, 43, No. 85, who fails to mention his source.

¶ 476. In a report—copy of which I have—made to your Excellency under date of August 14, 1766, by the deceased captain of Fronteras, Don Gabriel Antonio de Vildósola, he refers to the fact that opposite Terrenate and the settled Pimas Altos, the Rio de Santa Cruz or the Rio de Sobaipuri flows quite close by towards the north to enter the Gila, and that it can be settled because of its being abundant in water and lands for raising wheat.

¶ 477. Finally, Adjutant Inspector Don Roque de Medina accompanied the documents of the review of the presidio of Santa Cruz[122] with a table of its settlers, in the notes to which Lieutenant Colonel Don Pedro de Fages sets forth that in the year '78 settlers of the presidios reaped grain, barley, corn, chick peas, frijol, lentils, chicharos, cotton, chile, and all kinds of garden stuff in irrigated lands without a scarcity of water because of the permanent flow of the river. The adjutant inspector corroborated this report, proposing various means for encouragement of the settlements of Santa Cruz and for the cultivation of many lands which the Sobaipuri Indians sow, as he recognized by means of the mother ditches which remain open and which at a little cost could be put into use.

¶ 478. According to the contexts of the reports concerning the recommendable circumstances of the Rio de San Pedro, Terrenate, Santa Cruz, or Sobaipuri, by which names it is known, only those of the military governor, Don Jacobo Ugarte y Loyola, and Lieutenant of Engineers, Don Gerónimo de la Rocha, differ, and I have seen myself under the necessity of preferring them.

¶ 479. The reasons which have obliged my deference to the reports and findings of these two officers are: First, the terror instilled in the troop and settlers of the presidio of Santa Cruz that had seen two captains and more than eighty men perish at the hands of the enemies in the open, rolling ground at a short distance from the post, and the incessant attacks which they suffered from numerous bands of Apache, who do not permit cultivation of the crops, who surprise the mule trains

[122] A.G.I., Guad., 272, Croix to Gálvez, No. 589, Arispe, December 23, 1780.

carrying effects and supplies, who rob the horse herds and put the troop in the situation of not being able to attend to their own defense, making them useless for the defense of the province. Second, the general hunger suffered in the year just passed, perforce greater and more acute in the distant presidios of the frontier. Third, the lack of mule trains, as the small number of those which pass over the roads make more risky and dangerous the transportation of provisions and make it difficult to use the troop in other maneuvers more useful than those of these escorts. Fourth, the line of presidios which is directed through the rest of the spots that the military governor and the engineer propose, adapted (although with the increase of a presidio) to that which Lieutenant General Marqués de Rubí describes and the royal instruction provides for, taking into consideration the best possible defense of the province with respect to the deplorable condition in which hunger, pestilence, and war keeps it. Fifth, the fact that if one considers the convenience with which the Rio de San Pedro may be occupied, it will be easier to do it when the territory breathes freely from the present rigorous calamities. Finally, the fact that, since communication remains open with the new pueblos of the Rio Colorado through the presidio of Altar in the rainy season and through that of Tupson in the dry, the establishments of the Gila will have an effect at a suitable time.

¶ 480. An additional, powerful reason, according to my belief, is the fact that the company of the presidio of Santa Cruz is occupying today, in provisional barracks, the terrain near the arroyo of Las Nutrias and not the old site of Terrenate because of the inconvenience which the *cañada* of San Mateo offers and because the houses of that settlement have become ruined.

¶ 481. For the building of the new presidio and encouragement of its settlers there is a little less than ten thousand pesos (the same amount which was provided for Fronteras), made available by equal contributions from Captain D. Joseph de Vildósola, officers, and troops of Santa Cruz. I have taken proper measures so that the building may proceed and the crops be sown as copiously as the present scarcity of seed permits.

¶ 482. This presidio located in Las Nutrias is closer by two leagues to the sierra of Chiguicagui, which is opposite it, and to those of Magallanes and Mavavi, located on its right side. The distance of twenty-six leagues from Fronteras facilitates the union of these forces, their mutual aid, and prompt advice. The greater proximity to the pueblo of S. Ygnacio Ymuris and others is facilitating the most prompt provision of supplies until the presidio does not need this assistance.

¶ 483. The military governor and Engineer Rocha consider it certainly necessary that the presidios of Santa Gertrudis del Altar, San Miguel de Orcasitas, San Carlos de Buenavista, and San Agustín del Tupson remain in the present sites, and as there are no others in the province, it will be necessary to occupy with a new presidio the spot which is called La Estancia de Buenavista and to consult regarding the continuance of the line.

¶ 484. This increase offers difficulties, but before treating them, I am supposing that the presidio of Tubac, transferred to Tupson, exists today in its old terrain of Tubac, and that we are considering retiring it towards the west to bring it closer to Altar and nearer to Santa Cruz de Terrenate for the purpose that Lieutenant General Marqués de Rubí set forth in his *Dictámen* and in accord with what was ordered in the royal instruction.

¶ 485. I say, then, following the method which I have proposed for the most instructive and clear explanation concerning the point of the establishment of the line of presidios of Sonora, that the presidio of San Ignacio de Tubac was erected in the year 1753 because of the general revolt of Pimería Alta, Don Diego Ortiz Parilla then being governor of the province; and that there was considered and agreed upon the transference of this presidio to Tres Alamos or Optupo or Optuavo, on the banks of the Rio de San Pedro.

PROVINCE OF SONORA

¶ 486. To give effect to what was provided for in the royal instruction, D. Antonio Bonilla found no location to the west of Tubac except the valley of Arivaca, swampy, unhealthy, and scantily supplied with resources for the location of a presidio. He indicated the location of a detachment in the abandoned mission of El Búsanic, which divided the distance of forty-one leagues fromAriyác to the valley of Escomác, where he considered that the presidio of Altar should be moved. But attending to the establishment of the line that he considered indispensable along the banks of the Rio de San Pedro, he proposed for the transmigration of Tubac the valley of E. Quiburi, twenty-three leagues distant from the headwaters of the river, where he had recommended that Terrenate be located, and three from the valley of Santa Cruz, where the establishment of this presidio was made.

¶ 487. Commander Inspector D. Hugo O'Conor adverted to the same defects in the valley of El Ariyác, and not encountering any other spot in the western direction in which to locate the presidio of Tubac, he transferred it to that of San Agustín del Tupson, located to the north of Tubac, at a distance of twenty-one leagues from site, thirty-five from Santa Cruz, and nearly sixty from Santa Gertrudis del Altar.

¶ 488. The commander inspector rightly noted that the presidio of Tubac placed in Tupson was not forming the line advised in the royal instruction, nor that which was proposed along the banks of the Rio de San Pedro to the Colorado, but I considered that, notwithstanding he had petitioned repeatedly that the presidios of San Miguel de Orcasitas and San Carlos de Buenavista be transferred, the first to the junction of the Colorado and Gila rivers, and the second to the Gila and San Pedro, he believed these removals were as remote as was necessary for the occupation of a post to facilitate at the most opportune moment the new establishments and assist in the interim the frequent *entradas* of the missionary religious to the Yuma and the rest of the heathen nations that were being allured to accept Christianity.

¶ 489. If these were the ideas of O'Conor, as I persuaded myself at once they were, he could not have argued with greater correctness; for although the presidio of Tupson has not served to defend the province, it has conserved the mission of its name and that of San Xavier del Bac which it has nearby; it has contributed to the success of the establishment of the two new pueblos on the Colorado; it is the ladder or door to communication with California, and can be very useful in erecting the new presidio in the Estancia de Buenavista.

¶ 490. This spot, according to the reports of the military governor and Engineer Rocha, had the most appreciable resources for a settlement and makes possible repeopling and the erection of others in its shelter. It is distant twenty-one leagues to the northwest, quarter to the west from the post of Las Nutrias; ten from the abandoned presidio of Tubac to the northwest; and thirty-five from Altar to the southwest. Thus if a new presidio is established in the Estancia de Buenavista it will extend its hand on the right to Las Nutrias and on the left to Tupson. These three posts will be located along a line of forty-seven leagues. Their short extension will facilitate the best operations of defense and offense. Tupson will be the last presidio of the entire line. This will protect the new establishments of the Colorado; the new one, La Estancia, and Altar will end mutual support. The fulfillment of the royal decisions, which articles 2, 3, 4, and 5 provide for in the royal instruction, will be made in the direction of the line which they detail and all now possible will be secured of that which is considered necessary for continuing the line to the Colorado.

¶ 491. All these advantages consist, as I have already stated, in the increase of a presidio which the flying company of this province can garrison. But this company, that of volunteers, and the pickets of dragoons cannot be sufficient to reënforce the presidio of Fronteras, Santa Cruz, El Pitic, or San Miguel de Orcasitas, the first two of which suffered from repeated invasions of numerous Apache yet are the best barriers for the defense of the territory. Finally, if alone, a presidio cannot subject or contain the Seri, Tepocas, and Tiburones.

¶ 492. There being for the moment a really insuperable diffi-

PROVINCE OF SONORA

culty in the establishment of a presidio in the Estancia de Buenavista, I shall content myself with foreseeing the advantages which it offers. I desire to make, when my health and other grave matters of this command permit me, personal reconnaissances of the frontier, for although the military governor assures the usefulness of the new presidio, he has not seen the terrain proposed for its location, but recommends it because of the reports of Engineer D. Gerónimo de la Rocha, whom he commissioned to examine that site.

¶ 493. For the occupation of the junction of the San Pedro and Gila rivers, Adjutant Inspector Don Antonio Bonilla advised that the presidio of San Carlos de Buenavista be put there with the regulation dotation of fifty-seven units, including officers provided for in the regulation, increasing it with Opata Indians up to the number of ninety-nine units. Commander Inspector Don Hugo O'Conor proposed the same, but without the reënforcement of the Opata. Governor D. Francisco Crespo intimated that the presidio of Tubac be transferred to the junction with one hundred units. Father Fray Juan Díaz considered as a better place the junction of the Rio de San Pedro with the arroyo of Santa Teresa for the removal of Tubac with ninety-eight men. But the military governor, D. Jacobo Ugarte, and Engineer D. Gerónimo de la Rocha did not find the possibility for the establishment of the presidio at the junction of the San Pedro and Gila rivers. They referred to some spot at the junction of the arroyo of Santa Teresa, and even Engineer Rocha considered that it was necessary, in the case of continuing the line from Tupson, that the spot at Santa Teresa be garrisoned with competent forces and that the most prolix reconnaissance precede.

¶ 494. In the old *expediente* which paragraph 472 of this report cites, it appears that the Father Provincial of the ex-Jesuits, Cristoval de Escobar y Llamas,[123] begged his Majesty for the erection of the indicated presidio on the Rio Gila to protect the reductions of the Pima Cocomaricopas, Yuma, and the rest of the Indians who live along the banks of that

[123] See above, page 202, footnote 119.

river and of the Colorado as far as its debouchment in the Gulf of California. He asked that the new presidio be garrisoned with one hundred men so that their duties might be distributed in making war upon the Apache, and in cultivating the lands whose products they need at once because of the difficulty of providing themselves with supplies at points so remote from the province.

¶ 495. It appears also from a diffuse report of the governor, Don Agustín de Vildósola, that the Rio Gila has along its banks lands fertile for sowing and easy to irrigate; that to reduce the Apache it would be convenient to found a presidio in the neighborhood of the ford of the river which they call Todos Santos or that of La Casita; that when this presidio is located, it will be placed respectively distant eighty leagues from Terrenate, Fronteras, Janos, and Paso del Norte, with the Apache of the Gila thus surrounded on all sides; and that to garrison the presidio one hundred soldiers and one hundred Opata and their families—because of their established valor and fidelity —were necessary.

¶ 496. Other reports could be cited which are found in the *expediente* referred to but I omit them because in substance they are the same and because, to form an idea, the extract of the opinion of the Auditor of War, the Marqués de Altamira, will suffice.[124] He is not opposed to the establishment of the presidio, but he says that until then very few Spaniards had reached the Rio Gila; that they never had made a formal reconnaissance of those lands, and that it was not possible to determine the location of the presidio; that the number of eighty soldiers would be sufficient, to be recruited in New Vizcaya or Mexico, as it would not appear right to depopulate Sonora to populate the Gila; and that the support, also, of the one hundred Opata with their families would be convenient.

¶ 497. Auditor of War Altamira advises that along the banks of the Gila and the Colorado rivers, at the junction of the first with that of La Asunción, which comes down from the north composed of the Salado and Verde rivers, and with that of San

[124] See above, page 203, footnote 121.

Façade of Cathedral, Arizpe, Sonora

Pedro which runs from south to north and has its course through the plain of Terrenate, and at the junction of the Gila and the Colorado, various commodious sites offer themselves for the establishment of five or six missions, a settlement of Spaniards, and the presidio. But the selection of these spots ought to be made after extensively reconnoitering the terrain; for although various *entradas* have been made by Father Jacobo Sche del Mair, missionary of Tubutama, the diaries and reports of this ex-Jesuit do not give the necessary information to procede to the indicated selection.[125]

¶ 498. Altamira reports that already the usefulness and convenience of erecting missions on the banks of the Gila was indisputable because upon the missions depends the reduction of an extensive heathenism and the propagation of the Gospel; that in order not to risk failure, it was necessary that the presidio be situated in the best lands which the settlers merited; that these undertakings should not be embraced with only the view of founding missions, but every care should be taken to safeguard, encourage, shelter, and defend the settlers who are colonizing the land; and that without these considerations, reductions would not be achieved and what was discovered would be lost, principally in Sonora where there was no formal town population with the exception of San Miguel de Orcasitas whose settlers are to be first to enjoy the division of lands.

¶ 499. Throughout all the preceding statements, it is established that from the year 1745 until the past year of 1780, colonizing projects along the Colorado and Gila rivers were considered. But after many and extensive reports, official writings, and opinions, there has occurred in a period of more than thirty-five years no extensive examination of the country other than those which preceded my measures for the founding of the two pueblos of Spaniards on the Rio Colorado and territory of the Yuma Indians. Although Lieutenant Colonel D. Juan Bautista de Anza and Father Francisco Garcés have traveled along the banks of the Gila, Asunción, and San Pedro

[125] For a summary of Sedelmair's work, see H. H. Bancroft, *Arizona and New Mexico* (San Francisco, 1889), 365–66.

rivers[126] and have set forth opinions concerning the establishments of presidios and missions, they recommend, like all the informants, that examinations of the country be made before determining the locations of the settlements.

¶ 500. Therefore, Father Garcés, although his indefatigable, apostolic zeal has urged repeatedly the erection of the presidio on the Gila, restricts his reports and representations solely to the advantages of its establishment and does not attempt to name the spot where it should be erected.

¶ 501. In his representation of August 17 of the year '74, he advised the viceroy of New Spain upon the foundation of four missions on the Colorado, two among the Opata and two among the Gila Pima.[127] He indicated that the opinion of Adjutant Inspector D. Antonio Bonilla regarding the location of the presidios of Sonora on the rivers of San Pedro, Gila, and Colorado had fulfilled his desire and promised happy results.

¶ 502. The report was given to Lieutenant Colonel D. Juan Bautista de Anza when he was in Mexico.[128] The founding of missions on the Rio Colorado appeared proper to him, but not among the Opata and Gila Pima until the pride of the Apache was suitably punished as these Indians impeded the progress of the establishments. He set forth that by all means the missions of the Colorado needed for their defense, arrangement, and encouragement a presidio of larger forces than those of the regular dotation of the line, and that the repeated reconnaissances of the territory were indispensable to the location of the missions and the presidio.

¶ 503. When the little captain of the Yuma, Salvador Palma, received holy baptism in Mexico at the end of the year '76, he presented a petition to the viceroy begging missions and a presidio in his country because Anza had reported that the presidio of the Colorado could be situated at the confluence of that river and the Gila.[129] Regarding another presidio at the

[126] See above, page 175, footnote 104, and below, footnote 128.
[127] For reference to this report, see Bolton, *Guide*, XXIII, 88, item 6.
[128] Anza's opinion is translated in Bolton, *Anza's California Expedition*, V, 383–94.
[129] Palma's petition is translated in *Ibid.*, 365–76.

confluence of the Gila and San Pedro, he says that the pueblos of the Gila Pima are fifty leagues distant from those of the Colorado and Gila; that in these pueblos, designated as Zutaguizon and Juturilucan, which are so close to the rancherias of the Apache that they see their smoke daily, is proposed the location of the second presidio and missions; that the pueblos indicated can perhaps provide the supplies for the presidial troop, but that they would lack land for their horse herds; that this scarcity was greater on the Gila; that being informed that in the terrain of the Jalchedunes there were abundant pastures, it appeared to him proper that the presidio be situated there. He says, however, at the same time that Tupson is twenty-six leagues distant from the pueblos of the Gila Pima, and thirty-five from those of the Jalchedunes, while the Jalchedunes are a little more than fifteen from the Rio Colorado.[130] Thus Anza, illustrating the principal point of his reports, which is that of assuring a spot for the erection of the presidio, retires it to the great distance of sixty-one leagues and puts it little less than sixteen from the Colorado.

¶ 504. These propositions are not entirely in agreement with those of the last diary of Father Garcés, which he made under date of January 30, 1777, and which I sent to your Excellency on June 25 of the same year, letter No. 61. In point five of those which he puts at the end of his diary he says that the presidio of the Gila should be placed on the Rio de la Asumpción, or on another spot (if it were better), to divide the distance of the two rivers so that it may be close to the rancherias of the Tejua; that it should be garrisoned with eighty dragoons, fifty soldiers of leather, and as many, or a greater number, of presidials; that he is persuaded that on the Rio de la Asumpción there will be found abundant sites for sowing and that when there is none, recourse of finding them on the Gila remains.[131]

¶ 505. What is certain is (I repeat) that after thirty-five

[130] *Ibid.*, II, 375–92 for Garcés' journey among the Jalchedunes; also see Elliott Coues, *On the Trail of a Spanish Pioneer* (New York, 1900), II, Index.
[131] For a reference to a copy of Garcés diary, see Bolton, *Guide*, XXIV, 26, item 1; translated with the Note Five referred to by Croix in Coues, *op. cit.*, II, 457–67.

years during which the usefulness of the Gila presidio has been discussed, we do not yet know the most advantageous spot for its establishment. Although this may be determined easily by means of a formal expedition directed to reconnoiter the entire territory, preferential affairs of the province do not permit. The unhappy condition of the province and of its troops and presidios would not be improved measurably with the establishment of a presidio on the Gila, but rather, having been increased, the objects and cares and expenses of the province would be multiplied in proportion to the hostilities and afflictions. Out of this consideration, and at the cost of much anxiety, I have brought about the erection of two pueblos of Spaniards among the Yuma so that these fortunate Indians may embrace, voluntarily and happily, religion and vassalage. We are leaving aside for the present the Gila Pima, Cocomaricopas, and the rest of the heathen nations until the opportune time which God has destined for their reduction. We are going to conclude the affair of the line of presidios on the frontier of the Apache, namely the transference of Orcasitas to El Pitic, and the continuance of Buenavista in its present site.

¶ 506. With regard to the first, I have already tried to illustrate the advantages which the following offer: the new presidio of Opata in Babispe; the return of that of San Bernardino or Santa Rosa de Coro de Guachi to Fronteras; the transference of that of Santa Cruz de Terrenate to Las Nutrias; the erection of the new one in La Estancia de Buenavista; and the continuance of San Agustín de Tupson and Santa Gertrudis del Altar in their present sites.

¶ 507. Also I have spoken of the fact that to raise the company of Opata and put it in a state of service, I am awaiting the harvesting of the crops so that these Indians, supported by the forces of Janos and Fronteras, may persecute incessantly the Apache; that for the construction of this presidio and that of Santa Cruz, encouragement of its crops and settlers, I have twenty thousand pesos; that I shall reënforce them with the flying company, the volunteers, and pickets of dragoons, so that without diverting them from material works (as these

PROVINCE OF SONORA

will be done by Indians and day workers) they may be employed in the defense of the province; that I shall not proceed to the erection of the presidio of La Estancia de Buenavista until a second reconnaissance of the spot can be made, and until the hostilities of the Apache and the unrest of the Seri have diminished. This presidio can extend support to the company of the presidio of San Carlos de Buenavista or to the above mentioned flying company; Tupson will conserve the communication of the Rio Colorado and the Californias, and it is not impossible that it may contribute to the defense of the territory if the company which garrisons it undertakes in the year, assisted with a competent number of the Pimas Altos, some campaigns against the Apache; Altar will oppose wherever possible the incursions of these Indians into La Ciéneguilla, without failing to combine its movements with the interior forces destined to subject the Seri and the rest of the nations that do not remain faithful. Finally, it appears to me that I have demonstrated everything possible with method and clarity. I am not able to remedy the defects of my tedious explanations because no rationale satisfies the zeal with which I attempt to fulfill my duties, and because the affair of the establishment of the presidial line is grave. It has been discussed extensively. It embraces many points, different, minute, and prolix, which make interpretation, arguments, and solution of them difficult, and which are demanded by the view of the map that I am enclosing, drawn by Lieutenant of Engineers, D. Gerónimo de la Rocha, from the results of his reconnaissances. It does not however, embrace the territories of Janos and the pueblos of Opata. I shall say, in conclusion, that the presidios of the line of Sonora ought to be situated in the distances and directions set forth as follows:

PRESIDIOS	NOTE LEAGUES	DIRECTIONS
Janos		
San Miguel de Babispe	23	Southwest
Fronteras	29	West
Santa Cruz	25	West by Northwest
The new one of Buenavista	21	Northwest, one quarter west
Tupson	26	North northwest
	124	

Thus the length of the Sonora line from Babispe to Tupson will consist of 101 leagues; from Babispe to Santa Gertrudis del Altar, 110. With regard to this, Altar will be distant from the new presidio of La Estancia de Buenavista thirty-five leagues to the southwest.

¶ 508. At the beginning of the year 1740, the Indians—Yaqui, Mayo, Fuerteños, and Pimas Bajos—revolted. This revolt cost many lives, and more than one hundred thousand pesos to the royal treasury. The first governor of Sonora in his own right, D. Manuel Bernal de Huidobro, was removed from his office.[132] Sergeant major of militias, D. Agustín de Vildósola, succeeded him, and at the solicitude of this chief the company of Sinaloa was transferred in the year '42 to the spot of Buenavista to restrain the Indians mentioned. In El Pitic the presidio of San Pedro de la Conquista was founded with the intention of reducing and subjecting the Seri.

¶ 509. In the year '48, Governor Vildósola, suspended from his office, retired to Mexico and on the opinion of the Inquisitor, Judge don Rafael Rodríguez Gallardo, the cited presidio of San Pedro was transferred to S. Miguel de Orcasitas, taking this new name.[133]

¶ 510. The opinions of the auditor, the Marqués de Altamira, were opposed and Fiscal Andreu was quite converted to the point of this transference, but I have arranged that the presidio of Orcasitas return to its old terrain of Pitic where it is now.

¶ 511. This spot is, as the governor intendant, D. Pedro Corvalán, explained to me, the best barrier against the Seri and the most proper one on which to found a respectable settlement. Likewise the reports of the military governor, D. Jacobo Ugarte y Loyola, and that of Engineer D. Gerónimo de la Rocha, have supported it.

¶ 512. In consequence I determined that the other engineer, D. Manuel Mascaró, should reconnoiter the terrain and detail the works necessary for the construction of the presidio

[132] Bancroft, *North Mexican States and Texas*, I, 521–23.
[133] *Ibid.*, 528–36.

PROVINCE OF SONORA

and the construction of an irrigation ditch for the irrigation of the cultivated fields. He has done this, proving the usefulness of the transference of the presidio with his reports and maps, the documents of which I shall add to the file of papers which is in the possession of the Auditor, Don Pedro Galindo, and shall give an account to your Excellency when I am prepared.

¶ 513. In the meantime, I say that there are being gathered some settlers in the new establishment; that not having spent the four thousand pesos which his Majesty allowed for construction of the presidio of Altar, and which are now in possession of the official paymaster, I have arranged for the delivery of three thousand for the works of El Pitic; that the irrigation ditch, which is the principal work for the encouragement of the settlers, is going forward; and that the military governor desires the progress of the settlement.

¶ 514. I have referred to the fact that the company of Sinaloa occupied there in the year 1742 the post of Buenavista, and from there it was transferred to Altar, but because of the hostilities the Seri were committing in 1761, Governor Don Joseph Tienda de Cuervo proposed the creation of a flying company for the pueblo of San Joseph de Pimas.

¶ 515. Governor D. Juan Claudio de Pineda made the same proposition, preferring to garrison Buenavista with a presidial company. Viceroy Marqués de Cruillas condescended to favor this petition, erecting the presidio on August 1, 1765.

¶ 516. A little time after the erection of the presidio the Pimas Bajos revolted. There resulted and was concluded the military expedition.[134] These Indians, the Seri and Pimas Altos, surrendered, and both the presidial company of Buenavista and that of Orcasitas, experienced in the interior, and in aiding the maneuvers of war against the Apache, remained without other duties than those of maintaining the quiet.

¶ 517. For these reasons, Commander Inspector D. Hugo O'Conor and Don Antonio Bonilla proposed the transferences of the presidios to the Colorado and Gila rivers, putting some

[134] See above, page 140, footnote 78.

troop protection in El Pitic and Buenavista. Governor D. Francisco Crespo and Father Fray Juan Díaz gave substantially the same opinion, but the viceroy, Fray D. Antonio Bucareli, suspended the establishments of the two presidios until he could see results[135] (of the California undertaking).

¶ 518. The first, which proved the excellent opinion of the viceroy, was the revolt of the Seri in the year '77[136] and the well-founded fear that there might follow that of the Pimas Bajos and Altos and even other nations more faithful. But my opportune measures, prompt assistance, the operations of Lieutenant Colonel Anza, and the vigilance of Captain Tueros put out the fire of rebellion and avoided the serious injuries with which the province saw itself menaced. The second are the deaths and robberies which in the year '80 the Seri and Tiburones caused in the pueblo of Guaimas and Orcasitas, San Joseph de Gracia, San Joseph de Pimas, and territories of the jurisdiction Ostimuri.[137]

¶ 519. These reports, those of some suspicious movements which were noted among the Pimas Bajos, the continual desertion of the Seri from El Pitic, and the silence which the Tiburones maintained, since they had not really returned to promote their old petition of reducing themselves to mission or pueblo, oblige and force not only maintaining the presidios of Altar, Orcasitas, and Buenavista in their present sites, but demand continuing a detachment of the first in the Real de la Ciéneguilla, reënforcing the second with half of the company of volunteers, uniting the forces of the third, in order to avoid hostilities in the province of Ostimuri, and combining movements of the three presidios in order to punish the rebellious Seri and Tiburones, to restrain the Pimas Bajos, and to keep an eye upon the Piato and Pimas Altos.

¶ 520. It is possible that if the injuries which the Apache cause are lessened, the above Indians may be held back. In

---

[135] A.G.N., Provincias Internas, Tomo 88, 36–37, O'Conor to Bucareli. No. 491, Carrizal, December 2, 1775, acknowledged receipt of Bucareli's order to suspend transference.
[136] See above, page 27, footnote 75.
[137] A.G.I., Guad., 272, Croix to Gálvez, No. 525, Arispe, May 23, 1780.

this case I shall take measures which are proper either to increase the northern frontier forces or to transfer the Buenavista presidio to the Estancia of this name, or to improve the situation in San Joseph de Pimas, or to locate it on the Gila, reenforcing it with the troop which Altar and Orcasitas do not need.

¶ 521. From these two presidios and from Buenavista I have taken out the picket of a subaltern officer, a sergeant, two corporals, and eighteen men to garrison the new establishments of the Rio Colorado. Consequently the actual footing of each one of the three presidios is reduced to sixty-four units including officers.

¶ 522. In letters No. 52, 61, and 82 of May 26, June 25, and July 26, 1777, 359 of February 22, '79, and 505 of April 23, '80, I have given an account to your Excellency of all my dispositions relative to the above establishments.[138]

¶ 523. Father Garcés sought, as I have already stated, four missions on the Rio Colorado. Lieutenant Colonel D. Juan Bautista de Anza foresaw the necessity of defending them with a presidio of a greater number of forces than the regular ones. The Commander Inspector destined for this purpose the presidio of San Miguel de Orcasitas. The viceroy agreed but ordered suspended the transference of the presidio until seeing the results of the last expedition which Anza made to California to occupy the port of San Francisco, and his Majesty deigned to approve these resolutions in the royal order of February 14, '76.

¶ 524. In view of everything, the file of papers of which I remitted your Excellency a copy with the previously cited letter No. 505 was drawn up. Therein appears the impossibility of removing the presidio of Orcasitas or that of Buenavista to the Colorado and increasing greater expense for the treasury of the king; remembering what was provided for in article 14 of the royal instruction which governs me, I decided upon the

---

[138] A.G.I., Guad., 516, Croix to Gálvez, No. 82, México, July 26, 1777; for No. 505, see above, page 155, footnote 91; numbers 52 and 61 are not available; A.G.I., Guad., 516, Croix to Gálvez, No. 51, México, May 26, 1777.

establishment of two pueblos of Spaniards in the territory of Yuma Indians.[139]

¶ 525. For the security of these foundations, I took out from the two named presidios and Altar the picket of twenty-one men detailed in paragraph 521. I arranged that the families of these troops should compose the principal part of the settlers, who were increased with the recruiting of twenty other families of settlers not already located, and with those of the heathen Indians who docilely and willingly wished to congregate there.

¶ 526. I conferred the military and political command of the two pueblos upon the first ensign of the presidio of Santa Gertrudis del Altar, Don Santiago Yslas; and the spiritual administration of the Spaniards and catechising of the Yumas, upon fathers Fray Francisco Garcés and Fray Juan Díaz of the Apostolic College of Santa Cruz of Querétaro, with the salary of four hundred pesos annually for each one.

¶ 527. Likewise I arranged that each colonizing family should be given ten pesos monthly for the period of one year or more, if it were necessary, and twelve workers, or peons, for the constructions and custody of the herds, with their wages corresponding to the custom of the country; that on account of the same settlers, camping utensils, some stock, large and small, and other indispensable things be furnished them; and that lands and waters be divided among the three classes—soldiers, settlers, and Yuma—and the necessary rules for good government be provided to facilitate and encourage them.

¶ 528. The recruiting of the twenty families was made successfully in Pimería Alta. They were at their destination by December, '80, with Commander Yslas. The troop to complete the detached picket was lacking.

¶ 529. They were well received by the Yuma. They have begun to work in construction of their pueblos. The family of the little captain, Salvador Palma, and others of his nation are congregated in them.

[139] For an account of the Yuma missions, quite a hodgepodge, see Chapman, *op. cit.*, 389–413.

PROVINCE OF SONORA

¶ 530. The troop and settlers have elected a private quartermaster who must act with perception in the management of their interests under the rules of the Ordinance. Having remitted to them the allotments of herds and the rest of the assistance which they were lacking, to complete what was agreed and resolved upon in the file of papers of this establishment with the quartermaster of the presidio of Altar, D. Andrés Arías Cavallero, who incorporated his detachment in the expedition to the Californias which was treated in the report relative to this province, I only await the return of Arías to give an account to your Excellency of the condition and progress of the foundation of the Rio Colorado.

¶ 531. I do not doubt that they will be happy, because the respectable union of the two pueblos of Spaniards offers the advantage of attracting docilely the heathen Indians to reduction and vassalage, of protecting the communication with New California, of assuring that with Sonora, and of attempting at an opportune time that with New Mexico.

¶ 532. These establishments were to cost the annual amount of 18,998 pesos and six reals, if the presidio of San Miguel de Orcasitas were transferred to garrison them, but they amount to no more than that of the subsistence of the settler-families, which is 4,774 pesos annually. The subsistence will be used prudently until it is extinguished as the new settlements progress.

¶ 533. The truth is that the royal treasury does not get back the allotment which it provides for the above presidio existing in El Pitic. But since troops are needed for the defense of the province, and troops for the establishment on the Rio Colorado, which now cannot be postponed, are indispensable, it is clear that the treasury would be suffering a greater annual expenditure than the allotment for a new presidio if I had not restricted my decisions to the foundation of the two pueblos or military colonies defended by the settlers themselves, who occasion a temporary and redeemable expense, and by the pickets of twenty-one men whom I took from the three presidios of Orcasitas, Buenavista, and Altar, thereby lessening their respective dotations.

¶ 534. From these well-combined measures, in my opinion, not only the advantages referred to in paragraph 531 can result, but others that the seasonal establishments of the Colorado, the Gila missions of Jalchedunes, Opata, and Pimas Gileños, make possible. They are contributing, reënforced by the armed forces of the presidio of Altar, to the subjection of the Papago heathen, restraining as a consequence the unfaithful movements of the Piato and preventing their retirement to the Papago country. Finally, if the Yuma continue constant in their docile reduction, not many years will pass until the banks of the Rio Colorado may be themselves covered with grain fields, fruits, and herds, and settled with faithful vassals of the king, who may augment the forces of Sonora, and who will attend to their reciprocal defense and aid California. It appears to me that the new pueblos on the above mentioned river ought to be subjected to the government of California, because of their being on the bank opposite the jurisdiction of Sonora, and because their distance from Monterrey is less than that to this capital. [MARGINAL NOTE: With the greatest treachery the Yuma have murdered the religious missionaries, troops, and settlers. I doubted this catastrophe because of many well-founded reasons. But having verified it, I dispatched a formal expedition under the orders of Lieutenant Colonel Don Pedro de Fages, subject to the direction of the governor of California, Don Felipe Neve, who was at the mission of San Gabriel. I am awaiting news of the results to give an account of all. Rúbric of Croix.[140]]

¶ 535. In paragraph 324 I proposed, as a means of contributing to the benefit of this province, the better location of its presidios; the establishment on the Rio Colorado; the forma-

[140] *Ibid.*, 413–14; for Croix's account of the events, see A.G.I., Guad., 517, Croix to Gálvez, No. 718, Arispe, February 28, 1782, and *ibid.*, No. 749, Arispe, May 30, 1782; for the results of Fages expedition see A.G.I., Guad., 283, Croix to Gálvez, No. 844, Arispe, November 4, 1782; for Croix's investigations which established the fact that the site was not suitable for settlements, see A.G.I., Guad., 283, Croix to Gálvez, No. 845, Arispe, November 4, 1782; and A.G.I., Guad., 284, Croix to Gálvez, No. 870, Arispe, January 27, 1783.

PROVINCE OF SONORA

tion of militias; and the erection of new settlements. Having already set forth my measures and concepts concerning the first two points, I shall treat of the third and fourth in the second part of this report, affirming at once that the arrangement of militias and settlements in Sonora is more urgent than in the rest of the provinces of my command.

¶ 536. Meanwhile I qualify this assertion. I shall set forth to your Excellency particular points relative to the branch of war, which can be forwarded, and those which I am promoting at present for the defense and conservation of Sonora.

¶ 537. The expatriation of the Seri is becoming each day more imperative. The present military and political governor, D. Jacobo Ugarte y Loyola, Don Pedro Corvalán, Colonel D. Francisco Crespo, Lieutenant Colonel D. Juan Bautista de Anza, captains Don Pedro Tueros, Don Joseph de Vildósola, and other chiefs and informed subjects of this province since remote times—all demand it in all their reports.

¶ 538. I have subscribed to these well-founded opinions in my representation No. 525, which I made to your Excellency under date of May 23, '80, proposing the surprise of the Seri families congregated in El Pitic, the expatriation of the men to overseas destinations and of the women and children to California, and a formal expedition to the Isla del Tiburon to take similar measures with their inhabitants.[141] Although they are known by the names of Tiburones, they belong to the Seri nation, as the Tepocas who live in Las Marismas do. But not being able to undertake these operations without shedding blood and without occasioning extraordinary expense, I have never dared to arrange them until I could secure the royal approval of his Majesty which I have sought, although I know that these measures may aid the pacification of this province by freeing it from the hostilities of its domestic enemies, by restraining the rest of the reduced nations, and by making war upon the Apache with greater ease, fewer difficulties, and larger forces. There will be saved part, if not all, of the expenses which the royal treasury bears in maintaining the Seri at El

[141] A.G.I., Guad., 272, Arispe, May 23, 1780.

Pitic, and in support of the presidios of Orcasitas, Altar, and Buenavista for the defense of the interior of the province.

¶ 539. When Lieutenant Colonel Don Juan Bautista de Anza took charge of the province, he found it garrisoned with six presidios and one flying company, whose total forces amounted to 368 units, including officers and chaplains. In his report of July 31, '77, which I remitted to your Excellency with my letter No. 105, October 11, '77,[142] he proposed to me an increase of five hundred men, two hundred from the country, and the remaining three hundred from dragoons of mounted infantry, preferring to this class of troop the volunteer company of the command of D. Pedro de Fages. This was one third of all the existing force. He proposed that the increase be employed in the incessant persecution of the enemy within his country, and the other two forces in safeguarding our own, and locating besides one hundred men on the Colorado and Gila rivers.

¶ 540. Colonel D. Francisco Crespo, in his report of November 20 of the same year, which I also sent to your Excellency with my letter No. 217 of June 29, '78, states that there was not a doubt of the necessary, perhaps not small,[143] increase of forces. Without daring to provide the increases, he continued demonstrating that the project of punishing the Apache ought to be fixed in the principle of impeding their entrance into the province, and not in making campaigns into their country. The principle makes difficult the progress of these campaigns and facilitates campaigns of a mixed war of offense and defense carried out by three presidios located along the frontier of the north in the spots of S. Bernardino, Santa Cruz, and the junction of the San Pedro river with the arroyo of Santa Teresa. Each one should have the dotation of one hundred soldiers and twenty Opata to survey or examine incessantly their terrains in detachments of forty or fifty men with corresponding supplies, to follow the tracks of the enemies, and give prompt advice to the pueblos and interior troops.

[142] See above, page 30, footnote 89.
[143] Croix to Gálvez, No. 217. See above, page 36, footnote 108.

PROVINCE OF SONORA

¶ 541. The governor intendant, D. Pedro Corvalán, in the two reports which he made under date of January 28 and August 12, '78, copies of which I sent your Excellency with my letter No. 217, June 29, '78,[144] set forth his opinion of the necessity for the increase of 278 dragoons; for an offensive war persecuting incessantly the Indians in their rancherias; and for the establishment of two posts for the uniting of forces (El Pitic and San Joseph de Pimas) against the Seri, and of two others on the Apache frontier.

¶ 542. I approved the opinion of Anza in my previously cited representation No. 105, October 11, '77, concerning the increase of forces up to the number of 936 men. With royal approvals I have carried this out to the extent of 727, in the reenforcement of the six presidial companies with light troops, and with the two pickets of dragoons and company of volunteers. Thus this increase of 359 men exceeds by eighty-one that of the 278 dragoons which the governor intendant, D. Pedro Corvalán, proposed to me.

¶ 543. The union of forces which Minister Corvalán indicated in El Pitic and San Joseph de Pimas has not been necessary because he took prompt action against the general revolt of the Seri. But the transference of the presidio of Orcasitas to El Pitic and the recommendation I have made to your Excellency concerning expatriating the Seri are the consequence of his well-founded opinion as well as that of everyone else.

¶ 544. With regard to the war against the Apache, Corvalán proposes that it be incessant and offensive. Anza recommends it, but intimates that the larger number of troops should be employed in the defense operations. Colonel D. Francisco Crespo prefers confining these operations to patrolling the terrains of the frontier to impede the ingress of the Indians.

¶ 545. In the year '77, and part of '78, nothing could be undertaken against the Apachería because the duty of subjecting the Seri took precedence. Until the end of '79, some operations were carried out on the Apache frontier but were fruitless because of the poor condition of the troops and the worse

[144] See above, page 36, footnote 108.

location of the presidios. In '80 reconnaissances of the line were carried out; the establishment of the Rio Colorado was successfully made; the dispatching of supplies to the Californias was made possible; no unfortunate campaign against the Apache was made; the presidios of San Bernardino and Santa Cruz improved their location; and the troops of Sonora, in spite of general hunger suffered in the territory, discharged all these different duties, dismaying and tedious, conquering infinite difficulties. Their detailed explanation I omit in order not to annoy, and because your Excellency has a practical understanding of the country and the afflictions that the success of what is undertaken in it costs.

¶ 546. Since May, '80, following the opinion of the political governor, Don Pedro Corvalán, and supported by that of Military Governor D. Jacobo Ugarte, I considered initiating the union of forces in the presidios of Santa Cruz and Fronteras, but up until now I have not succeeded in taking the necessary measures because of the scarcity of supplies, and because the large detachments which escorted the expeditions to California and the Rio Colorado have not yet returned.

¶ 547. Considering the remedy of the scarcity of supplies proximate in the next harvests, expecting the early incorporation of the escorting parties into their companies, hoping soon to have the volunteers and pickets of dragoons in a condition of service, and having conquered the difficulties in the erection of the presidio of Opata in Babispe, I just resolved upon the union of forces in the presidios of Santa Cruz and Fronteras.

¶ 548. In the first, Santa Cruz, the assembly of 193 men must be made ready for war; in the second, Fronteras, that of 141; in Babispe, seventy Opata, twenty volunteers, and two officers. In all, the forces amount to 476 units; troops of leather, light soldiers, dragoons, volunteers, and Indian auxiliaries.

¶ 549. For the commander of the armed forces of this division I have appointed Captain D. Joseph Antonio de Vildósola, leaving to his judgment the detail and execution of the offensive and defensive operations, and offering him my exact opinions and the assistance which he asks, as far as possible.

PROVINCE OF SONORA

¶ 550. For the safeguarding of the interior of the province, there will be maintained in the presidio of Altar forty-four men, the same number in S. Carlos de Buenavista, and eighty-four in El Pitic, which amounts to the total of 172.

¶ 551. To conserve the establishment of the Rio Colorado and its communication with this province, I have in them a picket of twenty-one troops and twenty Spanish settlers. There must subsist in Tupson meanwhile, fifty men of the company which garrisons it, not only to aid the establishments in necessary cases, but to execute some sallies against the Apache with the aid of the Pima Indians.

¶ 552. These are the particular steps which at present I am taking for the defense of the province of Sonora, and the only measures for the present that can be taken with the hope of a successful outcome because they attend to the principal objects of restraining the Seri and punishing the Apache. The execution of the former in the interior of the province touches the zeal of the military governor, D. Jacobo Ugarte, and on the frontier of the north the experience, practice, and knowledge of Captain Vildósola. [MARGINAL NOTE: These operations have been suspended until the return of the expedition from the Colorado.[145]] But notwithstanding, I lack confidence to progress.

¶ 553. In a word, most excellent Señor, I am going to arrange the war against the Apache according to the rules which the general concept and understanding in these countries demand, but with the fear that they are opposed to the rules which your Excellency was pleased to send me in the royal order of February 20, '79, and with lack of confidence for good results.

¶ 554. My fear rests upon the fact that the operations must be offensive, and his Majesty wishes that they be purely defensive. My lack of confidence proceeds from knowing by practical experience the difficulties touching the collection and transportation of supplies to the frontier, and that the remounts which are continually brought from the interior of Sinaloa are noticeably defective, reaching the presidios in an

---

[145] See above, page 222, footnote 140.

unserviceable state and becoming useless in the first undertakings.

¶ 555. These indispensable and consequently necessary duties, founded even more upon necessity than upon the opinions which recommend them, dissipate the high hopes that my final measures promise. For if these same necessities have impeded up until now the defense of the country, the instruction and discipline of the troop, their good government, and the purely economical management of their interest, for reasons demonstrated extensively in my reports of January 23, '80, No. 458,[146] and which I shall qualify in the second part of this one, how can progress be possible in the offensive war which one considers making upon the Apache?

¶556. But whatever the obstacles are that oppose the favorable success of the operations of the troops of these provinces, they demand the prompt remedies that I have applied with efficacy and skill since the day on which I took charge of this command.[147] As they do not permit the achievement of their good effects for a period of some years, it is a clear and necessary consequence that necessity, and not the solidity of opinions and projects, obliges the continuation of the maneuvers of war, which up to now have been carried out. Although they may have been considered questionable in the opinion of many impartial subjects of character, honor, and intelligence, and although no advances may have been seen since the establishment of the first presidio, other than the addition of the twenty-one which garrison the provinces and the doubling of the number of auxiliary troops, yet there has been an increase in the hostilities, pride, and arrogance of the enemy Indians.

¶ 557. The vassals of the king rapidly occupied the immense territory of these provinces without opposition of the Indians, but since we experienced obstacles we have been losing progressively in spite of our boasted advantageous operations. Whatever they may be, I see myself under the necessity of ordering operations carried out because the hostilities of the

[146] See above, page 12, footnote 12.
[147] See above, page 17, footnote 25.

PROVINCE OF SONORA

Apache are so constant, bloody, and so deeply felt, as the recent destruction of the pueblos of Cucurpe testify. There really is no means other than offensive war for restraining them; public clamor prays for it with the greatest anxiety, although I know that the operations that can now be made will not produce the successes that are spoken of and desired. I also note that my measures, ideas, and projects, founded upon the most zealous desires of seeing fulfilled the king's sovereign, pious intentions to improve the maneuvers of this war, are future risks, but they are achievable and will forestall, in the meantime, the ruin of the country by the causes which chance and the unhappy condition in which I found this province would permit.

¶ 558. I have always looked upon Sonora as the first object of my attention. While I was visiting the distant provinces of Texas, Coahuila, and New Vizcaya in order to understand their woes, and to provide, with my measures, for their remedies, I could not give my personal attention to Sonora, but confided the defense of this important dominion to the zeal, practice, and experience of Lieutenant Colonel D. Juan Bautista de Anza. I sent him suitable and extensive assistance, which he asked of me, for the discharge of his interim command. I conceded him ample authority so that, taking advantage of his knowledge, he might not execute badly his operations and my comprehensive orders and advices. They had the effect which I had hoped for in the fortunate extinguishing of the fire of rebellion among the Seri, which, it was feared with good reasons, might communicate itself to the rest of the reduced Indian nations.

¶ 559. Because of my grave sickness and the presence of Anza and the military governor, D. Jacobo Ugarte y Loyola, at the council of war at Chihuahua, Captain Don Pedro de Tueros took charge of the province with the same authority and forces as his predecessor.

¶ 560. Both commanders did everything possible to alleviate the weakening sufferings of Sonora. I, who came at the time of its greatest affliction of war, pestilence, and hunger, to find it without a line of presidios and without troops in condition for its defense—if I have not been able to arrest enemies so powerful, I have desired to do so with the liveliest anxieties with which I am dedicating, and will dedicate, myself, until my powers achieve the conservation and prosperity of this province.

PROVINCE OF CALIFORNIA

¶561

I HAVE written much of California in the particular report on Sonora, without having treated the important points of the creation of the militia, settlements, minerals, the establishment of the capital of these provinces, and various other matters of which I shall speak in their places since the report regarding California belongs here.

¶ 562. It is appropriate that, concerning the measures wisely taken since the year '67 for the occupation of the new establishments of the peninsula, the arrangement of them and of the older ones has fallen to the careful observance of the governor, D. Felipe Neve. His zeal and skill are also responsible for maintaining the tranquillity of the territory and advancing its defenses, conservation, and encouragement.

¶ 563. With regard to the first, not only has he observed the rules prescribed for the discharge of his government, but he has integrated them extensively, making possible their important execution in the formation of the new interim regulation.[148] With respect to the second, he has known how to avoid the disturbances of the subjected Indians, and those of the heathen who can cause difficulties. Regarding the third, he has taken well-founded measures for the establishment of the new pueblo of San Joseph de Guadalupe and Porciuncula, the occupation of the canal of Santa Barbara with a presidio and three missions, and the detail and arrangement of the troops of the peninsula.[149]

[148] A.G.I., Guad., 277, Croix to Gálvez, No. 506, Arispe, April 23, 1780.
[149] See below, page 231, footnotes 150 and 151.

PROVINCE OF CALIFORNIA

¶ 564. In a letter of August 23, '77, No. 89, I advised your Excellency of them; in another of September 23, '78, No. 269, I gave an account of my first dispositions, and in No. 477, February 23, '80,[150] I gave an account to your Excellency of the council which I held in this capital with the governor intendant of Sonora, D. Pedro Corvalán, and Assessor D. Pedro Galindo, with the assistance of the secretary of the commandancy. Agreeing with the verbal opinions of those attending this council, I approved the proposals of the governor of California. I dispatched instructions and orders to Captain Don Fernando de Rivera for recruiting troops and families, the equipment of the latter, collection of remounts, and transportation of all to the peninsula. I sent the necessary orders to the above governors of Sonora and California and the corresponding ones to the viceroy of New Spain, Regent of the Royal Audiencia of Guadalajara, and royal officers of these coffers, enclosing to your Excellency a copy of these documents and an extract of all relative to the opinions of the governor of California up to the time of those which I made at the date of my last decision.[151]

¶ 565. The orders touching the recruiting of the troop and settler-families appear difficult of fulfillment, but Captain D. Fernando de Rivera completed the number of the first and almost that of the second. He carried out successfully the gathering of horses, mules, goats, and burros, and dispatched by sea to the presidio of Loreto the larger part of the settler-families. He began his march by land with the expedition of supplies in February of the current year.

¶ 566. Thus, by sea and land, I have supported the new establishments of California with fifty-nine recruits, presidial sol-

[150] Croix to Gálvez, No. 89. See above, page 26, footnote 68; A.G.I., Guad., 270, Croix to Gálvez, No. 269, Chihuahua, September 23, 1778; A.G.I., Guad., 278, Croix to Gálvez, No. 477, Arispe, February 23, 1780; see also, A.G.I., Guad., 275, Croix to Gálvez, No. 270, Chihuahua, September 23, 1778; A.G.I., Guad., 267, Croix to Gálvez, No. 271, Chihuahua, September 23, 1778; and A.G.I., Guad., 278, Croix to Gálvez, No. 498, Arispe, March 26, 1780.
[151] A.G.I., Guad., 272, Croix to Gálvez, No. 463, Arispe, January 23, 1780; *Ibid.*, No. 499, Arispe, March 26, 1780. For expenses of animals sent to California in 1779, see A.G.I., Guad., 268, Croix to Gálvez, No. 728, Arispe, February 28, 1782.

diers, and sixteen settlers, sixty-five women, and eighty-nine boys and girls that compose the total of 170 souls, with almost a thousand head of horses and mules and the necessary supply of munitions, clothing, supplies, and the rest of the things indispensable, the expenses of which, in the larger part repayable by the troop and settler-families, are occasioning very little burden to the royal treasury.

¶ 567. To accredit this economical measure and the infinite, minute, and tedious details that I have taken in the midst of my afflictions and cares in Sonora, which really could make impossible the remission of such opportune assistance to California,[152] the instructive orders which I sent to Captain Rivera and to the governor of the peninsula under date of December 18, '80, are recopied to the letter.

¶ 568. "Informed by letter from your Grace at the first of the current month of the aid that you need to transport recruits and families and remounts to the new establishments of California, I approve that Lieutenant D. Diego Gonzales be sent by sea to Loreto accompanied by Ensign D. Ramón Laso and the families of soldiers and settlers indicated in the margin of the notice which your Grace enclosed in your letter of November 29 just passed. It appears to me well that they continue their journey from that presidio in the three launches and the little sloop to the bay of San Luís, and from there, after giving notice to the presidio of San Diego, they go to their destination, with the escort and baggage that may be needed. All this is in accord with what the señor governor, Don Felipe Neve, has proposed to me concerning the affair.

¶ 569. "So that this may be done, I advise in the adjoined order to the boatswain of the "Xebec," Santiago de Castro, anchored in the port of Santa Cruz de Mayor, that, holding the boat of his command at the disposition of your Grace, he agree to receive on board the officers, families, and the supplies and provisions that your Grace may consider sufficient, which are to be taken to Loreto by the bay of San Luís. The collection of these supplies must be arranged for; and your Grace may ap-

[152] A.G.I., Guad., 267, Croix to Gálvez, No. 712, January 26, 1782.

PROVINCE OF CALIFORNIA

ply to me if the "Xebec," because of its smallness, cannot transport the people and the supplies in a single trip. He may make two trips, or ask the commander of Loreto at once for the sloop and some of the launches. This way can perhaps also be useful for carrying some provisions to the presidio if it is in need of them.

¶ 570. "In any event, I leave to the judgment, experience, and knowledge of your Grace the measure that you esteem convenient concerning this point, and suggest that your Grace send your instructive orders to Lieutenant D. Diego Gonzales for guidance in his voyage and navigation.

¶ 571. "According to the notice which your Grace sent me with the previously cited letter of November 29, last, there ought to go by land the forty-two soldiers of the recruits which, together with the twenty-three men of the detachment of these presidios that your Grace has at your orders, amounts to sixty-five.

¶ 572. "Considering the larger number of the first dedicated to the care of their families and escort of the mule trains, your Grace ought to count upon the second for the duties of the remount. I am persuaded that they may discharge this duty because of the understanding they will have acquired from having gathered the animals.

¶ 573. "To this party of twenty-three men, twenty others and the ensign, whom your Grace asks of me, will be added. This officer, D. Cayetano Limón, is coming with the indicated troop increase to this Real. So that this may be done, I am sending under this date the corresponding order to the military governor, Don Jacobo Ugarte y Loyola.

¶ 574. "It appears to me that the eighty-five men detailed are sufficient so that your Grace, taking the required precautions, may go safely to Tupson.

¶ 575. "The twenty men of the increased allotment ought to remain. Ensign Limón ought to march with the twenty-three of the first detachment which your Grace now has at your orders. To those will be added twenty men from the presidio of Tupson and Santa Cruz, and twenty-two others from the same presidios and from Altar, although these latter are going for the escort of the herds and other supplies for the Rio Colorado under the command of Lieutenant D. Andrés Arías Cavallero. But in any event, under the command of your Grace, the expedition will be composed of 107 men from Tupson, excluding officers. In this number will go some of those who accompanied Lieutenant Colonel D. Juan Bautista de Anza on his discoveries, to serve as guides as far as the new establishments of California.

¶ 576. "As soon as your Grace reaches the Colorado River you will dispatch with Lieutenant Don Andrés Arías Cavallero, the troop of this province, giving him, if conditions demand, the troop necessary for continuing his march. In case Álferez Limón follows, this officer ought to return with the troop by land with all possible speed, or whatever is best or appears proper to Señor Governor D. Felipe Neve.

¶577. "Your Grace, informed of my resolutions according to everything your Grace has set forth to me and asked for in your cited letter of the first of the current month, should in the first place advise me of any difficulty that occurs so we may take timely steps to overcome it.

¶ 578. "In the second place your Grace ought to take measures for the prompt march of the officers and families that must be transported by sea, taking particular care that they go with all possible accommodations, and with abundant provisions and supplies, so that without scarcity or anxiety they may reach their destinations happy.

¶ 579. "In the third place your Grace ought to arrange the march by land with a similar view to ample supplies to insure a comfortable journey, taking care that the women and little children may not be fatigued, and that the remounts are kept in good condition without exhaustion or loss. Finally, there should be sufficient supplies in order that the troop may discharge completely its obligations, maintaining contact on the marches, and executing with vigilance and zeal the orders of your Grace to prevent attacks from the Indian enemies and

PROVINCE OF CALIFORNIA

avoid irritating in the slightest way friendly and peaceful nations who live between the Colorado River and New California. Knowing its importance, I am charging your Grace strictly with this particular duty.

¶ 580. "Fourth, your Grace ought to economize in expenses wherever possible both so that the royal treasury may not be burdened by any expense which can be avoided, and so that the officers, troop, and settlers may not contract increased obligations.

¶ 581. "In the fifth place, your Grace ought to resort to the royal officers of these coffers so that they may provide for your Grace the funds you need. Under this date I am advising them, so that they may forward to your Grace the necessary campaign tents for the families that are going by land.

¶ 582. "Sixth, your Grace ought to try to keep watch on the tents, mule-train equipment, leather bags, leather trunks, and the rest of the items that may be delivered, with an account and statement after the marches by sea and land are achieved, to the señor governor of California, who may arrange everything as I am advising him in a letter of this date.

¶ 583. "Seventh, your Grace should render with the greatest clarity and accuracy, before undertaking your march, the three general accounts of the expense of the remounts, settler-families, and recruited soldiers, provided for in the fortieth article of the instruction of December 20, '79, to the señor governor intendant, D. Pedro Corvalán, accompanying them with supporting documents.

¶ 584. "Eighth, your Grace ought to carry, with the same clarity and accuracy, the particular accounts of the soldiers recruited and the settlers in the corresponding master books and service sheets, so that having delivered these to the ones interested they may have due notification in detail of what they have received, and of their obligations. Thus, just and prudent discounts will not restrict what must be made them for reimbursement. Your Grace must put the master books in the hands of the señor governor of California, so that he may examine and approve them.

¶ 585. "Finally, your Grace ought to give me an account (from whatever point possible) of the particular events that attend your Grace on your marches, according to the understanding that I have. I am satisfied with the zeal and skill with which up until now your Grace has discharged your important commissions. I am waiting to see them concluded happily, to send to the king this agreeable news and recommend to his Majesty the particular merit that your Grace has earned in the last third of your life, so that he may deign to dispense to you the privilege and thanks that may be his sovereign pleasure."

¶ 586. [MARGINAL HEADING: Letter to Governor (Neve). A copy is sent to him of the instruction given to Moncada.] "The subjoined is a copy of the order which I am sending under this date to Captain D. Fernando de Rivera y Moncada. It will inform your lordship of my active measures for the transportation to the peninsula by land and sea of the settler-families, recruited soldiers, and remounts.

¶ 587. "For my part I have done what has been possible for the success and prompt remission of these supplies. Captain D. Fernando de Rivera has discharged his commission up until now with zeal, activity, and skill, and your lordship has contributed to everything with your opportune advice and circumstantiated reports, very proper from your experience, understanding, and love of the royal service.

¶ 588. "Thus I shall present to his Majesty, when your Lordship may communicate it to me, that agreeable news of the happy arrival of the transports, as I am now giving news of the early departure to the most excellent señor viceroy, so that he may not delay sending whatever your lordship has solicited, which ought to be sent from Mexico and the ports of San Blas.

¶ 589. "In the meantime I am hoping that your lordship may take measures so that nothing may be lacking on the arrival of the transports referred to and so that the officers, the troop allotments, settler-families, and allotments of horses and mules may be distributed without delay to their respective destinations. The presidios of that province are to be governed from the first of January next by the new regulation. As I have already advised your lordship the officers of the allotment are serving under the regulation from the day upon which they ceased their previous assignments, while the troop and settlers serve from the day of their admission into the presidio.

¶ 590. "Captain D. Fernando de Rivera should deliver to your lordship the regimental registers of all the master books of accounts so that you can pass inspection upon them yourself or by means of Adjutant Inspector D. Nicolas Soler (who I am hoping is now continuing his march with Captain Rivera). Your lordship will take care that the troop and settlers understand the legality of the charges and obligations they have incurred. Prudent and moderate discounts may be made against them until these are covered.

¶ 591. "Also your lordship ought to arrange for the receipt of the campaign tents, mule-train equipment, leather side-bags, leather trunks, and the rest of the effects that the royal treasury has paid for. You may have distributed what can be used on presidial campaigns. The corresponding charges will be made to the gratification fund and the extra equipment will be deposited in some of the royal warehouses where it may be cared for and preserved. It appears to me proper that where there is an opportunity, the campaign tents may be returned to the Real de los Alamos for other transports of families that might occur in the future.

¶ 592. "As Captain D. Fernando de Rivera should give an account to your lordship, as he has to me, of his early departure and of the time in which his arrival can be made at that province, I add only what has been referred to, namely, that I am keeping the reports of your lordship to govern my future arrangements."

¶ 593. These orders having been dispatched, I have seen my measures well executed up until now. According to the context of the three last letters which I have received from Captain Rivera, two written from the Mission of San Xavier del Bac, and the third from the Gila River, dated 18, 20, and 29, of April just passed, no other particular news has attended him except an attack of the Apache at Sicurisuta before reaching the presidio of Tupson. But although the Indians fought four hours they did not succeed in stealing a single thing and it is certain that three of them died in the combat.

¶ 594. Rivera is thinking of wintering on the Colorado in order to strengthen the horses and goats, dispatching without loss of time the mule herd and families, and sending ahead a party of troop to explore the sierra between the Colorado and the presidio of San Diego. If this road is shorter, it will free him from going via the Mission of San Gabriel, which is lacking in pastures and water. [MARGINAL NOTE: Beaten to death like all the unfortunate others who were on the Colorado, Captain Moncada, a sergeant, and six soldiers of the presidios of the Colorado died. When the misfortune occurred, the families, recruits, and the rest were safe in the mission of San Gabriel with the exception of 257 horses and mules that could not continue the march.][153]

¶ 595. In any event, the expedition, already beyond the risk of enemies, has conquered the greatest difficulties and the important supplies are very close to New California where they are needed.

¶ 596. The qualities of Captain Don Fernando de Rivera are constant. No one could have been better fitted for the discharge of the commissions that I entrusted to him by proposal of his governor, D. Felipe Neve. The fatigues of Rivera, made at the age of seventy with its own difficulties, justly merit that I recommend them to your Excellency so that the king may deign to dispense to him who is interested the graces and honors that may be his royal pleasure, as well as the retirement which he solicits and which he will pray for as soon as he concludes his command and renders the accounts of those interested, which have come into his possession.

¶ 597. The viceroy has supported my decisions completely;

[153] A.G.I., Guad., 517, Croix to Gálvez, No. 719, Arispe, February 28, 1782, on the arrival of the settlers; see A.G.I., Guad., 267, Croix to Gálvez, No. 725, Arispe, February 28, 1782, on the expedition against the Yuma; for a discussion of the massacre see "Historical Introduction," pages 59 f.

PROVINCE OF CALIFORNIA

the zeal of the governor has made them possible in the matters touching him. The establishments of New California provided for, I am devoting myself now to those which concern old California.[154]

¶ 598. Concerning these and others relative to the government and arrangement of the missions under date of November 21, '78, Father Missionary Fray Nicolas Muños, of the order of Santo Domingo, made me a diffuse representation in the name of the Father President Fray Vicente de Mora.

¶ 599. In view of that report, after I had recovered from my sickness and had entered this capital, I gave various orders, with the verbal opinion of the intendant of this province and the assessor of the commandancy-general, to the governor of California on February 14, '80, asking for circumstantiated reports.

¶ 600. This chief satisfied these on July 4 of the same year and drew up a file of papers. I sent it, with a decree of October 27 following, to the assessor, D. Pedro Galindo, in whose possession it now is, as is the one regarding the new mission of S. Vicente Ferrer, founded in the spot of Santa Rosalía. But the dispatching of both files of papers being tedious, I shall give an account to your Excellency as soon as they are concluded, with the necessary copies. Thus, although one could make an extract of them, I do not consider it urgent in consideration of the fact that the new regulation attends to the solution of the principal points that Father Muñoz advances in No. 45 of his previously cited petition.

¶ 601. The new regulation has begun to be observed since the first of January of the current year, as I stated to your Excellency in a letter of April 23, '80, No. 506,[155] with the concordance of the viceroy of New Spain and in accordance with the direction that I gave the governor of California under date of September 21 of the same year.[156] I am copying this as follows:

[154] A.G.I., Guad., 278, Croix to Gálvez, No. 527, Arispe, May 23, 1780, and A.G.I., Guad., 281 Bis, Croix to Gálvez, No. 692, Arispe, November 30, 1781.
[155] See above, page 230, footnote 148.
[156] A.G.I., Guad., 267, Croix to Gálvez, No. 721, Arispe, February 28, 1782.

¶ 602. "Notwithstanding not having received the replies of your lordship to my letters of February 10 and 12 of the present year, I have resolved that from the first of January next, '81, there be observed for the interim the new regulation formed by your lordship. For the purpose, I have asked of the viceroy that he be pleased to send the orders and corresponding advices to the offices of the royal treasury of Mexico, commander and commissary of the port of San Blas, factor of the Peninsula, and the reverend fathers, prelates of the religious of Santo Domingo and San Fernando, who administer these missions. On my part, I shall direct soon the necessary orders to the governor intendant of this province, and to the royal officers of Los Alamos; and to your lordship I shall direct the necessary copies of the new regulation as soon as they are printed in Mexico by order of the viceroy who is to remit them to me.

¶ 603. "With this understanding your lordship can at once arrange and combine your measures for the effective fulfillment of the new ordinance, so that the presidios of this peninsula may be informed at a suitable time of everything that they need, and that the present commissary of Loreto, the guards of the warehouse, and the rest of the presidios may have adjusted and liquidated their accounts by the end of the current year, in order to make their respective deliveries to the official paymasters.

¶ 604. "The arrival of these reports at this province can be postponed if the departure of the expedition for the Colorado River is not made at the end of next October or the beginning of the following November, as with your reports must be incorporated those of the above mentioned officers. But in any event, in my opinion since the difference of time that can intervene between the last day of the year and that of the arrival of the paymasters from their respective destinations is small, it will be necessary that until then the commissary of Loreto and the warehouse officials continue with the management of the interests of the rest of the presidios and that their salaries be credited them.

PROVINCE OF CALIFORNIA

¶ 605. "These measures and others that may be needed must govern the future events which depend upon the commissions entrusted to Captain D. Fernando de Rivera. As it is not possible to attend to these matters because of my distance from him, the difficulties of recruiting troops and settlers and gathering supplies for the dispatch of the expedition, with the particular needs that are increased, and incidents that occur each day on this beleaguered frontier, I do not find a secure foundation to dictate now any fixed resolution other than that of the execution of the new regulation at the beginning of the next year of '81. Thus, with this notice your lordship will take corresponding measures and I shall continue advising those which are conformable to the cases which occur.

¶ 606. "In the meantime I am sending to your lordship the adjoined index with the enclosures of documents that are set forth in it so that, informed of the resolutions that I have taken on the points of government, and internal discipline and management of the troops of the provinces, your lordship may be pleased to declare the observance of those that can be adapted to the new regulation of the Peninsula."

¶ 607. It appears to me, most excellent señor, that my measures with relation to California have been efficacious and diligent, and that from them ought to be expected the increase of its population, the security of its defenses, the union and free communication of the old possession and the new ones by the important establishment of the presidio of the Santa Bárbara Canal, its three inchoate missions, and pueblos of Guadalupe and Porciuncula.[157] These successes have been achieved with a minimum of expense, and those promised by a regulation, made up of methodical points of easy and simple practice, will lessen some part of the expenditures of the annual allotments. It will eliminate the fearful apprehension of the old discounts and charges, amounting to 150 per cent in the presidios of northern California, and one hundred per cent at Loreto.

[157] Croix to Gálvez, No. 725. See above, page 238, footnote 153; A.G.I., Guad., 272, Croix to Gálvez, No. 729, Arispe, February 28, 1782; A.G.I., Guad., 517, Croix to Gálvez, No. 814, Arispe, August 23, 1782; *ibid.*, No. 815, Arispe, August 26, 1782.

It is increasing the number of officers, troops, and settlers; sets up for them the observance of the particular good rules of government and discipline; assures the pure management of their interest; redeems the royal treasury in this region from bankruptcies, losses, damages, and waste; facilitates, though in small amount, the circulating of money; and creates the pleasing prospect of permanency and increase of the military and colonizing establishment. Finally, with the most minute points clarified, the door is opened wide to the erection of new missions for propagating the voice of the Gospel and reducing docilely the numerous small bands of barbarians that are vagrant in the territory and on the coasts of California as far as the boundaries of the province of Sonora and New Mexico. Thus I conceive it. I repeat that the new regulation is the result of the zealous work of Governor D. Felipe de Neve, reënforced with my opportune suggestions and put into execution with the desire that the good results that it promises be achieved and with the hope that time may prove them.[158]

¶ 608. Most excellent señor, may all the provinces have the happy aspect of that of the Californias! However, your Excellency already sees that Texas is surrounded by a numerous heathenism that it cannot resist without uniting its weak forces, dispersed settlements, and few and dissident settlers; that Coahuila, experiencing the sufferings of Texas, produces its own because of its friendship with the Lipan Apache whom it protects in its bosom without being able to protect itself from their devastation of a territory that would be opulent in agricultural resources, mineral riches, and advantageous sites for settlement. The well-known riches of New Vizcaya would be destroyed shortly by the incessant hostility of all Apache that it resists, were not the Apache forestalled by my efficient measures of covering the extensive frontiers of the province with the number of troops that I have at my orders, by increas-

---

[158] For later significant data on Croix's relations with California, see A.G.I., Guad., 517, Croix to Gálvez, No. 722, Arispe, February 28, 1782; A.G.I., Guad., 268, Croix to Gálvez, No. 728, Arispe, February 28, 1782; A.G.I., Guad., 283, Croix to Gálvez, No. 847, Arispe, November 4, 1782; A.G.I., Guad., 283, Croix to Gálvez, No. 862, Arispe, December 30, 1782; A.G.I., Guad., 284, Croix to Gálvez, No. 885, Arispe, February 24, 1783.

ing the provincials, and by operations which make possible its defense and conservation. New Mexico, because of its distance and because of the proximity of all the barbarous enemy nations, will always offer grave cares. The unfortunate province of Sonora, afflicted notably with the cruel plagues of war, pestilence, and hunger, is beginning to breathe in alleviation from its sorrows and in the hope of their remedy. I am devoting myself to all, aiding, succoring them as far as forces and resources reach, and maintaining vigilance by seeking all exact means for establishing the zeal that animates me in my profound loyalty to the king and my humble gratitude to your Excellency, who I beg may be pleased to place me at the royal feet of his Majesty. Meanwhile, until the four reports[159] are completed, of which this is the preliminary one, may he be pleased to advise me of his sovereign resolutions.

May our God guard your Excellency many years. Arizpe, October 30, 1781. Most excellent sir, your most attentive and loyal servant kisses the hand of your Excellency.

EL CAVALLERO DE CROIX
(rúbric)

Most Excellent Señor Don Joseph de Gálvez.

[159] Apparently only the second was completed. See above, page 11, footnote 10.

BIBLIOGRAPHY

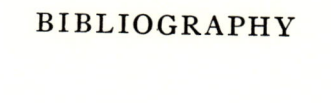

BIBLIOGRAPHY

FOLLOWING is a chronological list of the chief manuscript materials used in this study arranged under their respective headings. The abbreviations utilized herein with their meanings are:

A.G.I.	Archivo General de Indias, Seville, Spain.
A.G.N.	Archivo General de la Nación, México City.
A.H.N.	Archivo Histórico Nacional, Madrid.
Aud. de Méx.	Audiencia de México, A.G.I.
Guad.	Audiencia de Guadalajara, A.G.I.
Sparks.	Sparks Collection, Harvard College Library.

MANUSCRIPT MATERIALS

ORGANIZATION OF THE COMMANDANCY-GENERAL

Testimonio de la Ynsp.n de Presidios que se cometió al Marqués de Rubí, Mariscal de Campo de los Reales Exercitos de S. M. el Año de 1766. Pral. No. 12. A.G.I. 103–4–15.

Informe dado por el Señor Marqués de San Juan con fecha de 1768 sobre la creación de una capitanía general comprehensiva de la península de Californias y provincias de Nueva Vizcaya, Sonora y Sinaloa. 1768. A.G.I., Guad., 252.

Testimonio de los Dictámenes dados de Orden del Exmo. Señor Marquéz de Croix, Virrey de este Reyno por el Señor Mariscal de Campo Marquéz de Rubí en Orden à la Mejor situación de los Presidios para la defensa, y extensión de sus fronteras en los confines de este Virreynato. No. 1. Superior Gobierno, Año de 1771. Pral. A.G.I. 103–4–15.

Reglamento é instrucción para los presidios ... 10 de Setiembre de 1772. A.G.I., 106–4–24. Instrucción para el establecimiento de un gobierno y Comandancia General en las Provincias de la Nueva Vizcaya, Sonora, Cinaloa y Californias (copy unsigned and undated, 1774?) A.H.N. Estado, 2314.

Charles III to José de Gálvez enclosing appointment of Croix as Commander General of the Provincias Internas de Nueva España. A.G.I., Guad., 301.

Consejo de Indias No. 5. Real Orden y copias que la acompañan de la Instruccion dada al Gov.or de Sinaloa, Sonora y Californias. The King to José de Gálvez, August 22, 1776. A.G.I., Guad., 242.

BIBLIOGRAPHY

CORRESPONDENCE OF EL CABALLERO DE CROIX, COMMANDER GENERAL

[NOTE: During his term as Commander General of the interior provinces of New Spain, Croix dispatched to José de Gálvez, Minister of the Indies, 944 letters. Confidential communications were so indicated and numbered separately. For convenient reference in this bibliography, the number of each letter used is given first.]

No. 1. Croix to Gálvez. México, February 25, 1777. Dice el dia en que sale de México para la Vizcaya el nuevo Comandante-Ynspector. A.G.I., Guad., 516.

No. 5. Croix to Gálvez. México, February 26, 1777. Expone los motivos que le han obligado a la providencia de hacer cesar en sus funciones a various officiales de los presidios y ... pide la real aprobación, A.G.I., Guad., 516.

No. 17. Croix to Gálvez. México, February 26, 1777. Con motivo de las instancias repetidas del Governador del Nuevo México sobre su relevo, pide y recomienda al Teniente Coronel Don Pedro Garibay. A.G.I., Guad., 516.

No. 31. Croix to Gálvez. México, March 24, 1777. Remite extracto de las n.des de Yndios ocurridas en la Nueva Vizcaya y refiere sus provid.as para contener la hostilidades. A.G.I., Guad., 516.

No. 32. Croix to Gálvez. México. March 26, 1777. Acredita con documentos el deplorable estado de la Provincia de Sonora y dice sus disposiciones para contener la sublevación general que se recela. A.G.I., Guad., 516.

No. 37. Croix to Gálvez. México, April 26, 1777. Remite copias de oficio y indice que pasó al virrey pidiendolo varios documentos y papeles, y solicita R.1 orden para que se le entreguen todos los correspondientes a las Provincias de su cargo que se hallan en los archivos que cita. Sparks Mss. 98, (III), Harvard College Library, Cambridge.

No. 38. Croix to Gálvez. México, April 26, 1777. Expone el concepto que le merecen aquellas provincias, y el metodo con que piensa executar sus primeras operac.es. Sparks, 98 (III), Harvard College Library.

No. 43. Croix to Gálvez. México, May 26, 1777. Incluye copias de ordenes é Ynstrucción que ha dado para la compra y transporte

BIBLIOGRAPHY

de mil y quinientos cavallos al Nuevo México. Sparks, 98 (III), Harvard College Library.

No. 47. Croix to Gálvez. México, May 26, 1777. Da cuenta con documentos de las sensible desgracias ocurridas en la Provincia de Coaguila. A.G.I., Guad., 516.

No. 48. Croix to Gálvez. México, May 26, 1777. Dice los fines que le estrechan a emprender su marcha a las provincias de Coaguila y Texas. Sparks, 98 (III), Harvard College Library. [Note: Robertson has this listed under date of August 23, 1777.]

No. 51. Croix to Gálvez. México, May 26, 1777. Ofrece atender y distinguir al Indio Yuma Salvador Palma a su Nación, y los Gentiles que acepten nuestra amistad comercio y trato. A.G.I., Guad., 516.

No. 59. Croix to Gálvez. México, June 26, 1777. Da cuenta con documentos de las providencias que se ha tomado para defensa de la Nueva Vizcaya. Sparks, 98 (III), Harvard College Library.

No. 65. Croix to Gálvez. México, July 26, 1777. Incluye copia del vando que piensa publicar a su ingreso en las provincias internas par la formación de milicias. A.G.I., Guad., 515.

No. 69. Croix to Gálvez. México, July 26, 1777. Acompaña copia de informe del governador de Coaguila sobre el estado de esta provincia. A.G.I., Guad. 516.

No. 72. Croix to Gálvez. México, July 26, 1777. Remite documentos que acreditan el deplorable estado de las Tropas de Sonora y Nueva Vizcaya. A.G.I., Guad., 516.

No. 75. Croix to Gálvez. México, July 26, 1777. Refiere las novedades que had ocurrido en la Provincia de Coaguila. A.G.I., Guad., 516.

No. 76. Croix to Gálvez. México, July 26, 1777. Da cuenta con documentos de las novedades ocurridas en Sonora, de las providencias del Teniente Coronel Don Juan Bautista de Anza y de las suyas. A.G.I., Guad., 516.

No. 77. Croix to Gálvez. México, July 26, 1777. Acredita con documentos el estado del Real de la Ciéneguilla y las Providencias dadas para su resguardo, conservación y beneficio. A.G.I., Guad., 516.

No. 78. Croix to Gálvez. México, July 26, 1777. Da cuenta de las novedades de Nueva Vizcaya de sus oficios que a consecuencia pasó al virrey, y de sus disposciones. A.G.I., Guad., 515.

BIBLIOGRAPHY

No. 79. Croix to Gálvez. México, July 26, 1777. Acompaña copia de informe que le pasó el Brigadier D. Hugo Oconor y ofrece satisfacer al Real orn. de 12 de Abril en que se le incluyeron dos cartas de este oficial. A.G.I., Guad., 516.

No. 80. Croix to Gálvez. México, July 26, 1777. Continua el detail de las primeras operaciones que ha meditado y piensa poner en practica desde su llegada a Durango. A.G.I., Guad., 515.

No. 81. Croix to Gálvez. México, July 26, 1777. Remite copias de Diario y Mapa que hicieron dos religiosos del Nuevo México en demanda del camino por tierra el puerto de Monterrey. A.G.I., Guad., 516.

No. 82. Croix to Gálvez. México, July 26, 1777. Avisa la llegada de los Indios Yumas a S. Miguel de Orcasitas, la continuación de su marcha y deseos de que se establezca la Religion en su pais. A.G.I., Guad., 516.

No. 88. Croix to Gálvez. México, July 27, 1777. Expone las causas de llevar en su compañía al Padre Lector Fray Juan Morfi del orden de San Francisco y pide se le dispense el corto tiempo que le falta para su jubilación. A.G.I., Guad., 267.

No. 89. Croix to Gálvez. Querétaro, August 23, 1777. Refiere los auxilios que solicitó el governador de Californias y las novedades ocurridas en los nuevos establecimientos. A. G.I., Guad., 515.

No. 90. Croix to Gálvez. Querétaro, August 23, 1777. Incluye documentos que acreditan la sublevación de los Yndios Seris y sus providencias para contenerlos. A.G.I., Guad., 515.

No. 91. Croix to Gálvez. Querétaro, August 23, 1777. Refiere las desgracias ocurridas en la frontera de la Pimería Alta. A.G.I., Guad., 515.

No. 92. Croix to Gálvez. Querétaro, August 23, 1777. Da cuenta con documentos del estado de la Ciéneguilla. A.G.I., Guad., 516.

No. 93. Croix to Gálvez. Querétaro, August 23, 1777. Con documentos justifica la providencia de haver dejado al arvitrio del Teniente Cor.1 D.Juan Bautista de Anza la remoción ó subsistencia de los presidios de Sonora. A.G.I., Guad., 515.

No. 94. Croix to Gálvez. Querétaro, August 23, 1777. Da cuenta de las quejas que promovio la nación Opata y de sus providencias. A.G.I., Guad., 515.

No. 98. Croix to Gálvez. Querétaro, August 23, 1777. Acompaña copia del oficio que pasó al virrey pidiendole el aumento de dos mil hombres. Dice los motivos que tiene para haver solicitado

BIBLIOGRAPHY

este auxilia, y repite el plan de sus proyectadas primeras operaciones. A.G.I., Guad., 515.

No. 105. Croix to Gálvez. Durango, October 11, 1777 (Confidential) General summary of provincial conditions causing him to ask for increase of two thousand men and a statement of his ideas regarding the needs of the provinces. Sparks, 98 (IV), Harvard College Library.

No. 108. Croix to Gálvez. Durango, October 10, 1777. Acompaña copia de carta del gov.or de Coaguila sobre hostilidades y malos procedimientos de los Yndios Lipanes. A.G.I., Guad., 516.

No. 109. Croix to Gálvez. Durango, October 10, 1777. Remite extracto de las principales operaciones de los destacamentos de campaña. A.G.I., Guad., 516.

No. 118. Croix to Gálvez. Hacienda de Patos, November 20, 1777. Remite el diario de su marcha desde México a Durango, y ofrece dirigir el de la que quedava executando luego que a Chihuahua. A.G.I., Guad., 516.

No. 119. Croix to Gálvez. Hacienda de Patos, November 24, 1777. Da cuenta de sus primeros reconocimientos; del estado de las provincias; de la necessidad del aumento de tropas, y propone el modo de crearlas. Sparks, 98 (IV), Harvard College Library.

No. 123. Croix to Gálvez. Hacienda de Patos, November 24, 1777. Da cuenta con documentos del estado de la Sonora y de sus providencias. A.G.I., Guad., 516.

No. 124. Croix to Gálvez. Hacienda de Patos, November 24, 1777. Da cuenta de las novedades de la Nueva Vizcaya y Coaguila. A.G.I., Guad., 516.

No. 137. Croix to Gálvez. Saltillo, November 27, 1777. Acompaña copia de las ultimas cartas que ha recivido y acreditan el estado infeliz de las provincias de su cargo. A.G.I., Guad., 516.

No. 149. Croix to Gálvez. Valle de Santa Rosa, February 15, 1778. Da cuenta con documentos de las pazes pretendidas por los Apaches del Gila y Sierra Blanca y de sus disposiciones. A.G.I., Guad., 276.

No. 150. Croix to Gálvez. Valle de Santa Rosa, February 15, 1778. Da cuenta de aumento de Tropa que le ha franqueado el virrey de sus consecuentes disposciones. A.G.I., Guad., 276.

No. 151. Croix to Gálvez. Valle de Santa Rosa, February 15, 1778. Da cuenta del auxilio de raciones en dinero que ha dispuesto se

BIBLIOGRAPHY

subministran a la compaña franca de voluntarios de Catalonia destinada a la Sonora. A.G.I., Guad., 276.

No. 152. Croix to Gálvez. Valle de Santa Rosa, February 15, 1778. Acompaña una extracta y resumen de novedades ocurridas en ellas y pide se le prevenga si en lo subcesivo deve remitir ambos documentos ó solo el resumen. A.G.I., Guad., 276.

No. 153. Croix to Gálvez. Valle de Santa Rosa, February 15, 1778. Incluye copia del detall de servicio que deven hacer las tropas de la prov.ia de Coaguila. A.G.I., Guad., 276.

No. 154. Croix to Gálvez. Valle de Santa Rosa, February 15, 1778. Remite copias del vando que mando publicar en la provincia de Texas y prevenciones que hizo al Gov.or. A.G.I., Guad., 276.

No. 155. Croix to Gálvez. Valle de Santa Rosa, February 15, 1778. Yncluye copia de Ynforme del governador de Nuevo México sobre el estado de aquella provincia y refiere el auxilio que le ha franqueado. A.G.I., Guad., 276.

No. 156. Croix to Gálvez. Valle de Santa Rosa, February 15, 1778. Refiere sus providencias para la defensa de Sonora. A.G.I., Guad., 276.

No. 157. Croix to Gálvez. Valle de Santa Rosa, February 15, 1778. Acredita con documentos los efectos favorables que had producido sus providencias en beneficio de la nación Ópata. A.G.I., Guad., 276.

No. 159. Croix to Gálvez. Valle de Santa Rosa, February 15, 1778. Da cuenta de las disposiciones que ha dado para que concurran en Chihuahua a la junta de Guerra reservada los governadores que expresan. A.G.I., Guad., 267.

No. 170. Croix to Gálvez. Chihuahua, April 3, 1778. Extracto de todas sus operaciones desde el dia en que llegó a México y dice el methodo que se ha propuesto para las subcesivas. A.G.I., Guad., 267.

No. 171. Croix to Gálvez. Chihuahua, April 3, 1778. Remite un plan del aumento de Tropa de que avisó en carta No. 150 y dice los motivos que le han obligado a variar el primero. A.G.I., Guad., 276.

No. 174. Croix to Gálvez. Chihuahua, April 3, 1778. Remite extractos y documentos sobre las prevendidas paces de los Apaches del Gila, refiere el modo y circumstancias con que ha dispuesto sean admitidas. A.G.I., Guad., 276.

BIBLIOGRAPHY

No. 176. Croix to Gálvez. Chihuahua, April 3, 1778. Remite extracto y resumen de novedades ocurridas en Sonora, Vizcaya, y Coaguila. A.G.I., Guad., 276.

No. 189. Croix to Gálvez. Chihuahua, April 3, 1778. Pide que el Coronel D. Jacobo Ugarte y Loyola se le continue el abono de sus sueldos desde que sesó en el gobierno de Coaguila y hace presente su situación triste. A.G.I., Guad., 276.

No. 198. Croix to Gálvez. Chihuahua, May 1, 1778. Refiere y funda las providencias que ha dado para defensa de Nueva Vizcaya. A.G.I., Guad., 276.

No. 200. Croix to Gálvez. Chihuahua, May 1, 1778. Acompaña extracto de las ultimas ocurrencias sobre paces con los Apaches del Gila. A.G.I., Guad., 276.

No. 202. Croix to Gálvez. Chihuahua, May 1, 1778. Acompaña estado del armamento que comprehende necesario para la defensa de dichas provincias y pide su mas pronta remisión. A.G.I., Guad., 276.

No. 207. Croix to Gálvez. Chihuahua, June 1, 1778. Remite el diario de sus primeros reconocimientos. Sparks, 98 (V), Harvard College Library.

No. 208. Croix to Gálvez. Chihuahua, June 1, 1778. Remite noticias de población correspondientes a la provincia de Coaguila. A.G.I., Guad., 267.

No. 217. Croix to Gálvez. Chihuahua, June 29, 1778. Incluye los documentos de la Junta de Guerra que celebró en Chihuahua y pide varios auxilios en el interim se le puede conceder el de los dos mil hombres que ha solicitado. A.G.I., Guad., 276.

No. 219. Croix to Gálvez. Chihuahua, June 29, 1778. Incluye noticia del buen estado en que se halló la creación de milicias de Nueva Vizcaya. A.G.I., Guad., 276.

No. 221. Croix to Gálvez. Chihuahua, June 29, 1778. Refiere las condiciones con que se ha rendido la nación Seri en la provincia de Sonora. A.G.I., Guad., 276.

No. 222. Croix to Gálvez. Chihuahua, June 22, 1778. Dice los nuevos cuidados que ofrece la Sonora y sus providencias. A.G.I., Guad., 276.

No. 223. Croix to Gálvez. Chihuahua, June 29, 1778. Recomienda el merito que nuevamente ha contraido el Teniente Coronel D. Juan Bautista de Anza, contribuyendo a la rendición de los reveldes Seris. A.G.I., Guad., 276.

BIBLIOGRAPHY

No. 224. Croix to Gálvez. Chihuahua, June 29, 1778. Da cuenta de haber mandado recomponer el quartel del Pitic. A.G.I., Guad., 276.

No. 225. Croix to Gálvez. Chihuahua, June 29, 1778. Avisa el dia que llego at Pitic la compañia de voluntarios y la utilidad de esta tropa. A.G.I., Guad., 276.

No. 236. Croix to Gálvez. Chihuahua, July 27, 1778. Remite copia de las juntas de Guerra que ha tenido sobre el arreglo de milicias del Paso del Norte establecimientos del destacamento de Robledo, y providencias relativas a la Nueva México. A.G.I., Guad., 267.

No. 267. Croix to Gálvez. Chihuahua, September 23, 1778. Da cuenta de la feliz voluntaria redución de los Indios Xaramanes apostatas de la mission de la Bahia de Espiritu Santo en la provincia de los Texas. A.G.I., Guad., 275.

No. 268. Croix to Gálvez. Chihuahua, September 23, 1778. Advises campaign against Karankawan or their removal beyond the seas. A.G.I., Guad., 270.

No. 269. Croix to Gálvez. Chihuahua, September 23, 1778. Da cuenta de las primeras prov.as que ha dado coresp.a a la provincia de Californias. A.G.I., Guad., 270.

No. 270. Croix to Gálvez. Chihuahua, September 23, 1778. Acompaña estado general de población de California. A.G.I., Guad., 275.

No. 271. Croix to Gálvez. Chihuahua, September 23, 1778. Da cuenta de haverse erigido una nueva población sobre las margenes del Río de Guadalupe en la California septentrional. A.G.I., Guad., 267.

No. 279. Croix to Gálvez. Chihuahua, September 23, 1778. Refiere la carta 119 pide que si S.M. le concede el aumento de tropas se le embie la que nuevamente solicita para no gravar el r.l erario. A.G.I., Guad., 270.

No. 282. Croix to Gálvez. Chihuahua, September 23, 1778. Ynforme sobre algunos desordenes. ... en las missiones de Nueva Vizcaya, Coaguila, and Texas ... y los medios de corrijirlos y expresa los que ha tomado, y piensa tomar para el logro de este fin. A.G.I., Guad., 270.

No. 293. Croix to Gálvez. Chihuahua, October 23, 1778. Da cuenta de las resueltas que tuvieron por los Apaches del Gila de la infructuosa campaña que se les hize; de la que se queda practicando, exponde las causas que inutilizan ... tiempo. A.G.I., Guad., 270.

No. 297. Croix to Gálvez. Chihuahua, October 23, 1778. Expone con documentos las causas que se han movido a disponer la translacion del presidio de San Buenaventura del parage de Chavaria y las ventajas de esta providencia. A.G.I., Guad., 270.

No. 298. Croix to Gálvez. Chihuahua, October 23, 1778. Remite documentos de revistas, reforma, y nuevo pie de las milicias del Paso del Norte, y pide la rl. aprovación de sus providencias. A.G.I., Guad., 275.

No. 304. Croix to Gálvez. Chihuahua, November 30, 1778. A.G.I., Guad., 275.

No. 305. Croix to Gálvez. Chihuahua, November 30, 1778. Informe de piquetes de Dragones que sirven en aquellas fronteras. A.G.I., Guad., 270.

No. 315. Croix to Gálvez. Chihuahua, December 28, 1778. Da cuenta con documentos de todas las novedades ocurridas en la de Coaguila desde que se retiró del ella, y de la campaña que tiene meditada al Bolson de Mapimí. A.G.I., Guad., 275.

No. 316. Croix to Gálvez. Chihuahua, December 28, 1778. Acompaña copia de oficial del virrey y de otros documentos sobre hostilidades en Nuevo R.no de Leon. A.G.I., Guad., 270.

No. 317. Croix to Gálvez. Chihuahua, December 28, 1778. Informa el buen estado en que se halla de creación de milicias de Nueva Vizcaya. A.G.I., Guad., 270.

No. 323. Croix to Gálvez. Chihuahua, December 28, 1778. Dice que ha comisionado a los Gov.es de N. Mexico, Coaguila, y Texas para la creación resp.ta de militas y que se reserva la de Sonora que ha de correr por su cuenta. A.G.I., Guad., 270.

No. 329. Croix to Gálvez. Chihuahua, December 28, 1778. Da cuenta de sus ultimas prov.as para la translación del presidio de San Buenaventura. A.G.I., Guad., 270.

No. 330. Croix to Gálvez. Chihuahua. December 28, 1778. Dice sus providencias para la erección de una nueva villa en el presidio de Janos. A.G.I., Guad., 275.

No. 337. Croix to Gálvez. Chihuahua, January 23, 1779. Da cuenta del extrago y han hecho los Yndios del Norte en la Rancherias de Lipanes situados a la inmed.n de los presidios de Coaguila. A.G.I., Guad., 270.

BIBLIOGRAPHY

No. 341. Croix to Gálvez. Chihuahua, January 23, 1779. Manifiesta la utilidad de empleo de ayudante inspector y propone el aumento de oficial de esta clase. A.G.I., Guad., 270.

No. 3. (Confidential) Croix to Gálvez. Chihuahua, March 29, 1779. Dice que no ha podido remitir la relación concisa del estado de aquellas provincias en lo militar, politico, y economico. Sparks, 98 (VI), Harvard College Library.

No. 373. Croix to Gálvez. Chihuahua, March 29, 1779. Avisa las ocurridas en la provincia de Coaguila y sus providencias. A.G.I., Guad., 267.

No. 386. Croix to Gálvez. Chihuahua, April 26, 1779. Avisa su pronta marcha a Sonora y acompaña extracto y resumen de novedades. A.G.I., Guad., 267. Also Sparks, 98 (VI), Harvard College Library.

No. 387. Croix to Gálvez. Chihuahua, April 26, 1779. Da cuenta con documentos de las proposiciones que le hizo el governador del Nuevo Mexico en beneficio de aquella provincia. Sparks, 98 (VI), Harvard College Library.

No. 388. Croix to Gálvez. Chihuahua, April 26, 1779. Acompaña copia de carta del governador del Nuevo Mexico sobre difficultades de establecer el destacamento de Robledo. A.G.I., Guad., 267.

No. 394. Croix to Gálvez. Pueblo de Nombre de Dios, June 23, 1779. Da cuenta del lastimoso estado de su salud. A.G.I., Guad., 267.

No. 396. Croix to Gálvez. Pueblo de Nombre de Dios, June 23, 1779. Da cuenta de las ultimas novedades ocurridas con los indios Mescaleros y de sus providencias. A.G.I., Guad., 267.

No. 404. Croix to Gálvez. Pueblo del Nombre de Dios, July 23, 1779. Da cuenta de las disposiciones de su accidente, y refiere su prodigioso alivio. A.G.I., Guad., 267.

No. 405. Croix to Gálvez. Pueblo de Nombre de Dios, July 23, 1779. Avisa el cumplimiento que ha dado a Real Orden de 20 de Febrero de 79 sobre la guerra de los Yndios. Sparks, 98 (III), Harvard College Library.

No. 407. Croix to Gálvez. Pueblo de Nombre de Dios, July 23, 1779. Dice el estado de milicias de Nueva Vizcaya. A.G.I., Guad., 267.

No. 408. Croix to Gálvez. Pueblo de Nombre de Dios, July 23, 1779. Acompaña copia de expediente sobre donativo y arvitros con que contribuye la villa de Sta. Bárbara para la subsistencia de milicias. A.G.I., Guad., 267.

BIBLIOGRAPHY

No. 409. Croix to Gálvez. Pueblo de Nombre de Dios, July 23, 1779. Avisa la cantidad con que han concurrido de la Ciénega de los Olivios. A.G.I., Guad., 267.

No. 410. Croix to Gálvez. Pueblo de Nombre de Dios, July 23, 1779. Avisa la cantidad con que han concurrido de los del Valle de San Bartolomé. A.G.I., Guad., 267.

No. 434. Croix to Gálvez. Chihuahua, September 23, 1779. Remite copias de cartas del gobernador de Coaguila sobre sus sueldos y promoción a otro destino. A.G.I., Guad., 267.

No. 439. Croix to Gálvez. Chihuahua, September 23, 1779. Ofrece cumplir la Real Orden de 16 de Mayo sobre Ynspección de compañias milicianas de artillería. A.G.I., Guad., 268.

No. 458. Croix to Gálvez. Arispe, January 23, 1780. Informe General. A.G.I., Guad., 253.

No. 463. Croix to Gálvez. Arispe, January 23, 1780. Sends news that the governor of California has reported results of expedition to north. A.G.I., Guad., 272.

No. 477. Croix to Gálvez. Arispe, February 23, 1780. Refiere sus providencias para el establecimiento de un presidio y tres misiones en el canal de Santa Bárbara y de un Pueblo de españoles. A.G.I., Guad., 278.

No. 479. Croix to Gálvez. Arispe, February 23, 1780. Con documentos de revista de los piquetes de dragones de España y México acredita el cumplimiento de lo que se le previno en R1 orn. de 23 de Mayo de 1779. A.G.I., Guad., 278.

No. 481. Croix to Gálvez. Arispe, February 23, 1780. Da rendidas gracias por su promoción a Mariscal de Campo. A.G.I., Guad., 267.

No. 487. Croix to Gálvez. Arispe, February 23, 1780. Avisa el cumplimiento de la real orn. de 24 de Junio de 79 prohibiendo la comunicación, trato ó comercio con Ingleses. A.G.I., Guad., 278.

No. 488. Croix to Gálvez. Arispe, February 23, 1780. Avisa el recivo y cumplimiento de la real cédula en que S.M. autoriza a los vasallos de estos dominios para hostilizar a los subdidos del Rey de Ingleterra. A.G.I., Guad., 278.

No. 498. Croix to Gálvez. Arispe, March 26, 1780. Da cuenta del estado del Nuevo Pueblo de S. Joseph en la California. A.G.I., Guad., 278.

No. 499. Croix to Gálvez. Arispe, March 26, 1780. Reports his measures for rations for California missions. A.G.I., Guad., 272.

BIBLIOGRAPHY

No. 505. Croix to Gálvez. Arispe, April 20, 1780. Da cuenta de sus disposiciones para el establecimiento de dos pueblos en el Río Colorado, acompanado copias del expediente. A.G.I., Guad., 277.

No. 506. Croix to Gálvez. Arispe, April 23, 1780. Acompaña copia del nuevo provisional Reglamento formado por el Gobernador de Californias. A.G.I., Guad., 277.

No. 507. Croix to Gálvez. Arispe, April 30, 1780. Remite informe sobre el establecimiento de la Catedral del Obispado del Nuevo Reyno de Leon. A.G.I., Guad., 277.

No. 517. Croix to Gálvez. Arispe, April 23, 1780. Informa sobre la conducta y circumstancias del Capitan interino del Presidio de Santa Cruz de Terrenate D. Joseph Antonio Vildósola. A.G.I., Guad., 277.

No. 518. Croix to Gálvez. Arispe, May 23, 1780. Da cuenta de resultas de campaña executada en el año de '79 por la tropa de la Vizcaya y auxiliares Mescaleros contra los Lipanes. A.G.I., Guad., 278.

No. 519. Croix to Gálvez. Arispe, May 23, 1780. Refiere y acredita con documentos sus disposiciones relativas a la ejecución del plan que propusó en carta No. 458 para la seguridad de aquellos dominios. A.G.I., Guad., 278.

No. 520. Croix to Gálvez. Arispe, May 23, 1780. Da cuenta de sus primeros disposiciones para la egecución de su nuevo proyecto. A.G.I., Guad., 520.

No. 523. Croix to Gálvez. Arispe, May 23, 1780. Solicita aprovación de gastos que ha hecho con los Yndios de la Nación Lipana y Mescalera. A.G.I., Guad., 278.

No. 525. Croix to Gálvez. Arispe, May 23, 1780. Da cuenta con documentos sobre el estado de los Seris. A.G.I., Guad., 272.

No. 527. Croix to Gálvez. Arispe, May 23, 1780. Acompaña plan instructivo sobre el estado de la antigua California. A.G.I., Guad., 278.

No. 537. Croix to Gálvez. Arispe, June 23, 1780. Con documentos da cuenta de resultas de la quiebra del avilitado del presidio de San Buenaventura. A.G.I., Guad., 278.

No. 540. Croix to Gálvez. Arispe, June 23, 1780. Acompaña extracto y resumen de novedades. A.G.I., Guad., 267.

No. 581. Croix to Gálvez. Arispe, December 23, 1780. Remite cuenta de compra y transportación de cavallos con que ha socorrido a los vecindarios del Nuevo México. A.G.I., Guad., 277.

BIBLIOGRAPHY

No. 589. Croix to Gálvez. Arispe, December 23, 1780. Acompaña documentos de Revista del presidio de Santa Cruz y expone las causas de su translación al parage de las Nutrias. A.G.I., Guad., 272.

No. 590. Croix to Gálvez. Arispe, December 23, 1780. Remite documentos de revista del presidio del Tupson. A.G.I., Guad., 277.

No. 591. Croix to Gálvez. Arispe, December 23, 1780. Yncluye documentos de revistas del presidio del Altar. A.G.I., Guad., 272.

No. 592. Croix to Gálvez. Arispe, December 23, 1780. Remite documentos de revistas del presidio de Orcasitas y avisa su translación al Pitic. A.G.I., Guad., 277.

No. 595. Croix to Gálvez. Arispe, January 23, 1781. Acompaña Ynforme general sobre establecimiento de milicias de Nueva Vizcaya. A.G.I., Guad., 281.

No. 626. Croix to Gálvez. Arispe, March 26, 1781. Refiere la bizarra función que tuvó una partida de 16 homres presid.les de Coag.la con 300 Comanches y recomienda la hazaña de aquellos valerosos. A.G.I., Guad., 272.

No. 652. Croix to Gálvez. Arispe, June 30, 1781. Acompaña extracto y resumen de hostilidades de Indios. A.G.I., Guad., 267.

No. 8. Croix to Gálvez. Arispe, October 30, 1781. Dice que el Ynforme general ofrecido con fecha de 30 de Abril lo hara por partes. A.G.I., Guad., 253.

No. 692. Croix to Gálvez. Arispe, November 30, 1781. Avisa la erección de la mision de S. Vicente Ferrer en la antigua California. A.G.I., Guad., 281 Bis.

No. 693. Croix to Gálvez. Arispe, November 30, 1781. Acompaña documentos de revista de Inspección del presidio de Fronteras. A.G.I., Guad., 281 Bis.

No. 704. Croix to Gálvez. Arispe, November 30, 1781. Remite copia de documentos sobre translación de presidios de Sonora. A.G.I., Guad., 268; also Sparks, 98 (VII), Harvard College Library.

No. 712. Croix to Gálvez. Arispe, January 26, 1782. Incluye copias de tres expedientes sobre providencias económicas y relativos a la Sonora. A.G.I., Guad., 267.

No. 718. Croix to Gálvez. Arispe, February 28, 1782. Da cuenta con documentos de las lastimosas desgracias ocurridas en el Río Colorado. A.G.I., Guad., 517.

No. 719. Croix to Gálvez. Arispe, February 28, 1782. Expresa las bestias de que se apodaron los Yumas pertenecientes a la remonta destinada a California y la llegada a su destino de los reclutas y familias pobladores. A.G.I., Guad:, 517.

No. 721. Croix to Gálvez. Arispe, February 28, 1782. Acompaña copias de expediente ... para la observación del nuevo interino reglamento de Californias. A.G.I., Guad., 267.

No. 722. Croix to Gálvez. Arispe, February 28, 1782. Hace presente las causes que pueden obligar a la conveniente providencia de reducir las crias de ganados mayores en la provincia de California. A.G.I., Guad., 517.

No. 725. Croix to Gálvez. Arispe, February 28, 1782. Avisa que queda formado la compañia del Canal de Santa Bárbara, y que no ira a ocupar su terreno hasta que se concluya la expedición contra los Yndios Yumas. A.G.I., Guad., 267.

No. 728. Croix to Gálvez. Arispe, February 28, 1782. Dice su disposiciones para que se hagan los cargos correspond.tes del valor de las mulas y cavallos remitidos a California en el año de 79. A.G.I., Guad., 268.

No. 729. Croix to Gálvez. Arispe, February 28, 1782. Gives an account of the pueblo of Guadalupe in New California not injuring the nearby mission. A.G.I., Guad., 272.

No. 735. Croix to Gálvez. Arispe, April 23, 1782. Acompaña por duplicado la primera parte de sus informes generales, y por principal le Segunda, ofreciendo la oportuna remisión de las restantes. A.G.I., Guad., 253.

No. 737. Croix to Gálvez. Arispe, April 23, 1782. Incluye informe sobre el proyecto de minorar la dotación de caballos de las tropas presidiales y mantenerlos en caballerizas. A.G.I., Guad., 517.

No. 749. Croix to Gálvez. Arispe, May 30, 1782. Avisa las ultimas ocurrencias del Río Colorado. A.G.I., Guad., 517.

No. 814. Croix to Gálvez. Arispe, August 23, 1782. Da cuenta del establecimiento del presidio de Santa Bárbara y acompaña instrucción del Coronel D. Felipe Neve. A.G.I., Guad., 517.

No. 815. Croix to Gálvez. Arispe, August 26, 1782. Da cuenta de haberse establecido en el canal de Santa Bárbara a la parte del sur la mision de San Buenaventura. A.G.I., Guad., 517.

No. 835. Croix to Gálvez. Arispe, October 7, 1782. Da cuenta del estado de la Coaguila, remoción de sus presidios, reform y agregación a ellos de la compañia de el de San Savas, novedades y operaz.ns solicita la rl. aprovaz.n de sus providencias y pide que al gov.or Don Juan Ugalde se le promueva a otro destino, sir-

BIBLIOGRAPHY

viendo de introducir a su ynforme los cinco primeros parrafos. A.G.I., Guad., 282.

No. 836. Croix to Gálvez. Arispe, October 7, 1782. Da cuenta del rompimiento de los Mescaleros de Paz en el presidio del Norte y de las resultas. A.G.I., Guad., 282.

No. 844. Croix to Gálvez. Arispe, November 4, 1782. Avisa resultas de expedición contra los Indios Yumas, y pide grado de teniente coronel para el Capitan de Dragones D. Joseph Antonio Romeu. A.G.I., Guad., 283.

No. 845. Croix to Gálvez. Arispe, November 4, 1782. Remite informe sre que las margenes del Río Colorado no prestan proporciones para establecimientos. A.G.I., Guad., 283.

No. 847. Croix to Gálvez. Arispe, November 4, 1782. Incluye copias de las Instruy.es que dejó el coronel D. Felipe Neve al nuevo Governador interino de Californias D. Pedro Fages. A.G.I., Guad., 283.

No. 849. Croix to Gálvez. Arispe, November 4, 1782. Da cuenta de que el Governador de Coaguila no admitio la comisión de crear las dos comp.s volantes de Parras y el Saltillo, y de haverla instituido en el Capitan D. Luis Cazorla. A.G.I., Guad., 283.

No. 850. Croix to Gálvez. Arispe, November 4, 1782. Remite copia de un plan que forma el Governador de Coaguila, sus aumentos de tropa, sueldos y dotación de cavallos. A.G.I., Guad., 283.

No. 851. Croix to Gálvez. Arispe, November 4, 1782. Da cuenta de los motibos que le obligan a separar del Gov.or de Coaguila a Don Juan Ugalde y confirirlo interinam.te a D. Pedro Tueros. A.G.I., Guad., 283.

No. 852. Croix to Gálvez. Arispe, November 4, 1782. Dice que encargará la sub-inspección de las trops de Coaguila al nuevo gov.or interino. A.G.I., Guad., 283.

No. 853. Croix to Gálvez. Arispe, November 4, 1782. Remite estados de productos y gastos de Rl. Hacienda en las Prov.s de Sonora, Vizcaya y New Mexico. A.G.I., Guad., 283.

No. 862. Croix to Gálvez. Arispe, December 30, 1782. Incluye extractos de revista de los presidios de la Nueva California. A.G.I., Guad., 283.

No. 870. Croix to Gálvez. Arispe, January 27, 1783. Remite copia de Ynforme y Junta de Guerra sobre que las margenes del Río Colorado no prestan proporciones para esta establ.tos. A.G.I., Guad., 284.

BIBLIOGRAPHY

No. 881. Croix to Gálvez. Arispe, February 24, 1783. Remite extracto de providencias que ha tomado con los Yndios Mescaleros. A.G.I., Guad., 284.

No. 885. Croix to Gálvez. Arispe, February 24, 1783. Remite extractos de revista de inspección de los presidios de Monte-Rey y San Francisco. A.G.I., Guad., 284.

No. 891. Croix to Gálvez. Arispe, March 24, 1783. Expone lo que se le ofrece en repuesta a real orden de 27 de Junio de 82 en que se le hacen varias prevenciones sobre la guerra. A.G.I., Guad., 284.

No. 921. Croix to Gálvez. Arispe, June 2, 1783. Remite estado general de población de Sonora, y noticia particular de las jurisdiciones. A.G.I., Guad., 284.

No. 925. Croix to Gálvez. Arispe, June 2, 1783. Da cuenta de resultas de camp.a ejecutada contra los Apaches por el Cor.1 Dn Juan Ugalde y dice el estado inutil en que quedaron las tropas de Coaguila. A.G.I., Guad., 284.

No. 936. Croix to Gálvez. Arispe, June 23, 1783. En cumplimiento de real orden de 20 de Enero de esta año remite estado de las tropas de las provincias de su mando. A.G.I., Guad., 284.

CROIX MATERIALS—MISCELLANEOUS

D.n. Ph.e Barry. Durango, June 30, 1777. Resumen Gral de las hostilidades cometidas por los Indios Enemigos en las Jurisdicciones de las Alcaldias de esta provincia de la Nueva Vizcaya que se hallan en Frontera desde el año pasado de 1771 hasta fines del 1776 como consta por las relaciones testimoniales dadas por los mismos justicias, con toda individualidad, las que paran en esta secretaría de Govierno de mi cargo ... A.G.I., 103–4–16.

O'Conor to Croix. México, July 22, 1777. Copia del papel instructivo que pasó al Comand.te Gral de Provincias internas Dn. Teodoro de Croix, el Brigadier Dn. Hugo Oconor, Comand.te Ynsp.or que fué de ellas. A.G.I., 104–6–18.

Croix to Gálvez. Zacatecas, September 11, 1777. In regard to his petition to Bucareli for an increase in troops. Papeles tocantes a la Nueva España. Vol. II, 1772–1783. Eq. 1799. British Museum, London.

BIBLIOGRAPHY

Gálvez to Croix. Copia de R1. Orden de S. M. comunicada por el Exmo. Sor. Dn. José de Gálvez á el Sor. Comandante Gral. Don Teodoro de Croix ... El Pardo February 20, 1779. Archivo de San Francisco el Grande, Vol. 33, XI, 1779, pp. 33–39. University of Texas Library, Austin.

Mascaró, Dn. Manuel. Diario del Yngeniero dn. Manuel Mascaró desde la villa de Chihuahua al Pueblo de Arispe, en la Pimería Alta, Gobernación de Sonora, Año de 1779 (Chihuahua, September 30—Arispe, November 12). Bancroft Ms. 57, 326, pp. 97–106. Bancroft Library, University of California, Berkeley.

The King. Aranjuez, February—, 1794. No. 5. Ceremonial para el recivimto. de Sres. Comandtes. Grales. y la precede una real declaración sobre lo mismo. Archivo de la Iglesia de Arizpe, Sonora, Mexico.

CORRESPONDENCE OF OR CONCERNING VICEROY ANTONIO MARÍA DE BUCARELI Y URSUA

Bonilla to O'Conor. Chihuahua, August 14, 1774. Informe sobre la Provincia de Sonora. A.G.N., Procincias Internas. Tomo 88, ff. 10–33.

Crespo to Bonilla. No. 61. San Miguel, January 16, 1775. Expone a V.E. su dictamen sobre los puntos que promuebe en el informe de esta provincia el Ayudte. Inspector Dn. Antonio Bonilla. A.G.N., Provincias Internas. Tomo 88, ff. 142–161.

O'Conor to Bucareli. No. 449. Janos, August 29, 1775. Pasa á manos de V.E. el Informe que haze sobre lo observado en la provincia de Sonora y translación de sus presidios. A.G.N., Provincias Internas. Tomo 88, ff. 38–47.

O'Conor to Bucareli. No. 491. Carrizal, December 2, 1775. Dá cuenta á V.E. que en cumplimiento de su superior orn. de 18 de Octubre ultimo, dispondrá la pronta translación á demarcados terrenos de los quatro presidios removentes de Sonora, Altár, Tubac, Terrenate, y Fronteras suspendiendo la de los presidios de Orcasitas, y Buenavista hta. nueva orn. de V.E. A.G.N., Provincias Internas, Tomo 88. ff. 36–37.

Bucareli to Gálvez. No. 2638. México, December 27, 1776. Avisa la llegada del Brigadier Cav.o de Croix y providencias expedidas

BIBLIOGRAPHY

para la comandancia gral que le esta conferida. A.G.N., Bucareli. Tomo 86. ff. 16–17.

Bucareli to Gálvez. No. 2786. Remite testimonio del expediente formado sobre dudas ofrecidas para ejercer el Cabellero de Croix la Superintendencia de Real Hacienda en las provincias de su mando, y refiere la resolución que ha tomado y providencias dictadas a su consecuencia. A.G.I., Aud. de México, 1378.

Bucareli to Gálvez. No. 2819. México, March 27, 1777. Remite copia del papel instructivo que formó para el nuevo Com.dte General de Provincias Internas y otra del indice documentos que se le entregaron por la Secretaria de Camara. A.G.I., Aud. de México, 1378.

Bucareli to Gálvez. No. 2851. México, April 26, 1777. Contesta la Real Orden de 9 de enero de este año que manifiesta la intención de S.M. sobre el relevo que pidió del mando de aquel reino. A.G.N., Bucareli, Tomo 90. ff. 1–2.

Bucareli to Gálvez. No. 3217. México, August 27, 1777. Dá cuenta de los auxilios y tropa que le ha pedido el Comandante General de Provincias Internas, y acompaña copias de sus oficios y de los que le dirigió en respuesta, haciendo presente lo que sobre todo se le ofrece. A.G.N., Bucareli, 1777. Tomo 94, f. 59 vta.–62 vta.

Bucareli to Gálvez. No. 3218. México, August 27, 1777. Remite copias del oficio que le pasó el Comandante General de provincias internas, y de lo que le manifestó sobre separar de su mando alguna de ellas. A.G.N., Bucareli, 1777. Tomo 94, ff. 62–63.

Bucareli to Gálvez. No. 3338. México, October 27, 1777. Remite copia de la carta en que nuevamente pide auxilios el Comandante General de Provincias Internas y tambien acompaña la de la respuesta que le ha dado. A.G.N., Bucareli, 1777. Tomo 96, ff. 55–56; and ff. 443–447 vta., f. 449.

Bucareli to Gálvez. No. 3353. México, November 26, 1777. Satisface la Real Orden de 14 de agosto último, sobre entrega de documentos al Comandante General de Provincias internas, exponiendo que le ha franqueado cuantos pidió y no ha devuelto los que contiene la nota que acompaña. A.G.N., Bucareli, 1777. Tomo 97, ff. 19–20 vta.

Bucareli to Gálvez. No. 3354. México, November 26, 1777. Incluyendo copias de las dos cartas que expresa, informa haber dispuesto, a solicitud del Comandante General de Provincias Internas, que se traslade a la de Sonora la Compañía de Fusileros

BIBLIOGRAPHY

de Guadalajara. A.G.N., Bucareli, 1777. Tomo 97, ff. 20 vta.; 132–153; 154–156; 158–159 vta.

Bucareli to Gálvez. No. 3640. México, March 27, 1778. Acompaña copia de carta escrita por el Comandante General de Provincias Internas, sobre auxilios y providencias para su remedio. A.G.N., Bucareli, 1778. Tomo 101, ff. 16, 502–13; 500–501.

Bucareli to Gálvez. No. 3898. México, July 27, 1778. Dirige informe del Brigadier D. Hugo O'Conor, sobre las desgracias que refiere el Estado que remitió en 27 de octubre último. A.G.N., Bucareli, 1778. Tomo 108, f. 9.

Bucareli to Gálvez. México, July 27, 1778. Avisa que el Gobernador de California ha fundada el pueblo de San José de Guadalupe, con los pobladores que expresa la copia que acompaña. Ceballos, *Bucareli*, I, pp. 436–437.

Bucareli to Gálvez. México, January 27, 1779. Informa la indispensable que es el restablecimiento de la Compañia Presidial que antes guarnecía el Nuevo Reino de León, en igual número al de la Colonia del Nuevo Santander, para precaverlo de los insultos que padece de los bábaros, que no se had podido conseguir de otro modo ni con las providencias de que acompaña copia. Ceballos, *Bucareli*, I, pp. 445–447.

PUBLISHED MATERIALS

A. GENERAL WORKS AND MONOGRAPHS

Bancroft, H. H. *Arizona and New Mexico*. San Francisco, 1889.

———, *History of Mexico*, III. San Francisco, 1883.

———, *History of the North Mexican States and Texas*, I. New York, n.d.

———, *The Native Races*, I. San Francisco, 1883.

———, *Resources and Development of Mexico*. San Francisco, 1893.

Basauri, Carlos. *Monografía de los Tarahumaras*. Mexico, 1929.

Beals, Ralph L. *The Comparative Ethnology of Northern Mexico Before 1750*. Ibero-Americana: 2. Berkeley, 1932.

Bennett, W. C. and Zingg, Robert M. *The Tarahumara*. Chicago, 1935.

BIBLIOGRAPHY

Bolton, H. E. *Anza's California Expeditions*, 5 vols. Berkeley, 1930.

———, *Athanaze de Mézières and the Louisiana–Texas Frontier, 1768–1780.* 2 vols. Cleveland, 1914.

———, *Guide to the Materials for the History of the United States in the Principal Archives of Mexico.* Washington, 1913.

———, *Outpost of Empire.* New York, 1931.

———, *Texas in the Middle Eighteenth Century.* Berkeley, 1915.

Bolton, H. E. and Marshall, T. M. *The Colonization of North America, 1492–1783.* New York, 1925.

Caughey, John W. *Bernardo de Gálvez in Louisiana, 1776–1783.* Berkeley, 1934.

Ceballos, R. Velasco. *La administración de D. Frey Antonio María de Bucareli y Ursúa.* 2 vols. Mexico, 1936. (Publicaciones del Archivo General de la Nación, Tomos XXIX–XXX.)

Chapman, Charles E. *The Founding of Spanish California.* New York, 1921.

Coues, Elliott. *On the Trail of a Spanish Pioneer.* 2 vols. New York, 1900.

Hackett, Charles W. *Historical Documents Relating to New Mexico, New Vizcaya and Approaches Thereto.* II. Washington, 1926.

Humboldt, A. F. von. *Essai Politique sur le royaume de la Nouvelle-Espagne.* I. Paris, 1827.

Lumholtz, Carl. *Unknown Mexico.* 2 vols. New York, 1902.

McGee, W. I. "The Seri Indians." *Seventeenth Annual Report.* Part I. Bureau of American Ethnology. Washington, 1898.

Mecham, J. Lloyd. *Francisco de Ibarra and New Vizcaya.* Durham, 1927.

Morfi, Juan Agustín de. *Viaje de Indios y diario del Nuevo México.* Vito Alessio Robles, ed. Mexico, 1935.

———, *History of Texas, 1673–1779.* Carlos Eduardo Castañeda, ed. Albuquerque, 1935. Quivira Society Publications, Vol. VI in two parts.

Ocaranza, Fernando. *Crónicas y relaciones del occidente de México,* I. México, 1937. Biblioteca Histórica Méxicana de Obras Inéditas, No. 5.

Orozco y Berra, Manuel. *Apuntes para la historia de la geografía de México.* Mexico, 1884.

———, *Geografía de las lenguas y carta etnográfica de México.* Mexico, 1864.

BIBLIOGRAPHY

Priestley, H. I. *José de Gálvez, Visitor-General of New Spain 1765–1771.* Berkeley, 1916.

Robles, Vito Alessio. *Bibliografía de Coahuila, histórica y geográfica.* Mexico, 1927.

———, *Francisco de Urdiñola y el norte de la Nueva España.* Mexico, 1931.

Spier, Leslie. *Yuman Tribes of the Gila River.* University of Chicago Press, Chicago, 1933.

Swanton, John R. "Indian Tribes of the Lower Mississippi Valley and Adjacent Coast of the Gulf of Mexico." *Bulletin 43*, Bureau of American Ethnology. Washington, 1911.

Tamaron Y Romeral, Pedro. *Demonstración del vastisimo obispado de la Nueva Vizcaya, 1765.* Vito Alessio Robles, ed. Mexico, 1937.

Thomas, Alfred Barnaby. *Forgotten Frontiers: A Study of the Spanish Indian Policy of Don Juan Bautista de Anza, Governor of New Mexico, 1777–1787.* University of Oklahoma Press, Norman, 1932.

———, *The Plains Indians and New Mexico, 1751–1778.* The University of New Mexico Press, Albuquerque, 1940.

Thomas, Cyrus. "Indian Languages of Mexico and Central America. *Bulletin 44*, Bureau of American Ethnology. Washington, 1911.

Vivero, Domingo de. *Galería de Retratos de los gobernadores y virreyes del Perú, 1532–1824.* 2 vols. Barcelona, 1909.

B. SPECIAL STUDIES

Hackett, Charles W. "Revolt of the Pueblo Indians of New Mexico in 1680," in *Texas State Historical Association Quarterly*, XV, No. 2. 1911–1912.

———, "Visitador Rivera's Criticism of Aguayo's Work in Texas," in *The Hispanic American Historical Review*, XVI, 162–72, May, 1936.

Rowland, Donald (ed.) "The Sonora Frontier of New Spain, 1735–1745," in *New Spain and the Anglo-American West*, I, Lancaster, Pa., 1932.

Sauer, Carl. *The Distribution of Aboriginal Tribes and Languages in Northwestern Mexico.* Ibero-Americana: 5. Berkeley, 1934.

BIBLIOGRAPHY

Scholes, France V. "Church and State in New Mexico, 1610–1680," in *New Mexico Historical Review,* Vols. XI–XII, 1936–1937.

———, "Problems in the Early Ecclesiastical History of New Mexico," *New Mexico Historical Review,* Vol. VII, No. 1, January, 1932.

Thomas, Alfred B. "Antonio de Bonilla and Spanish Plans for the Defense of New Mexico, 1772–1778," in *New Spain and the Anglo-American West,* I, Lancaster, Pa., 1932.

———, "Governor Mendinueta's Proposals for the Defense of New Mexico, 1772–1778," in *New Mexico Historical Review,* VI, No. 1, January, 1931.

INDEX

INDEX

AGUAVERDE, presidio, 89
Aguayo, Marqués de, 60
Alegre, chief, 126
Allande, 150
Alonzo, chief, 126
Altamira, Marqués de, 203–16
Altar, dotation, 197; history, 195–97; locations near, 194; presidio, 194
Angel Nuñez, Fray, 140
Anza, Juan Bautista de, 106–14, 224; Comanche battle, 46, 109; Croix on, 141; Sonora proposals and reports, 134 f.
Apaches, 61 f., 105–74; attacks, 120, 146, 204; invasion, 118; location, 164; in Sonora, 143 f., 169
Arías Cavallero, Andrés, 234
Arivác, location, 171
Arizpe, ceremonies at, 44
Arroyo del Cíbolo, 85

BABISPE, 51, 158; presidio, 199
Bac, San Xavier del, 185, 193
Badeguachi, 200
Barri, Governor, report, 29 f.
Baserác, 156
Bejar, forces at, 78
Berroterán, Joseph, report, 23
Biquinete, 142, 145
Bocatuerte, Lipan, 101
Bolson del Mapimí, 117 f.
Bonilla, Antonio, Sonora proposals, 168–74
Borica, Diego de, 117
Bucareli, settlement, 77; location, 85
Bucareli, Viceroy, 22
Buenavista, Le Estancia de, locations, near, 192, 208–209

CABELLO, DOMINGO, 74; proposals, 77
California, account of, 231–43; Croix on, 232–37; forces, 231 f.; charges, 241; route to, 52, 174; regulation, 239–41; supplies for, 231–34
Carancaguazes, 75 f., 78, 81, 83
Carrizal, 101
Castillo, Luis de, 143
Chihuahua, 36-38, 119
Claudio de Pineda, Juan, Governor, 217
Coahuila, account of, 88–105; population, 88; Croix policy, 46; opposition in, 60 f.; defense, 101 f.; troops, 104; presidios, 49 f., 101
Coguiarachic, 145
Commandancy-General, creation of, 17
Comanche, 73–98, 105–14; description, 112 f.; attack, 111; defeat, 109; peace, 112; policy, 46
Corvalán, Pedro de, 153, 225
Crespo, Francisco Antonio, 224; report, 174
Crisanto, chief, 135
Chief, El Cavallero de, 44, 115-32; life, 17 f.; instructions to, 18–20; staff, 20, 123; routes, 36, 162, 164 f.; defense plans, 25–27, 39–42, 62–64, 117; and Bucareli, 28–35; reforms, 55–58; policy: California, 231–43; Coahuila, 59–65, 88–105; New Mexico, 105–14; New Vizcaya, 116, 120 f.; Sonora, 135–230, 225; Texas, 82–87; new policy, 43 f.; inspections, 128 f.; reports, 71 f., on Sonora, 137–41; on presidios, 50 f., 183 f., 196 f.; orders, 101 f., 147, 150, 232–36; illness, 122 f., 43
Cuchuta, locations near, 191

DIAZ, DOMINGO, 130
Diaz, Fray Juan, report of, 175–78

EL ARIVAC, 207
El Paso, 38 f., 106 f.
El Pitic, 52, 142, 194, 216 f.; locations near, 194 f.
England, war with, 44
Escomác, 197
Exploration, routes, 110 f.

FAGES, PEDRO DE, 153
Flying Corps, in New Vizcaya, 62 f.
Fronteras, presidio, 51, 146, 162–67, 189, 191; history, 197–99; locations near, 200

GARCES, FRAY FRANCISCO, 52
Gil, Nicolas, 119 f.
Gila, Indians, 124, 130, 164, 208 f.; settlements, 52; river, 175; locations on, 193; projects for 211 f.; presidio 213 f.
Gonzáles, Diego, 233

271

INDEX

Guadalupe, missions, 241
Guaivera, 202

HORSES, 55–57, 61 f.

INDIAN POLICY, in Coahuila, 94 f.; in Sonora, 193–95; work of, 214 f.; revolt of, 216; in Texas, 97 f.
Indians of the North, attack Apaches, 126 f.

JANOS, 162–67

LA BAHIA, 84
Lafora, Nicolas de la, 162
Lasaga, Lucas de, 60
Limón, Cayetano, 233
Lipan, 63, 73–98, 99–105; location, 99; and Mescaleros, 90 f.; in New Vizcaya, 125
Loreto, 240

MAGALLANES, road of, 191
Martinez, Francisco, 89 f.
Mascaró, Manuel, 52
Matagordo, shipwrecks, 76 f.
Matte, Nicolas de la, emissary, 80
Medina, Roque de, 143
Mescaleros, 63, 89–105, 128 f.; in Coahuila, 62; and Lipan, 90 f.; pueblos for, 125–27; customs, 129
Miera, map of, 55
Military settlements, 54 f., 128
Militia, in New Vizcaya, 54, 63
Monclova, council at, 35
Moqui, conditions among, 109 f.
Muños, Fray Nicolas, 239
Muñoz, Manuel, 125, 129

NATIONS OF THE NORTH, 76, 99
Navajo, 110–13
Neve, Felipe, 230, 236 f.
New Mexico, 24, 105–14; population, 105; settlers, 107 f., 111; defense, 55; forces, 106; contributions, 108; conditions, 63 f.; and Sonora, 110 f.; councils on, 39, 106; *see also* Anza.
New Spain (Northern), society, 6–10, 11–14; conditions in, 21–24, 26 f., 29–35, 39–42; forces in, 63; international influences, 15
New Vizcaya, account of, 115–32; population, 115; contributions, 121; boundary of, 164; policy in, 46 f.; attacks on, 131; to divide, 131 f.; patrols, 120; militias, 121; military settlements, 54 f., 128, 130; new settlements, 42–47; forces in, 52 f., 62 f., 116 f., 121; defense, 53 f., 118, 130 f.; presidios, 49, 53 f., 122
Nutrias, Las, 172

O'CONOR, HUGO, 31–34; work, 16, 48–50; ideas of, 206 f.; on Sonora, 178–182; in Sonora, 163; in Coahuila, 60 f.
Officials, weakness of, 42
Opata, 136, 157–62; conditions among, 199: presidio for, 155–58, 166; pueblos, 161

PARILLA, DIEGO ORTIZ, 206
Patule, chief, 101, 125
Paymasters, reforms for, 57 f.
Pericua, 202
Pima, 134–38
Pima, Gila, location of, 213
Porcuincula, mission, 241
Presidios, locations of, 48–50; Croix reorganizes, 47; criticism of, 146 f.; proposals for, 161 f.; discussion of, 160–62; report on, 151 ff.; bankruptcy of, 104; contributions, 103 f., 108; O'Conor on, 147 f.; in Sonora, 125, 137; at Santa Barbara, 214

RIVERA, FERNANDO DE, 231, 232–38
Robledo, 106 f.
Rocha, Geronimo de la, 148; survey of, 187–95; plans, 51
Rosario, mission, 85
Rubí, El Marqués de, survey, 16; in Sonora, 162–67

SAGUARIPA, 146
San Antonio de Bejar, 35 f., 77
San Bernardino, report on, 151; conditions, 146
San Buenaventura, presidio, 102; conditions, 128
San Fernando, Villa de, conditions in, 77
San Francisco, pueblo, for mescaleros, 129
San Pedro, Rio de, 149 f., 160–70, 175, 188, 190, 209; history of, 216

INDEX

Santa Cruz, presidio, crops, 204; locations near, 191 f. *See also* Terrenate.
Seris, 143 f.; revolt, 27, 35, 135–37; surrender, 142; expatriation proposed, 223
Settlements, by Croix, 42
Sobaipuri, location, 201
Soldiers, equipment of, expenses of, 241
Soler, Nicolas, 237
Sonora, account of, 135–230; population, 133; jurisdiction, 133; boundary, 164; report on, 137–41; problems, 47; crops, 153; frontier, 173, 179–95; and New Mexico, 53, 110; Apache in, 134, 138, 143, 218; conditions, 34, 142; forces, 52, 64, 134 f., 152–56, 224, 226 f.; defense, 52, 64, 204 f., 288 f.; presidios, 48 f., 51, 151, 154 ff., 160–230, 176 f., 178–82, 215

Taovayaces, 75, 80
Tarahumare, 122, 124, 128
Teopari, 146
Tepocas, 142
Terrenate, Rio de, 51, 167, 169, 170; locations near, 189; history, 200 f. *See also* Rio de San Pedro.
Texas, account of, 72–98; population, 72; Croix in, 35 f.; policy, 45 f., 82–88, 92–98; missions, 77 f.; presidios, 62, forces, 63; defense, 85 f.
Tiburones, 142, 145

Tienda de Cuervo, Joseph, Governor, 217
Tovar, Francisco, 151
Trade, Texas-Louisiana, 76
Troops, conditions in Coahuila, 94–103
Tubac, 170, 206–08
Tueros, Pedro de, 141, 142
Tuerto, Juan, chief, 125, 129
Tupson, 143, 152, 183, 185, 213–15, 238; locations near, 189, 190; presidios, 193

Ugalde, Juan de, 100–03; recommended, 100; opposition, 61 f.; removed, 62
Ugarte y Loyola, Jacobo, 151; in Sonora, 144; survey, 147, 184–87; reports, 51, 161 f.; instructions, 156
Urrea, Captain, 196
Ute, 113

Varela, Juan Manuel, 156, 158
Vicente de Mora, Fray, 239
Vicente Ferrer, San, mission, 239
Vildósola, Agustin de, 216
Vildósola, Antonio de, 200

Xaramanes, 85
Xebec, 232
Xaramanes, 85
Xebec, 232

Yuma, 219 f.; forces, 220; settlements, 220–23; massacre, 59 f.

TEODORO DE CROIX
AND THE NORTHERN FRONTIER
OF NEW SPAIN, 1776–1783

BY ALFRED BARNABY THOMAS

HAS BEEN COMPOSED IN ELEVEN-POINT
LINOTYPE OLD STYLE
NUMBER SEVEN

THE PAPER IS ANTIQUE WOVE